The Practical Hunter's
DOG BOOK

■

Second Revised, Expanded Edition

■

John R. Falk

Voyageur Press

ACKNOWLEDGMENTS

With sincere appreciation, the author wishes to thank the many persons who, over the years, have contributed materially, knowledgeably, and inspirationally to the total content of this book. Special gratitude is expressed to the late Pert Prince; the late George Fremault; Frank and Ellen Weed; the late Art Flick; Bill Bartlett; Bob Elman; Gene Hill; James Rikhoff; John Madson; Ed Frisella; and Dave Petzal.

Thanks also to the late Evelyn Monte, formerly of the Gaines Dog Research Center; the late William F. Brown, former editor of *The American Field;* as well as the secretaries and members of the various breed clubs that supplied photos for publication herein.

Printed in the United States

91   92   93   94   95   5   4   3   2

Library of Congress Cataloging-in-Publication Data

Falk, John R.
The practical hunter's dog book / John R. Falk.
p.   cm.
Reprint. Originally published ; Rev. expanded ed.
Piscataway, N.J. : Winchester Press, c1984.
Includes bibliographical references and index.
ISBN 0-89658-151-9
1. Hunting dogs.   I. Title.
[SF428.5.F35   1991]
636.7'52 — dc20   91-9317
                                                      CIP

This edition published in 1991 by
Voyageur Press, Inc.
P.O. Box 338, 123 North Second Street
Stillwater, MN 55082 U.S.A.
In Minn 612-430-2210
Toll-free 800-888-9653

Voyageur Press books are also available at discounts for quantities for educational, fundraising, premium, or sales-promotion use.
For details contact the marketing department.
Please write or call for our free catalog of publications.

DEDICATION

To those affectionate, loyal, hardworking and everlastingly wonderful suppliers of man's most golden moments afield—the hunting dogs of yesterday, today and tomorrow—this book is dedicated.

Foreword

A long, hard day, but a good one.

From early morning until sundown you and the old setter combed the back fields and side hills for late-season quail—nine hours of rough ground, briars, and shaggy field edges. You shot less than the limit but it was the kind of hunt that man and dog can take pride in, for you both hunted as well as you knew how, and you both did your jobs.

Supper is over now, and you sit by the fire. The old dog lies at your feet, as sore-footed and weary as you are, and just as content. He has been dried off, and some of the crud brushed out of his coat. He still isn't very presentable, but Ma'am doesn't object. In her house, there's always room for hard workers at the fireside, even if they are a little seedy.

So you two watch the logs burn down, each with his own thoughts. And since you and that old dog both love birds and rough country and hard hunts and firesides afterward, and hold so many values in common, it occurs to you that you may both be thinking of the same things.

How often, back to the Stone Age and beyond, has it been thus? The Egyptian nobleman and his hounds, hunting gazelles and lion together; Mongolian hunters crossing the Bering Land Bridge into a new world, their wolf-dogs laden with hunting supplies; black Australians and their yellow dingos, hunting with stick and fang and incredible skill.

For as long as man has made fire, there has been a man-dog hunting partnership.

It has endured because it is one of those perfect mixes, like October frost and gunsmoke. As a hunter, the man can take pride in a pursuit that entails skill and tradition. He is also recapturing some of the best parts of his racial boyhood, and during a good hunt he is probably as free as it is possible for modern man to be.

The hunting dog shares this pride, and the ancient tradition. Here is no pampered pet, fat and ailing and snappish. A good hunting dog has self-respect—and it is possible for a dog to respect himself, make no mistake about that. He is a professional, bred for the job, and paid in love and pride and action for what he wants to do most.

My old friend John Falk understands this as few men do. He knows the gun dog and the hunt, and in this book he does as good a job of fitting them together as anyone ever has. It's a fine piece of work, practical and complete, and the sort of thing we'd expect.

Let me put it another way: if there's such a thing as reincarnation, you and I could do a lot worse than being reincarnated as a bird dog owned by John Falk. No one who loves hunting—man or dog—could ask much more than that.

JOHN MADSON

Preface

The first edition of this book was published more than a decade ago, and we take some pride in the fact that it has remained so popular through the years. All the same, we feel that this new edition will be even more useful, as we have taken pains not only to update it but to expand it in significant ways. We have, for example, added important material on first aid afield, on photographing your dog at work, and on keeping a field-dog diary that will bring future pleasure and will also help you evaluate your dog's performance. In addition, we have updated the appendix on suggested reading, breed registries, equipment suppliers, and so on. We have tried to omit nothing that might help you get the most out of your hunting dog.

If most folks were aware of the many practical considerations that go into hunting dog ownership, just as they are aware of the considerations that go into buying, operating, and maintaining an automobile, there would be no need for *The Practical Hunter's Dog Book*. The fact that a dog is a living animal — a companion and working partner rather than a machine — in no way cancels the need to be practical in such matters as selection, purchase, training, care, and field techniques. On the contrary, only a practical, well-informed approach is likely to result in the ideal bond that can be formed between man and dog.

The American public has reduced to a science the complicated process of choosing and purchasing the family chariot. Despite a spate of models, makes, and styles, a plethora of power plants, and a wealth of optional equipment, the average American is unconfused and virtually unhesitating in pinpointing the car that best fills his individual bill of particulars.

In a sense, hunting dog ownership can be viewed in much the same way. Like a car, the type and breed of gun dog you choose deserves a studied approach from every angle. Objective considerations prevent the man who needs a station wagon from buying a sports car simply because he admires its sleek lines or the way it hugs the road. Forethought is equally important to avoid buying a flushing breed when a pointer is needed, for example, or a show dog when a field dog is required, a puppy when a trained adult animal is the answer, an all-purpose utility dog when only a specialist can do the desired job. Providing the informational food for forethought is one of the principal aims of this book.

Not only is our goal to assist you in the initial selection of the most suitable type and breed of dog for your particular circumstances and brand of gunning, but also to familiarize you with the fundamental considerations involved in making future canine decisions – decisions on such significant matters as the proper age to begin training, whether professional training is a good idea, when and how to breed your animal to the most suitable mate, and whether your dog should share your home or be kenneled outdoors.

What to do before and after a litter arrives may turn out to be important to you, and that's here, too. Also covered in detail are such crucial topics as training equipment, conditioning your dog for the field, transporting him safely and efficiently, and how to care for him after the hunt is over. There is a thorough analysis of the pup's first season afield and what you should – and should not – expect of him, and there is ample discussion of the training refinements that mark the performance of a fully finished field dog, as well as their practical value, if any, to the hunter. Even the commonly overlooked merits of field trials are investigated from the hunter's point of view.

We make no pretense that every answer to every question can possibly be contained in any single book. But it is our sincere belief that what is between these covers provides the broadest possible span of practical information to set the average gun dog owner on the proper path to derive the maximum pleasure, benefit, and satisfaction from his hunting dog.

JOHN R. FALK

South Salem, N.Y.

Contents

— CONTINUED —

Part IV: Training and Performance

Part V: Your Dog at Home

Part I

Preliminary Planning

Every hunter finds the idea of an "all-purpose" hunting dog inherently appealing. Such a dream dog—the kind that does everything—simply doesn't exist, however, and most sportsmen wouldn't be able to do full justice to him anyway.

1

What Kind of Dog?

THE DOG THAT NEVER WAS

IN AN AGE so distinctly characterized by specialization, it's paradoxical that in choosing a first hunting dog substantial numbers of American gunners seek to by-pass the specialists in favor of the multi-purpose breeds.

Somehow, the idea that exceptional versatility should transcend specialization in a shooting dog remains a popular notion. In most cases, the only basis for such a conclusion stems from glowing hand-me-down accounts from bygone eras when game, in boundless quantity and variety, was brought to bag with the aid of "almost any old kind of huntin' dog." In others, the intensive promotional campaign that, not too many years ago, heralded the arrival here of certain "general-purpose" breeds from abroad can doubtless be credited for spreading the infectious idea.

This promotion proved to have a potent influence on American sportsmen, softening us up for not only general acceptance but fervent support of a breed variously known as a "multi-purpose," "general-purpose," and even "all-purpose" hunter. The campaign's immodest success was hardly surprising, since its persuasive premise was one which any man who follows dogs afield would desperately like to believe is possible.

Every hunter finds the "all-purpose" hunting dog inherently appealing. And why not? The description conjures up infinite images of a dream dog: effortlessly conquering icy waters to fetch downed ducks; boldly bucking impenetrable briers to root out cottontails; stylishly snapping into head-high point on elusive coveys of bobwhite quail or skulking ring-necked pheasant; diligently unraveling the complicated scent trail of bobcat, fox or coon, and probably even scrapping courageously with boar or bear at bay.

Unfortunately, such versatility, however inspirational to contemplate, is still unattainable within any single breed of hunting dog. It is true that certain breeds can, if judiciously trained, manage to perform several different functions in the field. But, at best, these pinch-hit propositions always mean a compromise with even average standards of quality, style, and efficiency of performance. A far cry from the image of all-around perfection we'd all like to own, the jack-of-all-trades gun dog inevitably mirrors the rest of the adage: "master of none."

If you recognize the fact that no one breed of hunting dog is capable of performing many diverse field jobs with anything close to the precision and efficiency of the specialist, you can spare yourself almost certain disappointment in choosing your first hunting dog. Furthermore, when you think about it objectively, you'll probably be surprised to discover that, honestly, you neither need nor want that illusory "all-purpose" breed anyway...and for a very practical reason.

Like virtually every hunter, you can name, without the slightest hesitation, your favorite game: that one bird or animal you'd rather, and usually do, spend most of your time hunting for in the field. If you're a bird hunter, you probably seldom bother with rabbits; if essentially a rabbit hunter, you aren't likely to gun many birds, besides a few you occasionally run across during a cottontail hunt. Over an entire season you might make one or two special trips after some sort of game other than your favorite. So, in the final analysis, it becomes apparent that you are actually pretty much of a specialist yourself, favoring a specific type of shooting and sticking with your preference most of the time.

So it doesn't make much sense for you to compromise the quality of work obtainable from a dog bred to specialize on the game you prefer, merely for the sake of using him on several additional species which you rarely hunt anyway. By basing your considerations primarily on the type of game that most interests you and that is, of course, native to your area, you'll effectively narrow down the field of choice to the breeds of hunting specialists that are most suitable for you.

Depending upon the species of quarry involved, you'll usually find you have an option among two or more breeds that specialize on the same game birds or animals but employ different hunting techniques. In other instances your choice may be extended to a number of breeds that share the same basic technique, but whose range, pace, and style vary considerably. In addition, your final selection may be dictated not only by your personal preference for a particular breed, but by geographical factors (the climate and physical composition of the terrain in which you live), as well as domestic considerations (the size of your home and its location in city, suburb, or rural environs).

The various breeds and their specialties, along with their characteristics and qualifications for the field and the home, are described in Part II of this book. But since your first step is to narrow down the potential candidates according to the kind of hunting you prefer (or, if you're a new hunter, the kind you believe you'll prefer) you'll want to consider first the four major areas of hunting interest by type of game and related hunting dog breeds.

The man dedicated to upland bird hunting finds himself in the catbird seat when it comes to the number of specialty dogs he can logically consider. In the northern half of the country, his quarry generally consists of three main species: the wary ruffed grouse, along the brushy fringes of the deep woods; the migratory woodcock, amidst the thick alder tangles; and the always rugged ring-necked pheasant, in the cornfields, hedgerows, swamps and brushlots.

Confronted with close cover conditions so much of the time, his dog must be a thorough worker, of medium range and moderate pace, with a coat substantial enough to ward off the punishment of brush, briers, and frequent spells of cold weather.

Should the pointing breeds prove his cup of tea, he can choose among the long-haired breeds, the English, Irish, or Gordon setter, or Brittany spaniel. For less rigorous cover work, he can opt for the Weimaraner, the German shorthaired pointer, the Vizsla or the English pointer among the breeds with short-haired coats.

The flushing breeds, as alternatives, offer a choice between the English springer and the English cocker spaniels. Although primarily specializing on pheasants, these long-haired breeds do very satisfactory work on grouse and woodcock. In fact, it was from the latter bird that the cocker (formerly cocking) spaniel derived his name.

Below the Mason-Dixon line, the upland bird hunter faces a some-what different situation. As a rule, he can forget about pheasants since, except in isolated instances, the ring-neck does not thrive in the southern states. Ruffed grouse and woodcock, though present in huntable numbers, are spotty and generally regarded as incidental game. Here, the bobwhite quail is *the* game bird, flourishing in the grain and grass fields of the big open spaces.

Fast, wide-ranging dogs, with lots of endurance and drive to cover miles of open terrain in quest of coveys, provide the only practical answer to the southern bird hunter's needs. A warm climate and relatively little rough cover tend to favor the short-haired dog. Though the option usually boils down to the English pointer—a short-coated pointing breed that is practically an integral part of quail hunting—the English setter, traditional northern favorite, must also be considered a strong contender, especially in the cooler areas of the southland.

The rabbit hunter has limited selection among the specialist breeds. Yet he suffers little hardship in his choice between beagle and basset hound, two rabbit-hunting breeds without peer anywhere in the world.

For the waterfowl hunter, north, south, east or west, the retriever breeds offer ample choice among the Labrador, golden and Chesa-peake Bay retrievers and the Irish and American water spaniels. In all of them a natural love of swimming is almost as highly developed as their fetching instincts.

The nation's coon and fox hunters have a ready-made choice in the hound strains named respectively for these two popular game animals. But they may also choose from among a large number of other equally popular hounds. While invariably used as specialists on a particular species of game, ranging from opossum and coon to mountain lion and bear, most strains of hounds can be successfully trained to trail any given quadruped.

In summary, whatever your preference in game and wherever you hunt it, your best bet will be a dog of the breed that was designed, and over the years—centuries, in some cases—used, for a single purpose. Let that elusive "all-purpose" dog continue to roam the mental coverts of the dreamers among us, while you make a practical choice of one of the specialist breeds. You won't be disappointed.

No matter which breed you eventually decide upon, however, you'll suddenly find a number of questions cropping up that call for addi-tional decision-making. The questions may not occur to you all at once or in neat and tidy order, but they will be important in assuring that the individual member of the breed you choose comes as close as possible to providing you with 100 percent satisfaction.

FIELD DOG OR SHOW DOG?

"Field dog or show dog, what's the difference, he's an English setter, isn't he? And English setters are hunting dogs, right? Who cares if his ancestors won twenty-eight best-in-show ribbons? I only want to use him for hunting, anyway."

Typical of the reaction of a majority of uninitiated sportsmen, this kind of statement sums up the general unawareness that there could possibly be any difference, functional or otherwise, among members of the same breed. It seems incontestable to most prospective buyers of gun dogs that any sporting dog is a *hunting* dog.

Yet, the difference between a dog of predominantly bench-bred ancestry and one from essentially working-field stock can be just slightly less apparent than the difference between night and day. A hunter who inadvertently acquires a pup heavy in show dog lineage will rarely come through the experience with a dry crying towel and a full game bag.

If you're the skeptical type, merely being told that such a difference

Field-type English setter, bred from hunting lineage, is built to hunt, has all the natural instincts, and demonstrates ability to find and point birds, in a stylishly intense stance. **Photo by Dave Petzal.**

Typical show-type setter is beautiful—note well-chiseled head, low-set ears, finely tapered tail—but often lacks the drive, stamina, and strong instincts a good hunting dog must possess. **Photo by Evelyn M. Shafer.**

exists may not convince you; it does seem incredible that all individuals of a given sporting breed can't be expected to embody the rudimentary potentials for which that breed was originally designed and developed. Why it happened still has people shaking their heads; but *how* such circumstance occurred is easy to explain.

Take, for example, the logical assumption that, because the English setter is a hunting breed, he should just naturally hunt. Several centuries ago, when this particular breed evolved from the "setting spaniels," it did just that. But in the nineteenth century the first dog shows were held as an incidental event at English field trials. Inevitably, the practice of conducting bench exhibitions completely separate and disassociated from field trials came into vogue. Limited at first to the hunting breeds, these shows eventually enlarged their scope, taking in entries representing all sorts and breeds of dogs.

As exhibiting dogs grew in popularity, soon extending to America and other parts of the world, dog shows became increasingly well-organized, highly competitive affairs. Stiffening competition brought with it greater incentive to win the prizes, as well as the prestige that accompanied them. This trend, in turn, spawned a whole new coterie of dog fanciers, persons who sought to make a livelihood, directly and indirectly, out of breeding and handling dogs strictly for exhibition. For many owners of the sporting breeds, bench wins began assuming precedence over their dogs' functional abilities.

In relatively short order, two distinct factions had arisen—one for field and another for show—where but a single one had stood before for each of most of the older sporting breeds. Little by little, with beauty their sole concern and criterion, the bench fanciers of the hunting breeds—their ranks continually swelling with new recruits who had never spent a moment hunting with a dog—began drawing up new standards, ever changing the physical structure of the various hunting breeds.

"Why not breed good-looking sporting dogs?" became their motto. And so, many of them did, with a resulting change in the physical structure of the various hunting breeds. But in the process of culling their litters of pups that failed to measure up to standards based on looks alone, they discarded some of their best hunting prospects. This was selective breeding of the highest degree. Unfortunately, the selectivity emphasized beauty to the exclusion of all the other qualities and instincts for which the sporting breeds had been originated and carefully developed, in many instances for hundreds of years.

Under this kind of breeding program it was not surprising that some of the best hunting attributes of many of our sporting breeds were drastically diluted. The fact that the degeneration of certain other hunting dog characteristics have been less rapid—scenting abilities, in particular—is certainly no credit to the show breeders. It just shows that some aspects of nature can withstand the follies of man a lot longer than others.

The American cocker spaniel is perhaps the most outstanding example of what the combination of overpopularity and breeding strictly

Most hunters contend that a gun dog's real beauty emanates from the zest, style and intensity of his functional field skills. The snappy ebullience of this Springer's delivery of a cock pheasant seems to support that viewpoint. **Photo by Gaines Dog Research Center.**

for show standards can do to what was once a merry-dispositioned, hard-working little gun dog. In their single-minded quest for beauty, the bench people changed the cocker standard from that of a medium-coated dog to one with coat so long that it literally dragged on the ground and had to be thinned continually to avoid matting. That, alone, might have been tolerable. But, in the rush to breed cockers able to meet the new standard, too many other considerations were sacrificed, including gentle temperament, and the breeders managed to bring forth a snappy, ill-tempered, often bug-eyed, chronic piddler as the typical representative of the new breed. Today's American cocker of bench-type bloodlines — and it's difficult to find any other kind — far from being a bird dog, can more aptly be described as "strictly for the birds."

The Irish setter is another sorry example of a fine breed that has been practically blitzed out of the hunting field by a bench-oriented fancy that took no account of this dog's working abilities. Fortunately a dedicated group of field breeders is striving to bring back the red setter as a gun dog.

In defending their philosophies show breeders naturally contend that they are breeding sporting dogs for soundness of body as well as beauty; that only by possession of sound structural build can a gun dog physically do the work he was originally intended for; and that they are, therefore, actually benefiting the sporting breeds as practical gun dogs over the long range. Furthermore, the show breeders criticize the field dog man for producing snipey-nosed, undersized specimens with short tails, high-set ears, and the like — which just happen to be able and willing to hunt their hearts out for hours on end. The sound bench dogs who fill them with pride and conviction are well up in leg and shoulder, with long, finely tapered tails, large, well-chiseled heads and low-set ears — from whom much of the heart, drive, and intense desire for the hunt have disappeared.

It can be argued that the true beauty of the gun dog stems not so much from mere physical conformation as from the manifestations of zest, style, and intensity in demonstrating the functional skills for which he was born and bred. If eye-appeal can be added, fine; field dog men are not against good-looking hunting dogs. Only when the practical, functional aspects of the sporting breeds are ignored or pushed into a secondary role in favor of mere physical beauty, does the question arise: Is the cart being put before the horse?

For too many years, this basic difference of opinion has kept field and show factions from agreement on the single standard that once existed and should now exist for every sporting breed. Some field and show standards, such as those of the English pointer and English setter, have drifted so far apart that there are virtually two separate breeds in each case; such a divergence is doubtless beyond all hope of compromise.

The field dog man's continued plea is to retain or return to realistic standards based on a sporting dog's original purpose—the strong instinct, desire, and ability to serve the gun. Fortunately it is not falling entirely on deaf ears in show dog circles. Fanciers of some sporting breeds recently introduced in America are demonstrating a desire to maintain close harmony between field and show elements. Among Brittany spaniel supporters, for instance, strict adherence to working type, by hunters and bench exhibitors alike, has not only created a strong, one-standard camp but has fostered an impressive number of dual (field and bench) champions for the breed.

The German shorthaired pointer is another example of practical collaboration between field and show interests who support a single standard dedicated to preserving the qualities and abilities for which the breed was originated. The rewards, as in the case of the Brittany, are graphically apparent in the number of dual champions produced to date—more, if memory serves, than any other sporting breed.

Such examples, representing increased awareness of the errors made in the past, are sources of encouragement for the future of sporting dogs in America. Someday, perhaps, the field and show factions of all our hunting breeds can be brought together. Should such a solid union become reality, there would no longer be a need to qualify any member of a sporting breed as being field or show dog type. With the prevalence of a single standard for each, we could once again refer, with conviction and pride, to any sporting dog as a *hunting* dog.

PLAIN OR FANCY?

Just as a preponderance of bench-bred lineage ordinarily will limit a dog's potential afield, so too can the quality of the bloodlines, or

Will this six-week-old English setter pup become a good hunting dog? "Fancy bloodlines" do provide a realiable yardstick by which his potential probabilities can be measured.

ancestry, of the working field dog you acquire exert profound influence on his prospective capabilities as a gun dog.

In any conversation among veteran hunting dog owners you sooner or later hear mention of the breeding of the dogs under discussion. Rarely is the reference a proposition by one owner to another in behalf of two matable canines. Rather, the subject is usually a previous "affair," or, more accurately, a number of past affairs and the resulting offspring. At least some of these will be known by reputation to hunting dog aficionados.

More succinctly, a dog's breeding refers to his family tree: the parents, grandparents and so on, whose bloodlines or genetic makeup have been combined to produce the present individual. The list of those individual ancestors is commonly known as a pedigree, which, despite the fanciful sound of the word, is still just a list, or record, of the puppy's forbears. Since even a mongrel would have a pedigree if anyone bothered to keep a written record of a mongrel's ancestors, the term "pedigreed dog" is meaningless; it's a misnomer often used by novices who think that it signifies quality breeding.

A pedigree is not a guarantee of excellent breeding but only a certified record of a dog's purebred ancestry over a specified number of generations. What makes a pedigree valuable is the information it can reveal about the individuals who have contributed to a puppy's inheritance. Reading a pedigree is simple. It is set up in chart-like fashion with two names, one above the other, at the extreme left-hand side. The upper name is the puppy's sire (father); the lower one, his dam (mother). Immediately to the right of each name a connecting line or symbol clearly links another pair of names, also one above the other. These are the grandparents of the puppy, the pair stemming from the sire line being the paternal grandparents, the other pair, the maternal grandparents. Depending upon how many generations are traced in the pedigree, the progression would continue in like order.

If this were all a pedigree could tell you, it wouldn't be very informative since the names of the puppy's ancestors alone would mean nothing to you. However, along with the names, you'll find various abbreviations that provide specific information about each individual dog's accomplishments, if any. For example, the prefix "Ch." denotes that the dog is, or was a Champion, while the suffix "U.D.T." indicates that he has earned his Utility Dog Tracker degree, the highest award obtainable in Obedience Training competition.

Most of the abbreviations are standardized and since any breeder or kennel owner can—and usually, without prompting, will—rattle off their meanings, we won't belabor them here, with one significant exception. In a pedigree certified by the American Kennel Club, the "Ch." title, which means that the dog has won his championship in the show ring, is valueless in terms of indicating a dog's hunting abilities. In fact, it may even serve as a caution light—especially if it appears several times within three or four generations—signaling a heavily bench-oriented ancestry. In an A.K.C. pedigree, the only prefix that's important to you as a hunter is "F.T.Ch.," which stands for Field Trial Champion and indicates that that particular dog distinguished himself in field competition.

In pedigrees issued or certified by any of the several other registering organizations, for example, the Field Dog Stud Book, the "Ch." prefix always means Field Trial Champion and has nothing whatever to do with bench show competition.

Many prospective gun dog buyers show only a cursory interest in the pedigree of the puppy they contemplate purchasing. A sense of embarrassment over their unfamiliarity with the document probably accounts for most persons' apparent disinterest. But, there are also fair numbers of sporting dog buyers who cynically claim that pedigrees are exaggerated in importance and that the fancy, titled ancestry serves only to inflate a puppy's value and has little bearing on his ultimate performance in the field. Their rationale is that any physically sound puppy from good, albeit uncelebrated, field breeding, can be turned into a good gun dog if he's properly trained. The kind of education he receives, not the number of field trial winners or champions in his background, is what really counts, they contend.

But even the pedigree skeptic admits that he wants "basically good field breeding," even though he disdains the titles and "fancy" bloodlines that offer one of the few other than personal ways of evaluating quality. In its most commonly understood sense, the term "good breeding" implies a high percentage of ancestors of tested and proven abilities whose natural hunting characteristics have been transmitted in strong measure to a majority of their descendants. In other words, the sire and dam—and their respective sires and dams, and so on for several generations back—will have demonstrated their own merits in the field plus a tendency to produce offspring with similar aptitudes.

Obviously, to make good breeding possible, an owner or breeder must be able to evaluate the ancestry of both the prospective sire and dam for several generations back, either from personal knowledge or by using some reliable yardstick. In earlier days, it was likely that the owner of a bitch had himself hunted over every one of the potential stud dogs available in his locality as well as over their parents, and even some of their grandparents. This personal familiarity not only permitted but encouraged sportsmen to breed their best bitches selectively, using only the best stud dogs in their area.

As the nation grew and life became more hurried and complex, the breeding process changed with the times. Rapid communications and transportation made long-distance breeding increasingly practicable. But personal familiarity naturally diminished. It is fortunate that at about this time field trials were steadily growing in popularity. Here was a sport that combined much of the flavor and excitement of the hunt with the thrills, suspense, and gratification of competition. And apace with the times, such field contests, previously limited by distance to neighboring communities, regularly began drawing entries from hundreds of miles away.

Attracting support from owners of some of the best gun dogs to be found in a given region, field trials soon brought about a vigorous sharpening of competitive spirit. As wins assumed ever greater significance, inevitably certain bloodlines which consistently produced winning dogs began to emerge preeminent.

Naturally, men who owned winners sought to breed them selectively to other winners. Eventually, the practice not only increased the number of outstanding individual performers, but, by wider dissemination of these field-proven bloodlines, also helped create and establish new lines or strains with superior hunting abilities all over the nation. Although still adhering to the earlier concept of breeding the best to the best, the hunting dog fraternity was no longer restricted to local sires and dams. Secondly, field trials were providing a higher but more uniform set of standards by which prospective breeding stock could be easily and accurately evaluated without the need of personal familiarity.

Since no more than a tiny minority of today's sportsmen are afforded an opportunity to hunt over several generations of the ancestors of the pup they purchase, only the records can provide proof of performance plus a reasonable measurement of quality. Thus, one of the definite

Pictured in oil, the immortal setter Sports Peerless was a prime example of "good breeding" and prepotency. **Photo by The American Field Publishing Co.**

Another example of the merits of "fancy bloodlines" was the English pointer field trial champion Tyson, shown here in an original oil painting. Tyson's official record: 8-240-1521. **Photo by The American Field Publishing Company.**

advantages offered by what the pedigree skeptics derogatorily dub as "fancy bloodlines," is their quickly identifiable field accomplishments.

Contrast this with the pup from several generations of unrecognizable forebears. With an absence of personal familiarity and no official records to indicate performance, the sum total of information on what sort of stock the puppy springs from is a big fat zero. Of course, his ancestors, even though uncelebrated, *may* have been very good hunting dogs; then, again, they may have been *duds*. The buyer of such a pup simply has no way of telling.

Going back to our "fancy bloodlines" offers a second advantage: a measurable indicator for both individual performance and prepotency—the ability to transmit similar good qualities to descendants. All of this information can be found in a detailed pedigree which lists certified field trial wins. In such a pedigree the official record of each ancestor is set down beside or underneath his name, in the form of three hyphenated numerals. These numbers indicate first, the individual's total field trial wins to date; second, how many winning offspring he or she has produced and, third, the number of field trial wins those offspring have accumulated so far.

For example, the figures: 19-168-608 would reveal that one particular dog had himself been a winner 19 times in field trial competition; had sired 168 puppies, who, themselves, had won a total of 608 placements in competition. A hypothetical example? Not at all, for it came, in fact, from the Field Dog Stud Book as the official record of the immortal English setter, Sports Peerless. And, should you think we've deliberately chosen a freakishly high record of individual performance and prepotency, just take a gander at the records of a couple of renowned English pointers: Ch. Spunky Creek Boy (25-231-1469) and Ch. Tyson (8-240-1521).

Thus, the strong quality inherent in the "fancy bloodlines" provides the buyer still a third advantage: greater probability of natural hunting potential in a puppy out of such breeding. The backing of this kind of field-proven ancestry considerably reduces the odds against your getting a pup that is woefully short of the necessary natural ingredients to become a fine performer in the hunting field. And if even the finest of championship bloodlines is not a gilt-edged guarantee against getting an occasional flop, how much greater must the odds be in choosing a pup from completely unknown breeding?

Of course, there is no disputing the importance of proper training in the ultimate making of any hunting dog; without it very few dogs ever live up to their full performance potentials. Yet, important as it is, even the best training can bring out only the inherited qualities that are there to be brought out.

MALE OR FEMALE?

The question of male or female puppy offers surprisingly small concern to a wide segment of the hunting dog buying public. Conventionally, the hunter about to choose a first gun dog shrugs off the idea that there's any decision to make where sex is involved. After all, he himself is male; his thinking is male; the average hunter is male; every dog he encounters — regardless of its sex — is referred to as "He," so what's to decide? Obviously, a male puppy is what he'll buy. Even the typical sportsman's wife supports this male-oriented thinking and generally opts without question for a dog of the masculine gender.

There are, of course, a good many reasons why you might select a male hunting dog. Ordinarily, males are bolder. They show greater physical endurance and tenacity. They can withstand rougher treatment and harsher training tactics. They exhibit considerably more independence and are not subject to the sometimes problematical twice-yearly heat periods that afflict the opposite sex.

Yet, it also should be pointed out that female canines usually possess more demonstrably affectionate natures and greater eagerness to please their owners. Since females also are more dependent, they generally accept training with greater willingness and, therefore, respond a little more readily than males to all the lessons that must be taught. And of course they are able to whelp a litter of puppies — a fact that can bring reproachful glances or joyful dances depending on the circumstances and degree of planning that preceded the blessed event.

But even though the hunter initially may not even be thinking of breeding this dog, the buyer should not bar that possibility from future

Most sportsmen automatically choose a male gun dog strictly out of habit. Females, however, offer many good qualities. The ability of a bitch to whelp a litter of pups — like the nursing Beagle below — is one of the obvious advantages.

Bitches, normally more sedate than dogs, often become increasingly tractable and affectionate after motherhood. Shoshone Princess Ruff, one of author's setters, was a typical example; on the right is her number one son, Shoshone Silver Rep, at 10 weeks.

consideration. Many a sportsman with a crackerjack gun dog will end up after two or three seasons wanting a junior version of the same. If he originally bought a female, or bitch as she is properly called, his breeding plans not only will be easier to effect but, nine times out of ten, will produce better results. The owner of a bitch can choose from any number of advertised, thoroughly tested and proven stud dogs, whose services are available at a fee, to sire the litter.

Conversely, the man who owns a young and uncelebrated male, no matter how gifted he may seem in his master's eye, has small chance of breeding him to a bitch of any renown. At best, he must usually settle for a "marriage of convenience" with some neighbor's pet that boasts of nothing more than the fact that she is of the same breed as the male.

Over and above her reproductive capabilities, a bitch offers other advantageous characteristics and benefits that, at least, under certain circumstances, might influence your choice in her favor. Besides her more tractable nature, the average female is smaller than the male of her breed, shaving his bulk and weight by as much as five to ten pounds and two to four inches in shoulder height. In a medium-large breed—the size of, say, the English setter—a typical field-type male of about fifty pounds and twenty-three inches high at the shoulder might prove to be a bit too much dog for some families. But the setter bitch, at roughly forty pounds and twenty-inch height, could well make the difference, where size and manageability were crucial considerations, between staying with your original preference and being forced to choose another breed, less desirable but smaller in stature.

The size differential between dog and bitch can also determine whether your hunting dog can conveniently become a close indoor companion or must be relegated to a kennel in the backyard. The more diminutive female, once housebroken, generally retains her ladylike manners with fewer slips than are likely from her opposite number. And the fact that a bitch's maternal instincts make her more protective than the male probably gives her a slight edge in the considerations of the family that still includes toddlers.

Overall, the only disadvantage of the female of the canine species, the single reason most buyers pass her up, is her semi-annual heat periods. These occur every six months and last for twenty-one days. These three weeks admittedly necessitate some extra care on the part of her owner, but the average female in heat does not present the burdensome difficulties some people believe she does.

Indoors or out, she must be confined and protected from potential Casanovas. The best insurance outdoors is a secure, covered kennel, the perimeter of which can daily be sprayed with one of the many commercially-made dog and cat repellents to discourage all animal visitors.

Protection and confinement is even simpler indoors, where the only problem encountered is the obvious one. Newspapers, spread on the floor of the one room to which she is restricted, offer an easy solution. Still another can be found in one of the harnesses or diaper-like accouterments specifically designed with disposable liners to alleviate the attendant complications. For all the fine qualities a female offers — her gentle nature and affectionate devotion—these few additional efforts seem a small price to pay.

But, if after carefully weighing the costs, you can honestly say that owning a bitch would still cause insurmountable difficulties, then, by all means, choose a male. No, I have not overlooked the fact that a bitch can be spayed—an operation that de-sexes her and eliminates the estral cycle. I simply do not advise or believe in spaying—and not for the reasons commonly cited: that spaying inevitably changes a bitch's disposition and leads to her becoming fat, indolent, and spiritless. In my experience, such results do not necessarily follow as direct effects of the spaying operation. (Rather, the combination of overfeeding, poor diet, and underexercise are responsible for the conditions usually ascribed to the operation.) I do not advocate sex alteration because, once done, it cannot be undone—often to the owner's later regret. Spaying is a safe, simple surgical procedure if performed during a bitch's puppyhood, but, unfortunately, it is ordinarily decided upon long before an owner has an opportunity to realize the potentialities of his bitch. There is a very real likelihood that he'll eventually want to breed her, and he will experience absolute frustration when he recognizes the finality of his premature decision.

In any event, whether you elect to buy a male or female pup, your mind should be firmly made up, and your decision irrevocable, *before* you visit a kennel to select your pup. For, unless you're psychologically prepared to face the additional responsibilities of being "father to a girl," picking out a lovable little female in a weak moment can prove to be mutually disastrous later on.

PUPPY OR TRAINED GUN DOG?

Is your choice to be a puppy or a trained hunting dog? In more than a decade as gun dog editor of a national magazine, I regularly received more reader inquiries on the subject than on any other single aspect of hunting dog ownership, save breed selection. The frequency of these requests for advice underscored not so much the common concern with the question itself, but the average novice's appalling lack of self-confidence in his ability to bring off a pup's training successfully.

The beginner, understandably, is apt to display a case of "buck fever" as he contemplates the job of turning a bouncing bundle of uncoordinated energy into an obedient, reliably serviceable, hunting field assistant. His anxiety can lead him to envisage dog training as a nightmarish project of mammoth proportions and unrelenting pressures, when actually it takes place in easy, unhurried stages over many months.

Training a puppy is a rewarding experience. But transforming these Brittany spaniels into finished gun dogs can't be accomplished without time, patience, and regular work. **Photo by American Brittany Club, Inc.**

Once he allows himself to be "psyched" into this frame of mind, any prospective gun dog owner will regard the training of a puppy as way beyond his capabilities. And so he will come to the hasty conclusion that buying an already-trained shooting dog is his only salvation. Numerous valid reasons can be cited for obtaining as your first hunting dog one that's already well-started, partially trained or fully-finished in his particular field specialty. But a baseless lack of confidence in your own ability to learn how to train a pup is certainly not one of them.

For the record, there is nothing mystifying or terribly difficult about the accepted techniques employed in successfully training any of the various types and breeds of hunting dogs. Nor are any special qualifications needed. If you are of at least average intelligence and normal temperament, physically sound and mentally stable, you should have no qualms about training your own hunting dog.

Far more significant than the concern over mastering the relatively cut-and-dried procedures of training, or the qualifications for the job, is a thoroughly realistic assessment of the time you can regularly and conscientiously devote to it. Transforming any hunting-breed puppy from a green, bubbly, potential-filled youngster into a polished, or at least functional, performer is never accomplished without the trainer contributing a great slice of time, patience, and perseverence.

But, neither is the process an endurance contest, with training accomplished through a giant burst of energy that overwhelms the pupil on a round-the-clock basis. In fact, fifteen- or twenty-minute sessions daily constitute an ideal training schedule, as long as the sessions are held to with regularity. A little every day over a long period is better than a great deal all at once.

Few sportsmen will experience difficulty maintaining such a regular routine; it is principally the man with a heavy travel schedule, irregular hours, considerable overtime, or an executive suite complex who will ordinarily find training a pup too problematical.

Aside from the time involved, training your own puppy requires some consideration of what facilities are available to you for conducting *all* of the training he must have. Although varying somewhat, depending upon the type and breed in question, much of the hunting dog's education can successfully be managed within surprisingly small training areas.

The accomplishments possible in the confines of the backyard should not be underestimated—especially when the numerous new training devices are combined with a bit of creative imagination. Backyard training has come a long way since Grandpa's day and is probably responsible for making gun dog ownership a practical possibility for so many of today's suburban sportsmen.

Nevertheless, a hunting dog's education can progress just so far without the opportunities to run, be exposed to, and make contact with game under natural hunting field conditions. It is an ancient but still valid proposition that the rabbit dog cannot attain proficiency until he has chased and learned the ways of the rabbit, or that the bird dog cannot live up to his name without knowing his quarry. So the hunting dog trainer must consider the accessibility of suitable open spaces where game—natural or stocked—is available to his dog. How close at hand are the open fields, the woods, the marshlands, the creeks and ponds, the places that hold the game you seek? How far must you and your pup travel to find them, and how often can you both visit them while he's in training? You alone will know or can uncover the answers and determine from them the feasibility of training your own puppy.

For many busy sportsmen, a trained shooting dog is the only practical answer. The Brittany shown here on point is Dual Ch. Belloaks Ibby, owned by Mrs. James B. Bell, Jr. **Photo by Morehouse.**

Should your answer be affirmative, you won't regret the time, patience, and effort put into the project. For bringing a pup along through all his schooling, with the tribulations as well as the moments of pride that accompany it, offers rewards that few other accomplishments can equal.

On the other hand, suppose that you are among that group of neophytes who, for a variety of reasons, decides that a trained shooting dog is the only way to go. This is not a decision that automatically brands you as inept. If, through lack of time or facilities, you can't justify undertaking the training of a puppy, then you're ahead of the game when you recognize reality and concentrate on buying a trained gun dog. This will, of course, require an initial outlay of cash substantially greater than even the best bred puppy would cost. Yet, the many and varied compensations of the trained shooting dog should more than outweigh the extra dollars spent.

Hunting dogs are customarily classified by the amount and progress of the training they have received afield — well-started, partly-trained or fully-finished, but regardless of their classification, all will offer very definite advantages over an untrained puppy. In fact, you can discount practically all of the chancy aspects generally associated with puppies when you purchase an older dog.

For openers, there's no puzzling over what the dog will look like; his size, physical development, coloring and characteristics, both good and bad, are apparent for the buyer to see, not wonder about or gamble on at the moment of purchase.

In addition, his health and physical condition are an important plus. If he is a fully or nearly matured dog, the chances of his contracting distemper or any of several other maladies often fatal to young, still growing puppies are largely eliminated. Having come safely through the period of highest mortality risk in the canine life cycle, he should, with continued proper care, live to a ripe old age, something that cannot always be guaranteed with a puppy.

Moreover, though it may seem inconsequential at first, it's often possible when buying an older dog to see some of the puppies he's sired. Nothing could prove a truer test of his merits as a stud dog for a possible breeding venture in the future.

Last, of course, is the most obvious advantage of all and your basic reason for choosing an older hunting dog—his training and field performance. This can vary, as previously mentioned, from well-started or partly trained to fully finished, depending on the dog's age and natural abilities, as well as on the man who's trained him. Often, even the classification terminology used to describe the degree of the dog's training progress will vary in accordance with the breed and geography involved.

Since the exact implications of each of these local variations may differ, it's always wise to get them spelled out by the trainer or kennel

Picking a puppy is always something of a gamble. What these 10-week-old English setter pups will develop into is anybody's guess. **Photo by Dave Petzal.**

owner before you begin any serious negotiations. This simple pre-caution will save needless heartaches and disappointment, to say nothing of irreconcilable argument, later on. Essentially, the buyer of a trained gun dog is offered three options, all of which are best outlined by means of specific examples. Taking pointing dogs, for instance, the three basic classifications can be illustrated as follows:

The well-started pointing dog should ordinarily be expected to hunt with enthusiasm, covering ground within the limits of his natural range, which may be close, medium, or wide. He should be hunting well enough to find at least a few birds—if they're present in fair numbers, and point and hold most of the tight-sitting ones long enough to indicate their presence. He also should show reasonable respon-siveness to basic directions from his handler and generally exhibit promise of developing his potentialities nicely as he gains additional experience. He'll vary in age from approximately nine to fourteen months.

The partly trained, or nearly broken pointing dog is ordinarily a notch or two further along in his training and performance. He should certainly do everything the well-started dog will do…and be just a bit better and more confident about it. When he finds birds, he should point and hold them staunchly, under most conditions, "bumping" only occasionally, and then seldom deliberately. His handler should be able to exercise fairly good control over him and demonstrate that the dog is essentially familiar with voice, hand, and whistle signals. The average age of this dog will be sixteen to twenty-two months.

Finally, the pointing dog described as fully trained or fully finished should be the "dog that does it all." With few pardonable exceptions, all his birds should be handled with the manners and confident effectiveness of the veteran performer. He should be able to find birds—especially planted ones—quickly and decisively, pointing and holding staunchly until the birds are flushed by the handler. He may or may not remain steady to wing and shot (that is, stand immobile as the bird is flushed and the shot is fired), depending on how he's been trained. Steadiness to wing and/or shot is an optional matter with every trainer; but, be certain to find out beforehand whether the dog is supposed to be steady so you can judge his performance accordingly.

In addition, the fully finished dog's responsiveness to all of his trainer's signals should be prompt and accurate at all times. The dog may retrieve downed birds, but fetching is not necessarily mandatory for the pointing breeds. Naturally, this kind of performer will have some age under his belt, averaging at least three years or older.

By no means, should the foregoing be considered absolute or rigid standards; they can and will differ from trainer to trainer, even when discussing the same type or breed of gun dog. And as the specifications or credentials of the trained gun dog differ, so too should the prices asked. Some rules of thumb on approximately how much you might expect to pay will be discussed in detail in a subsequent chapter, along with suggestions for locating and arranging purchase of precisely the kind of shooting dog you want.

For the moment, however, forget the cost factor; it has no place in your initial considerations of the decision to be made between puppy or trained hunting dog. For, if cost alone were to swing your otherwise logical choice from trained performer to raw recruit, your purchase of any hunting dog just might prove too premature. It would be far better in that case to defer buying a dog rather than to become involved in a situation certain to create frustration and unhappiness for all concerned—you, your family, and a pup whose chances at fulfillment of his natural heritage might be doomed from the start.

Aside from monetary considerations, the trained gun dog can be viewed as a sound and solid investment for any sportsman—even one who could objectively choose a puppy, instead. For the trained dog provides immediate dividends in hunting pleasure and at the same time acquaints his owner with the way an experienced gun dog performs. Perhaps, as has been said, you can't teach an old dog new tricks but if you're a new owner an *old* hunting dog can teach you plenty.

2

A Place to Live

CAN A GUN DOG BE A HOUSE PET?

WHERE YOUR HUNTING dog will live — indoors or out — may be dictated by circumstances over which you have no control. But having a choice and failing to recognize it can deprive you of a large part of the pleasurable companionship you and your gun dog can otherwise share year-round.

Of course, if you follow the example of some veteran owners, you'll elect to relegate your hunting dog to a kennel from one end of the season to the beginning of the next, never letting him set foot in the house, regarding him as little more than a canine hunting machine, and avoiding any close bonds of affection or real friendship with him.

The idea that a hunting dog belongs only in a kennel has prevailed for so many years that, even in this age of enlightenment, too many sportsmen still adopt without question the policy of keeping their dogs at arm's length, in the superstitious notion that fraternization spoils a gun dog's usefulness and efficiency in the field. Certainly, if that were true, most of our hunting breeds would have been ruined long ago.

Unquestionably, the earliest American settlers who were fortunate enough to count some kind of hunting dog among their valued belongings did not hesitate to share their meager digs with their dogs.

Most hunting dogs that are relegated to a kennel are denied house pet status solely by traditional misconceptions. **Photo by Dave Petzal.**

These animals helped not only to fill the larder but also to watch over and protect home, livestock, and family. And, if the frontier hunting dog's usefulness or efficiency had diminished from such close human association, he and his kind could not have survived long. In those trying times, anyone—human or animal—who couldn't pull his own weight was shunted aside or perished.

Perhaps the idea that man and his hunting dog should live apart from one another except during the chase sprang from the traditions of European nobility, who always maintained kennels to house hounds and spaniels that often numbered in the hundreds. But wherever and however the notion originated, it is sad that so many gun dogs today are needlessly denied the privileged status we so willingly give to virtually all non-sporting breeds, namely that of house pet and pal.

The premise that a hunting dog should never become a house pet is commonly supported by the belief that living indoors will ruin his nose; diminish his instincts and desire to hunt; make him fat, flabby, and lethargic; and promote contempt for obedience and mannerly behavior. But, a close inspection of the alleged results will show them up for what they are, either sheer poppycock or exaggerations that, with the exercise of a few simple precautions, are easily avoidable.

Consider, for instance, the possibility of ruining a hunting dog's nose simply by letting him live indoors. The idea makes just about as much sense as would the opposite proposal that keeping him outdoors will improve his scenting powers. Any dog's nose, or scenting ability, is as keen within the first few weeks after his birth as it will ever become. Nothing, other than the degenerative effects of serious disease or physically-inflicted injury can in any way alter the sense of smell he was born with.

Some observers may sincerely believe their dogs' noses improve with age, noting that they find game more frequently or easily than in seasons past. The natural assumption is that their dogs' scenting prowess has increased steadily over the years and will continue to grow stronger still. But in reality, all that has happened is that the dog has learned, through valuable experience in the field, to take more effective advantage of the scenting abilities he was blessed with at birth.

The only way to make a dog smell better, advises an ancient and wise adage, is to give him a bath. To that, we can add a modern postscript: keeping him in the house won't make him smell any different.

Almost equally nonsensical is the fear that a gun dog's instincts and naturally strong desire to hunt can be diluted by indoor living. Both the hunting inclination and the basic instincts that initially spark that urge are hereditary in all hunting breeds which stem from field-working parentage. And, even by denying an individual gun dog all opportunities to hunt, it would take countless generations — each one in turn kept from field work — to diminish even slightly the offsprings' naturally inherited instincts.

Plainly, then, no gun dog who is bred from proven field lineage and hunted several times a season will suffer the loss of his inbred love of the hunt merely because he shares his owner's home.

The third charge against keeping the gun dog indoors — that, as a pet, he'll inevitably become fat, flabby, and lazy — has at least some factual foundation. It can, and sometimes does, happen, but only when an owner is careless and permits it to happen.

Ordinarily, a dog puts on excess weight if he's fed too generously, either at regular meals or in between or both. He'll lose muscle-tone if he's not given proper daily exercise, he'll become lazy as a consequence of overfeeding and underexercising. Yet, none of these effects can be attributed solely to where he's quartered. Rather, they owe themselves strictly to the care given him by his owner. In other

It is easy to spoil your gun dog only if you neglect to learn the why's and wherefore's of proper care and discipline. Photo by Dave Petzal.

words, indoors or out, any dog will accurately reflect his owner's care and involvement. The marks of indifference and unconcern are just as often noted in the kennel dog as in the overindulged and poorly conditioned house pet.

Anyone can easily learn by trial and error to regulate the amount of food his dog requires. During hunting season, for instance, when your dog is out beating the brush for five or six hours at a clip a couple of times a week, he'll burn up energy far in excess of that provided by his normal ration. Obviously, a heftier daily meal will be needed just to keep him from losing weight too rapidly.

Later, during the off-season, he'll build up weight dramatically unless his portions are reduced, since the additional calories aren't being burned up through vigorous exercise in the field. If you make certain to feed your dog measured amounts, it will simplify the process of regulating the exact quantity he needs to keep in proper trim at any given time of the year.

But, diet is only part of keeping your gun dog in year-round condition; regular exercise assumes just as vital a role. Maintaining the proper balance between the two will enable your dog to remain healthy and in good shape no matter what the season, indoors or out. And, in fact, the house dog whose feeding and exercise regimen is conscientiously practiced will often put to shame his kennel-counterpart whose owner may be slipshod about these two vital responsibilities.

The final indictment against giving the hunting dog house pet status states that living indoors encourages contempt for obedience and mannerly behavior. But the real implication here is that the dog's owner—aided and abetted by the other members of the family—has fallen down on the job and become slovenly in enforcing normal discipline. Of course dogs, like children, will try to take advantage of you whenever they can get away with it. Any dog, if he feels testy, will seize upon the opportunity to disobey, and, once discovering he can ignore a command with impunity, react similarly to subsequent orders.

Naturally, then, it's entirely up to you to make your dog aware that you don't issue orders to him merely for vocal exercise. When you tell him to do something, make sure he does it immediately. Should he ignore the order, or follow it halfheartedly, go to him and firmly, but gently, physically enforce his compliance as you repeat the command once more. If you continually give orders and don't back them up, your dog soon will show his contempt by paying you no attention whatsoever...and that is guaranteed.

The line between kindness and overindulgence is set by the individual owner. From the look on this setter's face, the sofa would seem to be a "no-no" that will soon be reinforced by prompt punishment. **Photo by Dave Petzal.**

Often other family members are cited as the principal contributors to a house dog's delinquency; their tenderheartedness or inability to press discipline is blamed for undermining the dog's behavior. But, this sort of situation can be avoided, or at least mitigated, by the hunter who wisely resorts to a little psychology appropriately mixed with patience. Make it a point to involve every member of the family with your gun dog, impressing each one with the importance of the contributions they can make to the dog's overall well-being and ultimate performance. If you take the time to explain to the family how and why it's necessary to follow certain procedures and enforce discipline, you can foster in them a sense of sharing in the training and development of the dog. Then, instead of regarding him, with understandable indifference, as "the precious old hunting dog," everyone in the family can — and usually will — proudly claim him as their own.

Actually, when stripped of the superstitious half-truths and exaggerations, the case against making the gun dog a house pet really has very little substance. And the few minor inconveniences that accompany his presence indoors — brushing him more often to counter the shedding of his coat, brought on by warmer house temperatures; wiping his feet off after a walk in rainy weather — will soon seem inconsequential compared to the benefits his constant companionship affords.

How, for example, can one measure a little extra effort against the rewards of love, loyalty, and devotion: the slosh of a warm tongue across an owner's hand or youngster's chin, or the thumping of a merry tail on carpeted floor at the mere sound of your footsteps as you enter the house?

But even if sentimentality finds no place in your rationale, there are still practical advantages for the hunter who makes a house pet of a hunting dog. Only by living with your dog can you discover so many of the small personality traits that make him tick. Observing his little quirks, special mannerisms, and subtle reactions will often enable you to gain a quicker and deeper understanding of your dog, one that can save you hours, weeks, or, possibly months in formulating the most successful approaches to his future training in the field. Not a few seemingly unreachable pupils have responded only after their trainers took them out of the kennel and into the house for a while.

On average, the gun dog who shares the home of a conscientious owner will display a better rapport, be better understood and more disciplined than his counterpart who's kenneled the year round. And, in the final analysis, such a combination of significant factors is bound to affect the favorable quality of his performance in the field. So, if you have a choice, think it over carefully before deciding that your hunting dog *must* spend the rest of his days in a kennel.

THE BACKYARD KENNEL — A PROBLEM IN APPEARANCES

Not every owner can make a house pet of his gun dog. Some breeds are too large, some homes too small, and some owners too in love with interior decorating to make such a proposition even remotely feasible.

With no other option open, that handiest of facilities, the backyard kennel, suddenly becomes a life-saver. Without it, many a hunter, especially those in the suburbs, would have to forego hunting dog ownership entirely. And even if backyard kennel quarters are less desirable than a corner of his owner's home, the gun dog need not lead a forlorn existence, neglected and disassociated from those he loves.

Given ample regular exercise as well as frequent attention and affection, the kennel dog can live a comfortable, happy life, almost as full as that of his house-pet counterpart. So if the gun dog you purchase must be kept outdoors, you needn't feel guilty about his well-being unless you fall down in your responsibilities toward him.

Your first responsibility, of course, will be to provide him with a suitable kennel. Whether you build it yourself, hire someone to do it, or buy ready-made fence panels, the materials that go into your backyard kennel can vary as greatly as the design and dimensions you decide upon. Regardless of how large or small a run you erect — a factor mainly contingent on the breed involved — the materials used should be of the very best quality you can afford, selected to withstand years of weather and canine wear and tear.

The dog house you build or buy should also be designed and constructed to withstand the elements and provide shelter, spacious enough to stretch out in comfortably but sufficiently snug to be warmed efficiently by the dog's own body heat in cold weather.

*Stark and unsightly, the average backyard kennel stands out like a **sore thumb**, detracting from the appearance of home and property and comprising a legitimate source of annoyance to neighbors.* **Photo by Dave Petzal.**

Besides serving as permanent home to the dog who must be quartered outdoors, the backyard kennel frequently pinch-hits as a convenient part-time installation for the house-pet hunting dog, offering a handy, safe place in which to confine him securely during those hours when the family is away from home.

But although its practical value is indisputable, the average backyard kennel has one singularly glaring drawback: it is almost always unsightly. Standing out like a sore thumb, conspicuously detracting from the otherwise neat and tidy appearance of your home and property, it can also be a legitimate source of annoyance to neighbors. It's easy for the gun dog owner to become conditioned to the unsightliness of his backyard kennel. Yet his neighbors, who may not

With a bit of planning and imagination, the backyard kennel can be attractively concealed. Here, green canvas and cedar plantings plus an old-fashioned mail box make a neat job. **Photo by Dave Petzal.**

share or even understand an enthusiastic owner's love of dogs, deserve some degree of consideration.

Admittedly, it may initially seem impossible to make a bunch of six-foot fence posts and fifty feet of turkey-wire or chain-link fencing attractive. Yet by combining some thoughtful planning with a bit of creative imagination you can transform the average backyard kennel from an object of neighborhood scorn into a pleasingly decorative part of the natural landscape. Trees, shrubs, climbing vines or any growing greenery that can be employed naturally and artistically will camouflage the stark, unattractive outline of kennel fence posts and wire. Screened by such plantings, the backyard kennel can, at least, be less conspicuous and, at best, merge into near invisibility in the natural landscape of your property.

The less obtrusive you can make your outdoor dog enclosure, the better off you'll be, both from your own and your neighbors' viewpoint. Moreover, attractive concealment isn't the only advantage offered by natural landscaping. If, for instance, a line of thick shrubbery prevents looking into the enclosure, it also blocks the dog's outside view. The routine trafficking of neighbors, their children and pets, passing cars, delivery men, and the numerous other distractions that can send a dog into a frenzy of barking are effectively cut off from sight.

Such greenery also serves as a natural protective shield against the elements. In summer it provides cooling shade from the heat of the sun, and in winter, a buffer against biting winds, hail, and snow.

What type and how much landscape planting is called for will depend on the physical dimensions of your kennel, as well as on its position in the yard. For example, a small run situated just outside the back door between the house and an unattached garage might most easily be concealed by placing a trellis, with ivy or one of the other climbing vines, at either end.

A larger enclosure in the middle of the yard, with all four sides plainly visible, presents a more difficult problem in camouflage. Regardless of the type or amount of landscaping, such an ill-chosen site would make virtually any plantings look out of place. Relocating the run to a more suitable area of the yard would seem the easiest solution.

In general, the best location for a kennel run will be the corner of your yard. There, near the boundary, some form of hedge, shrubbery, or trees often exists as part of the original landscaping, setting off property lines and separating one yard from another. Taking advantage of this existing landscape not only saves time, work, and money, but also assures a more natural backdrop, against which supplementary plantings can be blended in artistically.

In many areas, property owners are required to maintain specified distances between any kind of structure and the property lines. Since these regulations vary widely, you should be sure to check your local zoning laws before planning your kennel run.

Longer view of the same kennel shows how effectively it's made to blend into near invisibility with the natural landscape. **Photo by Dave Petzal.**

For runs under six feet in height, such as might normally be used for beagles, bassets, cockers and some of the other smaller gun dog breeds, the flowering shrubs — mountain laurel, forsythia, hydrangea — can be used to good effect, either by themselves or in combination with smaller evergreens.

For the amateur horticulturist, camouflaging the backyard kennel can become a highly interesting project. For the rest of us, myself included, the helpful advice of a local nurseryman can always be solicited to plan and get the job done successfully.

In any event, should additional camouflage prove necessary, a few yards of waterproof cloth attached to the outside of the kennel's fence can work wonders. Ordinary military shelter-halves, the green-and-brown splotched variety obtainable in any army surplus store, make excellent supplementary blinders for the backyard kennel. And if they are wrapped around the entire enclosure, they'll also keep the dog from noticing and noisily reacting to outside distractions. The fact that they also provide effective wind-breakers adds still another bonus to their value.

There's almost no limit to the decorative, practical ideas you can come up on the subject of backyard kennel camouflage. And, even if it does involve expenditure of a few extra dollars, some time, and a little perspiration, you'll find the end results worthwhile. You'll have eliminated an eyesore; enhanced the appearance of your yard; added to your dog's comfort; and given every evidence that you're a considerate neighbor to those who live around you.

If you do select a corner location already planted with some trees or shrubs, you need be concerned only with camouflaging two sides of your dog's pen. Depending on the dimensions of the run you've planned, any number of variations in type and layout of landscaping, ranging from the simplest to the most ornate, are possible.

For example, such conifers as spruce, pine, or cedar, planted in a gentle arc around the two exposed sides of the run, form one of the most attractive designs imaginable. And, if the evergreens you buy are at least kennel-top high, they'll provide camouflage that will prove effective all year round. Check the maximum height to which these trees will grow, though. You may not want a small forest at that particular spot.

Part II

A Choice of Breeds

3

The Breeds That Point

THE ENGLISH SETTER

SPORTSMEN CAN ALMOST always find something to argue about—the best shot size for ruffed grouse, bucktails versus streamers for big trout, the toughest station at skeet—but there's one thing, at least, that seldom draws fire from any outdoorsman. Almost all will agree that the most dramatically exciting moment in hunting is that split-second when a slashingly fast bird dog suddenly skids into an intensely stylish point!

Seen once or a thousand times, it's a picture-moment that never fails to thrill, a sight that speeds the heartbeat, stokes the spirit, and refreshes the senses.

Of the nine or so breeds that instinctively point their game, none is more classically representative in this traditionally majestic stance on birds than the English setter. And, certainly, none embodies more harmoniously the hearthside qualities of companionable devotion and gentle temperament with the zesty spirit and unquenchable hunting desire so admirable in the field.

Staunch devotees of rival pointing breeds may dispute his bird-finding superiority over their own particular favorites, but most acknowledge, however grudgingly, that the setter's beauty and warmly affectionate nature are in a class by themselves.

Over many long years, the English setter has been the preferred pointing breed for the uplands in the upper half of the nation. In the tangled coverts that are home to the ruffed grouse and part-time residence to the transient woodcock, the setter is less a tradition than an institution. But, then, one look at his credentials reveals why.

The long-haired coat he sports is made-to-order protection for long hours of work amidst the typically dense, often thorny woodland edges of the north country. It also provides just the right amount of insulation against the mostly chilly and sometimes frigid weather common to the higher latitudes. And the fact that his coat is predominantly white makes him highly visible, whether moving or immobile on point, in the dim light of the alder swamps and shadowy evergreen thickets.

A strongly inborn pointing instinct, sensitive nose and predilection for close cover work—talents he comes by naturally—are absolute necessities for the job of finding and holding the usually cooperative woodcock and the always unpredictable grouse. Then, too, the close relationship he customarily establishes with his owner doubtless accounts for his willingness to constantly check back and keep in frequent touch with his boss during the hunt.

Traditional pointing breed favorite of America's northern upland bird covers, the English setter is unexcelled for stylish field work, close companionship and good looks.

As might be suspected, a breed with such qualifications did not develop by accident or overnight. The exact origin of the English setter is impossible to pinpoint, but at least there's never been a dearth of educated guesses about how and approximately when the breed began. Some conjecturers contend that the setter originated from a blend of cross-matings of the Spanish pointer, the large water spaniel and the springer spaniel, about two hundred years ago. Others place his origin two centuries before that, claiming that the setter had his roots in and was a natural outgrowth of the land spaniels, dogs that were known to have been around at least as early as the last quarter of the fourteenth century.

This latter school of thought points to the evidence contained in *Le Livre de la Chasse* (The Book of the Hunt), a book written in 1387 by Gaston de Foix, a French nobleman with an all-consuming interest in the joys of the hunt. Not only does the book discuss the land spaniels — whose job it was to flush or spring game for pursuit by the huntsman's hawks and falcons — but it also mentions the existence of a type of "setting" spaniel.

Further documentation is found in another volume, *Of Englishe Dogges,* penned by Dr. John Caius in 1570. In that work, the author details the technique used by the "setting" spaniels, making clear the fact that such dogs stopped and lay belly to the ground to indicate the nearness of game. At that point (no pun intended) the hunters threw or spread nets over the game's place of concealment.

The pointing instinct is generally conceded to be a natural, momentary pause taken by an animal — cats are an obvious example — just before springing on its prey. Thus, it would seem logical that selective breeding of only specific land spaniels who showed marked tendency to prolong this natural pause created an intensification and refinement of the pointing or "setting" instinct described in the old writings.

However diverse the opinions on the precise origin and age of the English setter, most authorities give the major credit for development of the modern setter to Edward Laverack, a wealthy Englishman of the nineteenth century.

In fathering the development of the modern English setter, Laverack, around 1825, obtained from the Reverend A. Harrison of Carlisle a pair of so-called "pure" English setters named Ponto and Old Moll. Reportedly, by means of an amazing — but still openly questioned — program of inbreeding, Laverack produced from them a strain bearing his name which later attained international reputation.

Gentle, warmly affectionate and deeply devoted, the English setter personifies the universal image of the outdoorsman's dog.

The Laveracks were certainly responsible for stimulating increased interest in, and further development of, what has come to be the present-day English setter. However, the fact is frequently overlooked that many of Laverack's less celebrated contemporaries also contributed significantly, if quietly, to that same foundation stock.

One of the major breakthroughs in setter breeding in England, in the 1860's, was the Duke-Rhoebe-Laverack cross. From this mixture, a Welshman named R. L. Purcell Llewellin obtained the basic stock with which to implement a strain — later to bear his name — of redoubtable field trial setters.

Although full credit for originating this strain, which pummelled all competition in British field trials, is invariably attributed to Mr. Llewellin, it more rightfully should go to Barclay Field, Sir Vincent Corbett, and Thomas Statter, the gentlemen who produced the original foundation stock.

The history of setter breeding, however, is less than reliably accurate in the days before the founding of the Kennel Club in England, in 1873, and initiation of its stud book a year later. Earlier, the veracity of pedigrees was open to serious debate. Authorities, both past and present, have suggested that breeders of that era were not above occasional surreptitious use of non-setter blood to freshen their stock. And, of course, it was known fact that Irish, Gordon, and Russian setter crosses were not uncommon in establishing some English setter strains. Statter's Rhoebe, a pillar of the early Llewellins, was herself a half Gordon, half English setter cross.

Inauguration of the Kennel Club's stud book, in 1874, made possible the recording of authentic, certified pedigrees from which the English setter's modern history can be meaningfully traced.

During the next decade, setters of the Llewellin strain were imported to the United States by the gross. In this country they met with widespread, often fanatic, public favor, proliferated, and were the basis for today's field-type American English setter. But the Llewellins' initial acceptance, although extensive, was far from unanimous; in some areas, competition of the highest caliber was provided by the native American setters, most renowned of which were the Gildersleeves, Morfords, Ethan Allens, and Campbells.

The native and Llewellin setter factions clashed decisively in a field trial battle shortly after the Llewellins began arriving in this country. Joe, Jr., representing the finest of the Campbell natives, was matched against Gladstone, cream of the American Llewellins, in a grueling two-day trial staged on December 15 and 16, 1879.

At the conclusion of the contest—judged solely on the number of quail each dog pointed—Joe, Jr., vanquished Gladstone, with a bird-score of 61 to 52. Maybe the native setter fanciers proved their point, but the Llewellin's popularity continued its upward surge, just the same.

So many setters of note, Llewellins and natives alike, left their mark on the present day field-type English setter in America, that it would take a separate book to compile a complete list of them. But, we'd be remiss not to include mention of a few of the indisputable stars recognized by all setter buffs: Gladstone, Count Noble, Ruby's Dan, Count Gladstone (who won the first National Bird Dog Championship held here in 1896) Eugene T., Rodfield, Feagin's Mohawk Pal (the only setter ever to win the National Championship three times) Phil Essig, Sports Peerless, Florendale Lou's Beau, Nugym and Mississippi Zev.

The English setter of yesteryear unquestionably held title as top pointing dog all over America, but today's setter must continually fight for the crown, even in his northern stronghold, against his most formidable rival, the English pointer. In fact, if major circuit field trial wins were the only measure by which to decide the issue, the setter

Working his birds by means of airborne body scent, the English setter zeros in on his quarry and assumes a rigid pointing stance to indicate the bird's presence and location.

would come in a low second. For some of the very qualities that most endear him to sportsmen as a good shooting dog and companion seem opposed to the standards of extreme range, super speed, and early maturity sought in the ideal, big-circuit field trial prospect today. Happily, at least for the setter and his steadfast supporters, field trial wins represent but a single jewel in a crown made up of many.

Probably the real strength of the English setter's inherent appeal springs from the balance he strikes between highly stylish and sheerly practical hunting field performance. Getting the game in the bag—the end result of the hunt—is the strictly practical measure of any pointing dog's merits. Some pointing breeds earn full marks in this respect, but they give the hunter little or no thrill in the way they work. Others, most specifically the English pointer, achieve essentially the same results but do so with often breathtakingly brilliant style. Some-

where between the two is the happy medium that usually characterizes the average setter's work in the field.

In performing his job the setter seeks to find birds and indicate their
presence and approximate location to the gunner by assuming a rigid
pointing stance. Quartering the cover ahead, he searches the breeze
for a whiff of airborne scent, zeros in on the source and then stops,
immobile in his tracks, awaiting the gunner's arrival to flush and shoot
the quarry.

Retrieving is not necessarily one of the setter's inborn talents. Some
individuals exhibit a strong natural instinct to fetch downed birds, but
others apparently couldn't care less, losing all interest once they
know the bird is dead. These dogs can, of course, be force-trained to
retrieve, or at least to point "dead." Either procedure will help salvage birds downed in heavy cover that might otherwise be lost to the
bag and needlessly wasted.

The setter's range and pace vary from close and fairly slow to
medium-wide and moderately fast. What type of setter you obtain depends primarily on the geography, cover, and game birds prevalent in
the region in which he is bred, raised, and trained. Yet, while he is a
specialist on ruffed grouse and woodcock, there are few upland birds
he cannot learn to handle successfully.

Most English setters obtained from good field-proven ancestry display an early desire to hunt, along with a well-developed pointing
instinct. The pointing instinct often displays itself almost as soon as a
setter puppy is able to waddle around. It's not unusual, in fact, to
watch six-week-olds abruptly quit playing in their kennel yard and
begin stalking a butterfly, grasshopper, or other insect slowly moving
across the ground. Often, when the "quarry" pauses, you'll see the
pup freeze on a solid and sometimes very stylish sight-point.

Nor is sight-pointing limited only to young pups. Joji, a male setter
I owned some years ago, made a lifelong game out of sight-pointing.
When he was still a pup, it was accidentally discovered that a flashlight beam drawn slowly across the floor could stiffen Joji into a point
every time. The more enticingly the light-spot was maneuvered, the
more stylishly intense were his points, and hours spent amusing ourselves with the flashlight only whetted his appetite for more. Long
years in the field, where he found and handled many a grouse, woodcock, ringneck, and quail, never diminished his love of our little
flashlight game.

Training and discipline, if given patiently and in good spirit, will be accepted willingly by the average setter, who, by virtue of his naturally affectionate, gentle temperament, normally strives to please the owner he reveres. Although he's not so sensitive that he can't take occasional harsh punishment—when he understands that it's deserved —a firm but gentle form of discipline ordinarily gets more consistent responsiveness from him.

When physically mature, at about eighteen months of age, the field-type English setter will stand approximately twenty-one to twenty-five inches high at the withers (the highest point of the dog's shoulders). His weight will range from about forty-three to fifty-three pounds, depending on his physical condition. (Unlike the field setter, the bench-bred variety is ordinarily a more sizeable dog, often weighing as much as sixty-five pounds and standing as high as twenty-six inches at the withers.)

In color, the field setter's long-haired coat should be basically white —for greater visibility—and flecked or patched with black, black and tan, lemon, orange, chestnut, or russet markings. His legs and his long, finely tapered tail are well fringed with hair, commonly known as "feathering."

In the United States, the breed is officially sponsored by the English Setter Association of America, a member breed club of the American Kennel Club. While most bench setters are registered with the A.K.C., working field setters usually are entered in the Field Dog Stud Book, the registry organization of the American Field Publishing Company of Chicago, Illinois.

Shoshone Ghost Dancer, the author's fifteen-month-old setter, racks up in classic style on a single Bobwhite quail.

Displaying the fire, intensity and style on point that makes him the indisputable number-one pointing breed in America, this English pointer nails down a covey of bobwhite quail.

THE ENGLISH POINTER

Pick a handful of the dozen or so requisites that comprise the most stringent standard set for the ideal bird dog—speed, style, stamina, intensity, natural bird sense—and you'll have a reasonably accurate, if incomplete, composite of the English pointer, the top pointing breed in America today.

Toss in about five more traits considered essential, such as range, pace, amenability to training, early development and indomitable spirit, and you can begin to understand why the pointer justly deserves the reputation of "the professionals' bird dog." Once contestable, there's no longer room for argument that the pointer has become number-one choice of the pros, the trainers and handlers who make their reputations and livelihoods largely on the number of major field trial placements their canine pupils accumulate every season.

The pointer's ability to win more field trials than any other pointing breed is beyond dispute. Skeptics and chronic gamblers might be well advised to go to the records before sounding off or making any rash wagers. And such impressive records as they will find were not, as might well be imagined, easily come by.

For many years the pointer, both in England and the United States, was obscured by the monumental shadow of the overwhelmingly popular English setter. Long after the world's first field trial took place in England in 1865, pointers could not even obtain the right to run in competition with their long-haired contemporaries. Reasoning that such field contests would have been far too one-sided in favor of the setters, sportsmen of that day were unshakable in their insistence on maintaining separate stakes.

Unsportsmanlike as it might seem to us today, such discrimination was in all probability a blessing *and* actually helped the pointer breed in two vital ways. Most importantly, it did spare the early pointers — many of them, at any rate — the ignominy of being drubbed unmercifully in the field by the generally far superior setters of the time. But even more significant, denial of the opportunity at least to try to compete with the high-class setters so rankled pointer men, that it spurred them to greater heights of determination to improve the hunting talents of their breed.

"Beat the setters" became more than just a high-spirited motto; it was, in fact, an obsession, an end toward which the majority of pointer breeders and fanciers labored unstintingly. And, though it may pain the steadfast setter man today to concede the pointer's annexation of the field trial crown, he cannot help but express sincere admiration for a bird dog that has fought terrific odds to prove himself. And that admiration extends as well to the persevering and dedicated men whose unswerving faith in the pointer's ability made such a climb possible.

The pointer, some authorities insist, originated in Spain at some time close to the start of the seventeenth century. The fact that dogs strongly resembling the pointer were pictured in oils by French artists very early in that century would seem to raise at least some doubt about the breed's exclusively Spanish origin. But, if the country of the pointer's birth is uncertain, so too are the theories as to how the breed first developed. Most popularly accepted, and apparently most rational, is the belief that the pointer evolved from one or more varieties of hound — foxhound, greyhound, and bloodhound, which were

Retrieving isn't the pointer's long suit, but many take to it naturally. Those that don't can be force-trained to fetch. **Photo by Sportsmens Service Bureau.**

crossed with the "setting spaniels."

However, the scene of the breed's ultimate refinement into the recognizable pointer we take afield today is clearly evident in his official designation, English pointer. Many of the men whose names are found among the relatively small nucleus of pioneering breeders of the pointer in England—names such as Thomas Statter, Sir Vincent Corbet and J. Armstrong—were the same men who contributed significantly to the improvement of the English, Irish, and Gordon setter breeds of the middle and late nineteenth century. And though perhaps there is not a spark of basis in fact, this dual association gave rise to the suspicion that some of the best setter blood of that time was unceremoniously pumped into the pointer to bring him closer to the standards of malleable temperament and good field performance displayed by the English gun dog breeds of the day.

The four dogs considered to be cornerstones in the ancestry of the modern English pointer were Brockton's Bounce, Statter's Major, Whitehouse's Hamlet, and Garth's Drake. These four were dogs of exceptional field prowess who were bred to extensively, and whose influence can still be seen in many pointers today both here and in England.

Probably the most famous of the early pointer imports to America, in the late 1870's and early 80's were Croxteth, King of Kent, Beppo III, and Mainspring, each of which holds the distinction of having established long lines of eminently successful field trial and shooting dog families here.

From such great dogs as Rip Rap (sired by King of Kent) and Jingo (sired by Mainspring), whose blood was later intermingled through the matings of many of their sons and daughters, sprang pointers of the type capable of competing with the long-haired bluebloods that, at that time, still ruled the field trials.

Though a pointer did not win the National Championship until Manitoba Rap accomplished this feat in 1909, the breed's true potential was fast becoming obvious right after the turn of the century, in the form of such dogs as Fishel's Frank and Alford's John. It was, in fact, a combination of this blood that produced the two pointer dogs generally credited with marking the real turning point for the breed's ascendancy to the field trial crown. Both Commanche Frank and John Proctor, sons of Fishel's Frank out of daughters of Alford's John, copped the National Championship in 1914 and 1916 respectively. Since the latter date, setters have won the National only seven times; pointers have claimed all the rest of the honors, indicative that the breed must have been doing something right.

It is fortunate for the bird hunter that many of the qualities that have helped the pointer push into the field trial limelight also contribute to his desirability as a high-class shooting dog capable of working practically all species of upland birds. His general style and hunting technique are similar to the English setter's, with the two exceptions being found in the pointer's usual tendency to range wider and run more speedily than the average setter. This speed and ranginess, plus the natural affinity for warm weather that his short-haired coat provides, ideally suits him for the work that has become his stock in trade: locating coveys of bobwhite quail in the fields of the sprawling southern plantation country.

Of course he has often proved his versatility in other parts of North America, handling the wily ring-necked pheasant, the tight-sitting woodcock and the toughest bird of all—the ruffed grouse. Equally significant are his capability on such northern prairie species as the sharptail grouse and the Hungarian partridge, birds whose natural habitat in the rolling cultivated grain fields of the region enables a hunter to take full advantage of the pointer's speed and big-going tendencies.

For the gunner who's long on results but short on time and patience, the pointer could hardly prove more ideal. He has an intense love of hunting—it is imbued so strongly in the breed that he will hunt for

Pointers seldom suffer from stern training methods, but patience and kindness are preferred in order to establish the kind of performance this stylish dog exhibits.

almost anyone carrying a shotgun — and he tends to develop early in the field. Both these qualities allow his education to progress without undue consequences no matter how fast an imprudent trainer endeavors to bring him along. Though it can be disastrous for many another breed of bird dog, a certain amount of mishandling by the amateur seldom retards a good pointer.

Nor does the breed seem to suffer at all from the somewhat sterner methods often used in bringing him under proper control. In fact, it's fortunate that he is not endowed with a soft, sensitive nature or "thin skin," as some trainers phrase it, for his exceptional spirit, energy, and drive in the field frequently require application of more drastic discipline to direct them properly into thoroughly polished performance.

Retrieving, considered by most hunters to be a requisite for a fully-finished gun dog, is hardly the pointer's long suit. Some take to fetching naturally, but force-training to retrieve usually produces the most consistent results with the average pointer.

Despite his increasing favor above the Mason-Dixon line in recent years, the probability is slight that the pointer can ever displace the English setter in the game coverts of the northland. Abilities aside, the pointer's shorthaired coat, for one thing, gives him insufficient protection against the sudden immoderate cold snaps often experienced late in the upland bird seasons up north. For another, his coat can't compare to the long-hair's for warding off the punishment of some of the heavier covers encountered in quest of northern pheasants, grouse, and woodcock. The pointer seldom lacks in "heart," and most pointers will plunge full tilt into even the most rugged of these covers, yet no hunter could be callous enough to ask a repeat performance after once witnessing the slashing job such wicked covers can do on the relatively unprotected hide of a short-haired dog.

The foregoing should not be construed as a total condemnation of hunting a pointer up north. As long as good judgment is exercised, with regard to avoiding especially harsh weather and cover, the pointer will more than hold his own in any latitude.

Some pointers make good pets. But it must be borne in mind that the term "pet" means different things to different persons. The majority of pointers cannot be classified as the same kind of pet as, say, a dog of the spaniel type. Generally bold, independent, and brimming over with spirit, the pointer is nearly always friendly. But, seldom can he be said to give or demand much more than token affection. A kind word or a pat of approval usually are sufficient to his emotional well being, and for these he, in turn, will trade a brief flurry of tail wagging and, perhaps, a whine or two of delight at seeing you.

As with every rule or generality, though, there is the inevitable exception. We have run across a few individual pointers whose affectionate natures could not be outdone by any breed. Sally, a big-running, hard-hunting pointer bitch who belonged to a shooting-preserve-owner friend of ours, was the most demonstratively loving pointer we have ever seen.

Put in a kennel after an arduous day's work on ringnecks, she'd sometimes howl the walls down, refusing to eat or take water or even lie down to rest her weary muscles. Only if her boss either got right in the kennel, reassuring her with lots of sweet talk and gentle stroking, or brought her into the kitchen—which was her real goal, just a step from the living room—would she cease her mournful serenade. Once indoors, her appetite and thirst miraculously returned, along

A shorthaired coat that adapts him to hot weather, plus a fast pace and generally wide range make the pointer an ideal bird dog for quail hunting in the South.

with normal signs of fatigue. But sleep would come only with what she considered her full and proper ration of loving, a commodity that finally induced her to curl up at her boss's feet.

Gone now, to the place where all good bird dogs must go eventually, old Sally is still fondly recalled as the only pointer we ever knew with the disposition of a lap dog.

Clean-lined, lithe, and powerful, with the stamina to go all day reflected in his sturdy but streamlined frame, the pointer is a large dog, weighing as much as seventy pounds and usually averaging close to sixty. Most dogs stand about twenty-four to twenty-six inches at the withers; bitches stand an inch or two shorter. Predominantly white, the pointer's short-haired coat is patched or ticked with liver, orange, lemon, or black secondary coloring.

Official sponsor of the breed in the United States is The American Pointer Club, a member breed club of the American Kennel Club. Pointers of bench lineage are usually registered with the A.K.C., while those of field breeding are registered in the Field Dog Stud Book, the registry of the American Field Publishing Company of Chicago, Ill.

Few men who have trod the uplands behind a good English pointer for a couple of seasons will ever be heard to complain about not getting their share of birds. And on the rare occasion when light game pockets provoke displeased mutterings, it's a fair certainty such grumbles are more traceable to slumping marksmanship than to poor dog work. In fact, when it comes to any question of their dogs' abilities, pointer men understandably are the last to raise it, and the first to fight it.

Perhaps the most classic concession we've ever heard uttered by a pointer man was one that most appropriately reflected the superior talents most pointer devotees ascribe to the breed. The remark was delivered in a Catskill Mountain hunting lodge by an old timer being kidded unmercifully about his and his pointer's failure to bring home a grouse in the midst of plenty.

"I'm ashamed to admit, men," the old gentleman said, dejectedly, "but, that fool dog of mine really fouled up, today. Could have left him home, for all the good he did. Sure, he found five or six grouse all right ...pointed and held 'em all, nice and stylish...but, you know, ever since I moved him down from 20-gauge to .410, he can't snap-shoot worth a damn!"

Exhibiting more style than most members of his breed, Ch. Adam von Feuhrer-heim, owned by Robert H. McKowen of Leacock, Penna., is a prime example of the dual bench and field type members of the breed. Photo by GSP Club of America.

THE GERMAN SHORTHAIRED POINTER

No pointing breed comes closer to fitting the real sense of the term "practical" than does the German shorthaired pointer.

However, don't immediately toss the book aside and, shouting "Hooray," race right out to buy a shorthair, confident that you now know which is the·one breed that will answer all your needs. It may very well be the shorthair; then again, it may not.

If your major gun sport is found in the expansive stretches of southern quail country, or in the wide, rolling grasslands that harbor the Hungarian partridge, the sharptail, and the sage grouse, then the German shorthaired pointer would doubtless prove a poor choice. Conversely, should your hunting world consist of ringnecks, grouse, and woodcock, and a mixture of small fields, swamps, and woodland pockets, the shorthair might be the finest thing that ever happened to you.

A veritable workhorse in the right cover and terrain, the shorthair is a practical pointing breed fully deserving of the description "meat dog." An onerous label in its original usage, the term as presently applied is complimentary. For the "meat dog" of today is the one who brings home the bacon, without letting any of it go to waste. The shorthair does this to perfection in the job that calls upon him to find, point, and, once the feathers disperse, retrieve promptly to hand the game birds his owner seeks. A tireless, dependable, close-working hunter of generally modest pace, he is far less concerned with displaying flashy style than in demonstrating a thorough, business-like dedication to productive results for the gun.

He is big and friendly...and he is rugged. Not many breeds, including even the fairly "thick-skinned" English pointer, can match his ability to take in stride the mistakes and often rough-and-tumble training methods employed by an over-anxious and unsophisticated handler. Yet because his feelings are not easily ruffled, he can general-ly stand the gaff—the shouting, the hacking—from an intemperate trainer without losing his instinctive devotion to his hunting job.

The breed reportedly had its beginning in Germany, as its name implies, about three hundred years ago. Most authorities and research-ers agree that the German pointers sprang essentially from the origi-nal Spanish pointer, a basic breed that had spread pretty well over the European continent by the early years of the seventeenth century. Beyona that fundamental fact, however, agreement about the German breed's early, and even later, development is rare.

There seems little doubt that somewhere along the way the Spanish pointers in Germany were crossed with hounds. Some historians con-tend that bloodhounds were used; others opt for the belief that it was really the St. Hubert hounds that contributed to the first German pointers. In any event, the early members of the developing breed showed improvement over the Spanish pointer but were still con-sidered to be too ponderous, slow-working, and lacking in nose when the era of wingshooting with firearms replaced hunting with nets and falcons.

Birds, although a significant quarry at the time, were not the sole interest of the seventeenth-century German hunter. He looked then, as now, for utility in his hunting dog. This criteria demanded a dog which, above all, has a fine nose, to find and point birds; he also wanted ability to retrieve from land or water, strong trailing instincts, for tracking large and small game animals, and sufficient courage and

Big, friendly and rugged, that's the shorthair. He seldom loses his "cool," no matter how many mistakes his owner may make. **Photo by Dave Petzal.**

sharpness to tackle and dispatch vermin and predators.

Still dissatisfied with the German pointer, the breeders of the 1860's continued experimenting with additional crosses. One of these was with the English pointer, which some researchers insist was used primarily to strengthen the German breed's scenting prowess, while others credit, besides nose, additional speed and pointing instinct as major contributions. Suspected, but never documented, crosses with setters may also have been made during the later years of breed development, adding perhaps a bit more point and gentility to what was pretty well-established, by the start of the twentieth century, as the modern German shorthaired pointer.

Something less than a standing ovation greeted the first shorthairs brought to the United States, in the mid-1920's. Regarded as essentially a novelty breed, they stirred little more than the usual brief flurry of interest accorded all curiosities. Chief stumbling blocks to the breed's initial acceptance here were American gunners' objections to its comparatively restricted range and slow, methodical pace. By comparison with the lively-running, stylish-hunting pointers and setters favored here, the newly imported shorthair's work was considered to be distinctly lackluster. To offset this stigma, the breed's backers bent assiduously to the task of producing dogs of increased speed and wider range. They did achieve a measure of success in these efforts, popularizing the shorthair as a bird dog, but they sacrificed some of the utility qualities for which the breed had originally been developed.

To be sure, the shorthair is still one of our most adaptable breeds, capable, if so trained, of serving the gun in a variety of functions. Nevertheless, it has been toward the bird-pointing specialization that the vast majority of his boosters have concentrated their attention.

As a bird dog, the shorthair cannot be considered a dazzling stylist. First of all, his physical structure—one of rather large frame and solid build—precludes his sustaining more than modest speed. Moreover, the hound blood coursing his veins still manifests its influence in the frequent tendency to rely too heavily on foot scent rather than the aerial or body scent by which the flashier bird dogs locate their quarry. And following foot scent means that the shorthair must run not only with his head carried low, but also at a slower pace.

This trio of shorthairs is eager to begin the hunt. Good nose, modest range and pace, as well as business-like dedication to his job, qualify the shorthair as a highly practical gun dog.

Yet, whatever he lacks in style, this practical pointer recoups in sheer determination and stamina. His slower way of going conserves a storehouse of energy that stretches itself nicely over the long, all-day hunt. And the legacy of a sensitive set of olfactories is something he applies with a thoroughness that invariably enables him to work out the most complex scent trails left by running birds.

He is especially esteemed by the gunner whose preference for a relaxed, unhurried hunt also extends to a casual, informal style of dog handling. Such a man can revel in the leisurely enjoyment of a close-working dog that requires scant formal direction from the gun. And should the shorthair inadvertently bump a bird, as can happen in any hunt, the error will customarily occur close enough to the gun to permit at least a reasonably fair shot at the flush.

Once downed, a bird seldom escapes or goes to waste unfound. For besides the shorthair's natural affinity for retrieving, his aforementioned knack for unraveling ground scent can usually be relied upon to produce even the best concealed cripple, and save him for the bag.

Highly subservient to the gun, the shorthair can, with a minimum of skillful formal training, be expected to turn in at least a very serviceable performance on birds. When astutely trained, to take maximum advantage of his adaptability and intelligence, a good shorthair comes about as close as is possible to that elusive ideal, the "all-around" shooting dog. Few American sportsmen have taken the time to put him through the kind of training required to develop and refine the full measure of his versatility.

Perhaps the best indication of the breed's talent as a "specialized" specialist can be found in the fact that he has become the number-one breed choice of commercial shooting preserve operators across the nation. In the generally restricted range and leisurely paced type of gunning most typical of the small-to-medium-size, pay-as-you-go shooting preserves, the shorthair is accepted and recognized as the ideal breed. In addition to his close-working and natural retrieving propensities, the shorthair's greatest asset to the preserve operator is the ease with which he can be handled.

Big as the German shorthaired pointer is—dogs stand as high as twenty-five inches at the withers and weigh up to seventy pounds— he has a mild disposition and an extremely even temperament. With strangers he is tolerantly friendly, if somewhat aloof, reserving his most demonstrative feelings strictly for his loved ones. Thus, only his size could possibly mitigate against accepting him as a house pet in some smaller households. Yet, if space poses no problem, the owner of a shorthair really misses out on a wealth of companionship, to say nothing of the benefits of an alert, loyal and highly effective watchdog, if he relegates his dog to a kennel.

Liver and white are the only colors acceptable in the shorthair, but they can be found in any of several combinations: solid liver; liver and white spotted; liver and white spotted and ticked; and liver and white ticked. His short-to-medium-length coat enables him to adapt well to all but the most extreme climates and makes grooming a quick and easy job. His docked tail (a simple and virtually painless operation performed a couple of weeks after birth) eliminates the hazards — carelessly slammed house or car doors and accidental tromping underfoot — that sometimes afflict the longtailed breeds.

The German Shorthaired Pointer Club of America, a member breed club of the American Kennel Club, officially sponsors the breed in the United States. As with most of the hunting breeds, the bench show registry for the shorthair is the A.K.C., while working field dogs ordinarily are entered in the American Field Publishing Company's Field Dog Stud Book. Many shorthairs, because of the dual interest encouraged by supporters of the breed, are registered in both the A.K.C. and F.D.S.B.

Keen, alert and intelligent, the shorthair is almost always eager to learn the lessons that will transform him into not only a highly practical gun dog, but a well-behaved, intensely loyal member of the family as well.

A setter without a tail . . . a springer that points? Neither. It's a Brittany spaniel, the only member of the spaniel clan that points rather than flushes its game. This is Fld. Ch. King Star, owned by A. R. Knowles. **Photo by American Brittany Club, Inc.**

THE BRITTANY SPANIEL

What man hasn't pondered the question, "Why so many brands of shaving cream, when they all give the same end result?"

Certainly, many a sportsman has worked himself into a lather trying to figure out the answer to a parallel question on the subject of pointing breeds.

And probably no more graphic example of the logical answer—and the reasons that spell it out—can be found than in the Brittany spaniel, the only member of the spaniel family that points rather than flushes game for the gun. Like all pointing dogs, the Brittany hunts by quartering the cover ahead of the gunner, inhaling the breeze for bird scent and, once his game is located, assuming a solid pointing posture that alerts the hunter to the bird's presence and approximate position. After the flush and successful shot, the Brittany will, on command, fetch the downed bird tenderly to hand before resuming his search for additional game. So too, will any well-trained pointing dog; what, then, makes the Brittany any different?

For one thing, his appearance. He is a long-haired dog with a naturally short tail, an unusual combination for a pointer. The average hunter confronting a Brittany spaniel for the first time may scratch his head in bewilderment: "Is this dog a setter without a tail...or a springer that points?" Closer and studied scrutiny will soon reveal, however, that the Brit is a little too small to be a tailless setter, yet, not heavy-boned enough or sufficiently feathered out to be a pointing springer.

Then too, the Brittany on the move will provide evidence that he is neither setter nor springer. Unlike the springers, he is not required to work always within gun-range, but neither is he as consistently rangy as the average setter. Although he compares more closely with the German shorthair in terms of normally restricted hunting range, the Brit is a livelier-paced worker, inclined toward more animated movement and less deliberate scenting technique. He's the smallest of all the pointing breeds so is, perhaps, the easiest to house, kennel, or transport.

Although achieving the same end results as all other pointing breeds, the Brittany embodies a number of differences, any or all of which might significantly influence a hunter's choice.

The fact that he *has* influenced so many hunters here since his arrival (in appreciable numbers) in 1931, is borne out by his tremendous, and still growing, popularity. The "bird hunter's beagle," is a description coined by his most avid admirers, and it most aptly reflects the esteem in which the little pointing spaniel is held. The label is imposing when one considers the parallel it draws. Without reasonably solid justification to back it, no such comparison could long hold up unchallenged; the fact that the Brit's practical values continue to attract greater numbers of fanciers every year would seem to leave little room for dissent.

Though comparatively new to the United States, the Brittany spaniel has for centuries been a well-known and much used gun dog breed in Europe. Like most hunting breeds, his exact origin is obscured in the hazy annals of time. It is theorized by some students of the breed that the Brittany's history dates back to the early fifth century A.D., when the Irish invaded Gaul. A good many of the hunting dogs that accompanied the Irish warriors doubtless were left behind, having strayed, or been stolen or simply left ownerless when their masters fell in battle. In mating with the native French breeds, these dogs of Erin may well have contributed to the original stock from which the Brittany spaniel evolved.

But whatever his primal ancestry, the Brittany, in all his diversified early forms, was revered by the French peasantry in the province from which he took his name. Although used to hunt rabbits, hare, and sundry game for the pot, the Brit acquired his most enviable stature pointing the big European woodcock.

It was at Pontou, a small valley town in Brittany, where what is probably the breed's most unique and distinguishing physical peculiarity evolved over a century ago. There the first tailless forbear of the modern Brittany was whelped. From the mating of a white and mahogany-colored bitch owned by an old hunter in Pontou, with a lemon and white dog, belonging to a visiting British sportsman, two bobtailed pups were produced. Only one of these tailless Brits grew to maturity, but, because of his noteworthy performances in the field and his ability to produce litters of tailless and stub-tailed pups, he became a much used and highly sought after stud.

A rare sight, this Brittany — owned by Jack Mayer of Moncton, N.B., Canada — stops while retrieving a woodcock to point a ruffed grouse. **Photo by J. Mayer.**

The Brit's modern history, most authorities concur, took shape in the early part of the present century with the breed improvement program inaugurated by a French sportsman named Arthur Enaud. Prior to Enaud's interest in the breed, the Brittany was feeling the degenerating effects of excessive inbreeding.

Enaud approached his self-imposed project thoughtfully and patiently, rejecting any expectation of accomplishing results overnight. His one neglect, however, was his failure to keep comprehensive records of his work.

It is known that he resorted to various crosses, after each of which he immediately returned to the original breed. What these outside infusions to the Brittany blood were, or precisely how many were made, is a matter of conjecture. Since restoration of the Brit's old orange and white coloring was among Enaud's chief aims, it is probable that he incorporated into the blood several Braques — pointing dogs of the period — which combined the desired coloration with intensification of both the scenting ability and the pointing instinct. It has also been suggested that he resorted to crosses with the Irish setter and English pointer.

Infinitely more important, though, were the results achieved by Enaud in restoring the vigor and freshness to the Brittany's blood. This he accomplished to the everlasting gratitude of the European and, subsequently, the American sportsman.

The first Brittany spaniels to reach the United States were a pair imported by the late Louis Thebaud in 1912. As far as is known, no others entered the United States until Thebaud's later importations in the early thirties. Thebaud and the late Allan Stuyvesant of Allamuchy, New Jersey, are generally considered the earliest and best known proponents of the Brittany spaniel in this country. It was they who were responsible for the formation of the Brittany Spaniel Club of North America, the sole organization representing the breed in the United States until 1942. In that year, the American Brittany Club was founded and ultimately merged with its predecessor, at which time a new standard for the breed was drafted. It was officially adopted four years later, in 1946.

Acceptance of the Brittany spaniel by American gunners was notably slow due to the onerous label "an old man's hunting dog," hung on the earliest importations of the breed. This was attributable to written accounts by Europeans who described the Brit as a dog of moderate range and slow pace, ideally suited to the middle-aged and elderly sportsman, and the label remained for some time. Unfortunately, this notion that identifying one's self with the little pointing spaniel was a public admission of advancing age and declining virility gained rather than lost impetus, keeping sportsmen away from the breed in droves.

In order to quash all basis for this popularity deterrent, and to better adapt the breed to American gunning and field trial requirements, the Brittany's range was widened and his pace speeded up through a program of selective breeding. And, though hardly the speed and range merchant that the field trial pointer or setter is, today's Brittany need take no back seat to the ordinary pointing dog

His active, business-like style, coupled with stamina and determination befitting a dog twice his size, make him a worthy contender for even the big-going breeds traditionally favored in pointing dog trials today. All too often the "horizon busters" lack the nose to match their speed. But nose is something the Brit is seldom short on; his consistently keen scenting ability more than makes up in thoroughness for whatever edge in speed the larger breeds may hold.

The Brittany's inordinately keen nose and persevering nature make a formidable combination in the field. These enviable assets sometimes prove a source of embarrassment to the owners of other pointing breeds who take their dogs afield with a Brit.

Two red faces were very much in evidence one December day, as a result of a Brittany's extra-sharp olfactories and unrelenting stick-to-it-iveness. Four of us were working an eight-year-old Brittany and a pair of English setters, aged four years and eight months, respectively, on a mixed bag of game-preserve pheasants and quail. Putting three dogs down at once is seldom advisable procedure. But, we felt that the experience of working with the older dogs would prove advantageous to the setter pup, whose owner was anxious to "bring her along" just as rapidly as her unusual precosity would allow.

Things went smoothly until one tricky little bobwhite, artfully dodging a couple of loads of 7½'s, managed a clean get-away up a gently sloping hillside into the hardwoods at the crest. Somebody yelled that he had the bird marked down accurately. So, whistling the dogs on, we trudged up the hill.

There, after a short search, the young setter made a nice find and staunch point. This time, the quail did not escape. Waving the dogs on, we swung down the hill toward the open field below. But not the Brittany…he was still busily casting about the spot where the bobwhite had been pointed and killed minutes before.

Typically spaniel in nature, the Brittany is always eager to please, but requires gentle persuasion for best results. **Photo by Nicky Bissell.**

We held up as his owner whistled, coaxed, cajoled, and finally succeeded in calling him off, but only briefly. No sooner did we start off again before the Brit stubbornly returned to the same spot. Immediately making game, he suddenly checked sharply, then froze on point, no more than twenty-five feet from the deceased quail's last hiding place.

No dog could have been stauncher, but we were skeptical as we hiked back to rustle the brush in front of him and tried to get it through that thick skull of his that we had already shot the bobwhite he only thought he smelled. The squawking cock pheasant that clattered into the air nearly made it to freedom while four surprised gunners stood gawking in disbelief. Finally, someone managed a killing shot. When the old Brit completed his retrieve, there shone in his eyes a certain uncomplimentary expression, the gist of which was better left untranslated. It was not certain if the red-faced setter men bowed their heads out of embarrassment or respect.

If his invariably good nose, instinctive bird sense and lively hunting style were less noteworthy, the Brittany would still command enormous respect and serious consideration as one of the most logical pointing dog choices for the average bird hunter. For the earlier-mentioned nickname, "bird hunter's beagle," accurately sums up the Brittany spaniel's practical qualities, many of which do parallel those that have made the little beagle hound America's most popular hunting dog.

As does the beagle, the Brit has working in his corner the assets of convenient size (17½-20½ inches at withers); keen scenting powers; inherent, enthusiastic desire to hunt; lots of determination and stamina; amenability to training and gentle nature. Typically spaniel in nature, the Brit instinctively takes to retrieving, needing only slight encouragement to fetch back any bird you down, on land or in the drink. While a duck is a pretty sizable package for him and not exactly his cup of tea he'll give it all he has and usually manages to swim back in with it, one way or another.

It is really in the uplands, though, that he does his most practical and serviceable work, on virtually any kind of game bird that lies to a pointing dog. There, the Brit's long-haired coat enables him to buck even the thorniest brush, and his small size gives him generally easier passage — under, rather than through, much of the thick cover that tends to slow up and tire out the larger breeds.

Whether the average Brit is easy or tough to train depends on the man involved. If your approach is brusque and your patience thin, the Brit will probably prove difficult for you. Conversely, if you can combine persistent gentle persuasion with vocal chastisement and, only when really needed, a stern but controlled hand, you should find that the job is fairly easy. For the Brit is a dog who wants to respond, even though he is a bit temperamental.

Basically white, with patches of either orange or liver secondary coloring, the Brittany weighs between thirty and forty pounds and presents a compact, functional appearance. While not dotingly affectionate, his devotion to master, mistress, and family is usually manifest in his desire to be near his people, and he is gentle enough to be submissive, if somewhat grudgingly, to those who must express themselves through constant fondling.

The fact that he is stub-tailed or completely tailless has rather obvious advantages where small children are concerned; the same holds true for carelessly slammed house or car doors and thoughtless missteps. The lady of the house can breathe easily knowing her precious coffee table bric-a-brac will be spared the rigors of an enthusiastic tail-wagging. In short, as a house pet, the Brit has it made, a situation of no small persuasion for the avid bird hunter who just happens to be a thoughtful family man as well.

A stylishly thrilling point—the exception where most Weimaraners are concerned—is struck by Fld. Ch. Fritz von Wehmann, owned by Gil Wehmann of New York. **Photo by Weimaraner Club of America.**

THE WEIMARANER

Of all the hunting dogs introduced to our shores in the past half-century, the breed with the most dramatic history is surely the Weimaraner. No other gun dog recently imported evoked such a stir of excitement among the hunting dog fraternity here as did the Weimaraner shortly after its arrival. Everything about the breed—from its history and reputation of "all-purpose" prowess in the field to its off-beat coloration and restricted ownership—smacked of the flamboyant, the exciting. Even the nicknames—"Super Dog," "Wonder Dog," and "Gray Ghost"—applied to the Weimaraner by his ultra-zealous backers were, if not actually concocted to heighten the already feverish aura of excitation, hardly sedative in their effect.

Touted as "the breed that could do everything...and do it all better than most," the Weimaraner, or at least the public image created for him, was eagerly embraced by American sportsmen. Here, at last, they believed was "The Dog That Never Was," the elusive ideal of perfection, for all types of hunting, that for ages had formed the covert longing of hunters everywhere.

Whether reflecting the powers of imaginative publicity, or the single foolish flight of fancy that every generation is entitled to—or maybe a little of both—the Weimaraner's image soared to fantastic, even ridiculous, heights. No gun dog breed could possibly live up to the promise that the unrealistically enthusiastic press attributed to the Weimaraner. But it was inevitable that the sporting press would latch onto the truly made-to-order story ingredients of the breed's background.

The Weimaraner originated in Germany, in the vicinity of Weimar, about 145 years ago and, according to the concensus of a majority of authorities, was developed during the reign of Grand Duke Karl August, as the exclusive shooting dog of the nobles of his court. Since the dogs were to be kept and used only by court members, the breeding was some sort of state secret which, if ever committed to written record, is now apparently lost to posterity.

Yet the pages of dog volumes old and new, European and American, are full of theories about the make-up of the Weimaraner's original bloodlines. Some contend that the breed simply sprang up as a fortuitous mutation of the St. Hubertus Brachen. But, this is only one among many notions; others have it evolving from each of such breeds as the Spanish pointer, the English pointer, the German shorthaired pointer, the Red Schweisshunde (literally translated, the red scent dog), and even the Great Dane.

We will probably never know which, if any, is correct. Nor, will very much light ever be shed upon the breed's development during the roughly fifty years after its purported origin under the Grand Duke. For, not until about 1870 did the Weimaraner become reasonably well known in Germany, and it did not gain official recognition as a true breed until 1896.

In June of the following year, the Weimaraner Club of Germany was founded and immediately invoked a set of stiff Prussianistic rules sharply limiting ownership to a select group of club members. Among the most stringent of the club's rules were the rigidly enforced breeding regulations, under which only approved dogs could be used to sire litters from approved bitches at specified periods of the year. Breeders were permitted to raise but six pups to a litter and could sell them only to club members.

Seemingly undemocratic on the face of it, the club's tight control was felt to be the only practical way to further the breed's improvement as a thoroughly functional gun dog, while safeguarding it from the stultifying effects that inevitably go with overpopularity. The system worked well and, for a number of years, succeeded in keep-

Devoted and keenly intelligent, the Weimaraner is an excellent companion and watch dog. This one is Tiger von Skyway, owned by Lewis H. Hodges of Ann Arbor, Mich.

ing the breed exclusively German.

But in 1929, Howard Knight of Providence, Rhode Island, with the aid of a friend from Germany, managed with considerable difficulty to become a member of the German club and subsequently import a pair of trained Weimaraners to this country. Both dogs were later found to be sterile, an unhappy circumstance which was reported to be no mere coincidence. However, Mr. Knight was permitted to import additional dogs later on, among which were a trio of pups and a bitch in whelp. Only one of the pups, Mars aus der Wulfsriede, survived a siege of distemper, but he went on to become one of the pillars of the breed in America, as did the bitch, Aura von Gaiberg, and her pups.

About 1939, Mr. Knight, who for personal reasons decided to give up upland shooting, gave his Weimaraners to Mr. and Mrs. A. F. Horn, owners of Grafmar Kennels. A short time later, with the formation of the Weimaraner Club of America, a breed program was formulated and the breeding activity stepped up by Grafmar Kennels. Though the Weimaraner became officially eligible for registration in the American Kennel Club in December, 1942, it was not until about two years after World War II, with the first sizeable imports of the breed from Germany, that the Weimaraner "craze" began here in earnest.

So effective was the promotion of the breed, and so relatively short the supply, that many of the nation's outdoor writers, many of whom had never even seen a Weimaraner in the field, rushed into print stories of the breed's "all-purpose" abilities that were based upon nothing more solid than hearsay. Gobbling it all up, their sportsmen readers hastened to spread by word of mouth the exaggerated claims of the "Super Dog" and set up a clamor for the breed long before it could be judged and evaluated by a reasonable number of competent field dog men.

To suspect that there were no unscrupulous souls giving impetus to the bizarre exploitation of the breed during this time, strictly for commercial profit, would be a little naive. And most of the honest and completely genuine Weimaraner supporters will readily acknowledge today that the breed was unscrupulously exploited during the post-war period. They look upon those years as having been a definite hindrance to the Weimaraner's development in this country.

But, what about the Weimaraner, today? Is there anything to the breed's "general-purpose" abilities? Will he retrieve from land and from water, trail rabbits, coon, fox, possum, and such, find, point, and handle grouse, woodcock, pheasant, and quail? Certainly he *could be trained* to do all these things, as *could many breeds* of shooting dogs; but, just as certainly, by doing all of them he would do none of them well enough to satisfy most hunters. For these are all jobs for specialists, jobs requiring not only certain highly ingrained aptitudes, but very specific and vastly different training approaches, too.

A rigid, no-nonsense-tolerated training system that establishes the sort of iron control so necessary in the making and handling of a crack retriever would hardly be advisable technique for developing a bold, hard-hunting, classy bird dog. By the same token, there never was an aggressive, independent trail hound worth his salt that could be considered under any kind of control while running hot scent. For these reasons alone, the so-called "all-purpose" hunting dog will never be anything but an unrealistic ideal.

The Weimaraner, like several of the other continental breeds imported at about the same time, has, therefore, been undergoing the customary metamorphosis from utility dog to bird dog. His ability to adapt to the peculiar demands of American hunters, as well as to the hunting field conditions that nurture those demands, is adequate proof of the breed's basic mettle. By concentrating efforts on breeding selectively for specialization in the upland bird covers, the

A fine litter of month-old Weimaraners. Note uniformity of size.

Weimaraner fancy has developed a number of strains that evidence a marked tendency toward greater range and speed, qualities that better equip the breed for the role of bird-finding specialist.

As a bird dog, the present-day Weimaraner is a great improvement over his forebears of fifteen or twenty years ago, and it may be that with continued astute selective breeding, the fancy will realize their ultimate goal of making the *average* Weimaraner a truly class bird dog, as we define the term today. That is not to say that most Weimaraners are not capable of turning in a serviceable performance that will put birds in the gunner's bag. Some I have seen, including a few National Field Trial Champions, could vie with the country's better pointers and setters. On the whole, however, one must sift through a great many members of the breed in order to find a few whose performances are truly outstanding.

No breath-taking stylist, to be sure, the average Weimaraner does have a good nose and can be trained to utilize it to best advantage for the gun by working him exclusively on birds. Conventionally, he is a bird dog of close to medium-close range, with an indefatigible stamina stemming from a pace best described as comfortable for a majority of gunners. Because he is endowed with a natural affinity for retrieving, this part of his training seldom needs belaboring by a busy owner.

Perhaps one of the breed's most ingratiating qualities is his ability to learn rapidly. This high degree of intelligence makes teaching him house, yard, and field manners a much easier task than it is with some breeds.

Though he is a large dog — males going up to seventy-five or eighty pounds and standing from twenty-five to twenty-seven inches at the withers — the Weimaraner is an excellent companion and family house dog. Space permitting, he is a far better house than kennel dog, since he is happiest only when close to those he loves. He is seldom unfriendly to people, yet he makes an excellent watchdog by virtue of his awesome size and hefty bark.

Sporting a striking silver gray, short-haired coat (another advantage in talking the wife into letting you keep him in the house) the Weimaraner jauntily carries a docked tail of about six inches in length. The unusual color of his eyes varies from light amber to blue-gray and, often they reflect the light in an eerie manner.

Distinctive in many ways, the Weimaraner embodies more than a full measure of individuality for the sportsman who delights in the unusual. Yet with his increasing popularity, what is unusual today gives every promise of becoming commonplace tomorrow.

A FEW ADDITIONAL POINTERS

If we're to believe the predictions of the folks who study and compute such complicated things, America is rapidly transforming into a suburban society, with the full transition anticipated by the close of the decade. Even allowing some leeway in the timetable, the premise of a shifting and constantly expanding population seems an inexorable eventuality. With it, of course, changes must come.

The hunter even now finds that much of his close-to-home hunting land has disappeared, traded for new housing developments, shopping centers, schools, and expressways, forcing him further afield in search of open gunning space.

Yet, change, however viewed, unfailingly generates its own compensating adjustments. Those same expressways that gobbled up local game covers enable today's sportsman to reach distant ones faster. And as crowding increases, federal, state, and county governments are increasingly recognizing the value of hunting and shooting recreation and are vigorously fostering acquisition of available land parcels for this purpose. These are to be set aside and kept open as sites for burgeoning commercial shooting preserves which will provide hunting for far more metropolitan and suburban gunners than local game covers ever could have accommodated.

Thus, despite pessimistic projections of a doomed and moribund sport, hunting—at least in palatable, if not strictly traditional, form— is destined not only to endure, but to grow.

With the changes in our hunting picture and the continuing adjustments that will accompany them, it would seem reasonable to assume that the kinds and breeds of gun dogs used may also change. Perhaps nothing so drastic as extinction faces most of our well-established hunting breeds. But, surely, the conditions and circumstances under which we will hunt will bring about progressive changes in the physical, temperamental, and performance qualities of the dogs we'll favor. Those breeds that successfully adjust by their nature and through selective breeding programs, will retain popularity and survive. Those that cannot make the transition will disappear, at least from the field.

But what, you may be wondering, do all these prognostications

A real pleaser, the wirehaired pointing griffon may not look like a bird dog, but he'll prove the point—as the one pictured is doing—to anyone who'll give him half a chance. **Photo by WPG Club of America.**

have to do with your selection of a gun dog breed for the present and immediate future? Perhaps very little—or, possibly, a lot. It all depends on whether or not your particular situation already mirrors the circumstances and conditions of the future. In other words, if you live in megalopolis; have little time, or really even little inclination, to devote to formal training of a gun dog; do most of your bird hunting on pay-as-you-go shooting preserves; and honestly figure that the dog you buy will turn out to be 75 percent family pet and 25 percent gun dog, what follows here will be of paramount significance in your considerations of breed choice.

For among the pointing breeds are three—not yet highly popular, but certain to become so—whose present overall qualifications will, by all odds, increasingly influence the standards for gun dogs during the next few decades. These "now and future breeds," as I choose to dub them, all meet at least three fundamental criteria in a changed and still-changing hunting picture. They are: (1) breeds better suited to the restricted cover conditions of present and projected hunting opportunities; (2) breeds more compatible, physically and temperamentally, with casual but functionally acceptable field training; and (3) breeds whose performance will be rated essentially on ease of handling and reasonably productive results on game, rather than on snappy style and class.

Such a trio of pointers is comprised of the wirehaired pointing griffon, the Vizsla, and the German wirehaired pointer; these, together with the Weimaraner and the German shorthaired pointer, are generically known as the "Continental" breeds. The threesome is examined here in the order listed above, since in my opinion, that is the order in which they rate, based on the earlier-mentioned criteria.

The wirehaired pointing griffon's looks are the antithesis of the classical pointing dog image. No clean, lithe lines or musculature rippling beneath sparkling white coat; no long feathered flag cracking proudly; no hint of a spirit barely bridled within a streamlined frame bursting with go, greets the beholder of a griffon.

Instead, the Griff presents an almost cobby frame, overlaid with a harsh, bristly coat of steel or whitish-gray, splotched with chestnut, and terminating in a six-inch stub tail, with the entire package weighing around fifty pounds. Yet, that half-a-hundred pounds of dog devotes every blessed ounce of himself to a single goal: pleasing the man who owns him. For, temperamentally, the griff is like nothing so much as an overgrown kid, starved for affection, and, literally, breaking his neck at every chance, in order to win his "hero's" approval.

The breed owes its development exclusively to the strong faith and tireless efforts of a single sportsman, E. K. Korthals, a Dutchman whose early interest and training in animal husbandry stemmed from his father's successful avocation as a cattle breeder.

When the younger Korthals' preoccupation with dogs, rather than cattle, caused his dismissal from paternal grace, he emigrated to Germany to continue his dog breeding activities with some of his original stock of rough-coated griffons. Most of these dogs were believed to be descendants of a strain that harked back to the griffon hounds of antiquity.

Poor record-keeping obscures definitive proof of the crosses Korthals used to accomplish his ultimate goal of a new breed. But piecemeal evidence indicates the incorporation into the Korthals' breeding program of spaniel, setter, Otter hound, and at least one infusion of German shorthaired pointer. During the 1880's, after Korthals moved from Germany to France, he completed his experiments, apparently satisfied that he had perfected the breed he sought. If popularity was any measure of his success, then his achievement was crowned, for so well established did the breed become in France that, even to this day, it is still known there as Korthals' griffon.

Although the first wirehaired pointing griffon in the United States was registered by the American Kennel Club in 1887, the breed was not imported in numbers before the turn of the century. Even then, the griffon remained, through the 1930's, more of an esoteric novelty than a serious entry into the American sporting scene. It was only after World War II that the breed acquired a new revitalized fancy here, largely due to the returning servicemen who had been exposed to the Griff in France and Germany.

Establishment of its own breed club—the Wirehaired Pointing Griffon Club of America—and monthly publication—*The Gun Dog Supreme*—has helped recruit sufficient numbers of supporters to the shaggy dog, to provide him his first real foothold here.

In common with most of the Continental breeds, the griffon was developed along utilitarian lines. But, like most imports, the emphasis laid on him here is as a pointer of upland game birds, augmented to some degree with retrieving from water. Although he's a strong, natural swimmer with a well-developed fetching instinct, don't expect him to match the water-working specialists. Neither can he, as a bird dog, approach the verve, pace, range, and stylish performance of most of the pointing dog specialists.

He is, however, a dog who'll get the job done. He's deliberate, slow, close-working, keen-nosed, but thoroughly dependable. Give him enough time, a few words of encouragement, and he'll find a bird...if it's there. He'll buck brush and briars — protected as he is by his bristly outer coat and dense, short undercoat—in any kind of weather, and do it all with a willingness that's bound to bring the words and pat of approval he's looking for.

The same nature and virtues that motivate him afield follow him home, where his affection and almost pathetic eagerness to please make him a fine family dog, requiring a minimum of formal training.

Second of our pointing threesome is the Vizsla, the only hunting dog in the United States who can lay claim to two somewhat contradictory distinctions. For, while he's the newest hunting breed eligible for registry in the American Kennel Club, having been accepted in 1960, he is reputedly one of the oldest sporting breeds in the world.

In fact, when the Vizsla was designated the official pointing dog of

The Vizsla, one of the world's oldest sporting breeds, has an inordinately good nose. This is Ch. Brok Selle Son of a Gun, owned by Dr. and Mrs. M. L. Wolfe, Montclair, N. J. **Photo by Heidersburger.**

Hungary, about 1825, the honor was hardly a spur-of-the-moment decision — since the breed had, at that time, been native to Hungary for some eight hundred years. Amazingly enough for such an ancient breed, he can be traced pretty accurately all the way back to the tenth Century. Profuse old records and artwork, some in stone etchings, depict the Magyar tribesmen with falcons and dogs that strongly resemble the present-day Vizsla. According to most historians, the breed apparently evolved from hunting dogs of those Magyar warriors who, around the eighth century, overran and settled the area that later became the Hungarian nation.

Preservation of the Vizsla's pure bloodlines through the ensuing centuries, became the tacit but implicit responsibility of the feudal warlords and later the aristocracy, whose ownership of the breed was rigidly restricted by custom, and perhaps even by force of arms.

The Vizsla's modern history began in 1825, with the establishment of the Magyar Vizsla Stud Book, which provided for recording and certification of pedigrees to safeguard the breed's continued purity. But, within less than a hundred years, war left the Vizsla on the brink of extinction. The breed narrowly escaped the second threat of total disappearance with the start of World War II, a scant twenty years later.

The Russian invasion of Hungary, in 1945, again imperiled the Vizsla's survival. But a handful of Hungarians fled with their dogs, to such countries as Austria, Italy, Germany, Turkey, and Czechoslavakia, snatching the breed from disaster just as their fathers before them had done. Those comparatively few remnants of one of the oldest sporting dogs in the world perpetuated the breed, in a postwar buildup, and the Vizsla soon found its way into the United States.

In adapting to his new home in America, the Vizsla has shown the makings of a good naturalized citizen, scoring well in the field on our native ruffed grouse, woodcock, and, to limited extent, quail, as well as on such immigrant species as the gaudy ring-necked pheasant. In range, pace, and what for him passes as style, the Vizsla is a fairly slow but industriously thorough and close-working pointing dog. Although it's never easy to say with certainty that a particular breed has a better nose than others, every Vizsla I've ever seen was blessed with uncommon scenting acuity. Perhaps his nose only seems sharper than it really is because of his deliberateness and tenacity. But time and again, I've observed Vizslas successfully untangle scent and eventually point birds that had been overlooked by much faster-working English pointers and setters.

The Vizsla's scenting prowess complements an inherent retrieving desire, a combination that seldom fails to salvage dead or crippled game birds for the bag. And, if his short-haired coat doesn't suit him for frequent immersion in excessively cold water, it certainly doesn't preclude his retrieving an occasional duck for the boss.

Standing from twenty-one to twenty-four inches at the withers, the Vizsla is a clean-lined, almost lean dog that weighs about fifty to sixty pounds. He has a docked tail and red-gold or cinnamon-colored short, smooth-haired coat. His disposition toward family is always gentle and affectionate but while he is appropriately well-mannered in the company of friends, his protective instincts cause him to view strangers suspiciously.

The Vizsla, because of his alertness and intelligence, ordinarily picks up training quickly, if he is handled properly. Definitely sensitive in nature, he seldom requires strong-arm tactics; if they are used on him, he can usually be counted on to turn off all positive response Lavish praise and hearty approval are the rewards he works best for, and if given in large doses, he'll reciprocate wholeheartedly, afield or at home.

The German wirehaired pointer, or drahthaar, as he is known in the land where he originated, is very similar, except for his whiskered chin and steel-wool-type coat, to his infinitely more popular cousin, the German shorthaired pointer. And, strangely enough, one of the principal deterrents to the wirehair's popularity standing — his scraggly coat — will probably prove to be one of his strongest redeeming qualities in the hunting picture of the future.

For although the wirehair's tough outer coat (which overlays a softer-textured secondary one) presents a somewhat unkempt appearance, it gives him several distinct advantages over his smooth-haired rival. A veritable suit of mail in even the wickedest covers imaginable, his coat not only provides solid insulation against hot and cold weather, but also enables him to withstand frequent exposure to icy water. Thus, he more than qualifies as a combination pointing dog and waterfowl retriever capable of functioning in almost any climate and weather.

Several cross mixtures are credited with having established the German wirehaired pointer before he was given separate and distinct breed status in Germany in 1870. These reputedly included the griffon, the pudelpointer (a cross of poodle and English pointer), the stichelhaar (a cross of pudelpointer, foxhound, English pointer and Polish water dog), and the German shorthaired pointer.

A ruffed grouse is tenderly brought to hand by a German wirehaired pointer, less popular but more graceful relative of the shorthaired pointer. **Photo by Jerome J. Knap.**

Well adapted in range and pace to hunting the ringnecked pheasant, the German wirehaired pointer can be used to find, point, and retrieve the occasional cottontail rabbit. **Photo by Jerome J. Knap.**

As with most of the German breeds, the wirehair was conceived and put together for use as a utility breed to point upland birds and hares, trail large game, vermin, and predators, and retrieve from land and water. The fact that he was able, with careful training, to handle these tasks is evident in his preeminence in German field trial records. He has consistently outnumbered all other breeds in the gun dog stud book in Germany since the mid-1920's.

It was at about that time when the first wirehairs set paw on U.S. soil. But before the breed could establish itself in sufficient numbers, the German shorthaired pointer arrived here, amidst drumbeats and fanfare extolling his virtues as a multi-purpose breed that would answer all the needs of the American hunter. Eschewing the free-wheeling promotional route, the wirehair backers chose to build support for their breed on a firmer foundation, relying on time to reveal the dog's true merits.

Later, with the shorthair established and his bandwagon retired to mothballs, the wirehair might have emerged from the shadows. But, history repeated itself as it so often does—this time with the introduction of the Weimaraner to our shores. Once more the door clanged shut for the German wirehaired pointer.

Finally, toward the mid-fifties, when the "Gray Ghost" fad has subsided, the wirehair began to realize slow but steady progress under the aegis of the German Drahthaar Pointer Club of America. Through the efforts of its dedicated backers, the breed was finally granted eligibility for registration in the American Kennel Club in 1959. With the A.K.C.'s opening of its stud book to the wirehair came the decision to anglicize the breed's name, changing it officially to the German wirehaired pointer.

A bit leggier than the shorthair, and somewhat more agile, the wirehair, as a bird dog, is a close-to-medium-close-ranging worker, with keen scenting powers and abundant stamina. On average, he displays more graceful style than any of the other "Continentals" hence is a more interesting dog to watch at work. With the exception of quail and other birds normally hunted in the big open country, the wirehair can successfully handle any species of upland game birds.

He is regarded by pheasant hunters, in all parts of the ringneck's territory, as particularly well-adapted in range and pace to hunt the semi-open and brushy tangles favored by the wild roosters. And his affinity for brush-busting makes him an excellent candidate for use on ruffed grouse and woodcock, especially in those small, thickly overgrown pocket-covers so often passed up.

A fairly good sized dog, he stands from twenty-two to twenty-six inches high at the withers and weighs an average of sixty pounds. In color his wiry coat is a bluish-gray overlaid with patches of liver or brown, and he sports a docked tail about six inches long.

Extremely companionable, the wirehair has a playful personality and gentle nature that lend themselves extraordinarily well to home life with his owner's family. Few breeds are more sensitive to their owners' moods than the wirehair or more responsive to training administered with patience and a masterly gentle touch.

Any of these three pointers are well worth your serious consideration under the previously detailed circumstances. In fact, they are often chosen over all of the more popular pointing breeds by sportsmen unrestricted by any considerations save the very special appeal of these breeds themselves.

4

The Breeds That Flush

THE ENGLISH SPRINGER SPANIEL

NO DOG IS more of a nemesis to the ring-necked pheasant than the English springer spaniel, a compact, energetic worker who has learned to cope with the unorthodox and frustrating tactics of the colorful immigrant from Asia.

When pointing dog owners throw in the sponge, whistle up their setters or pointers, and head for home in utter disgust over the run-squat-run antics of the dog-wise old roosters, springer men come in for their biggest innings. For, unlike the pointing dogs that must stand staunch, even as the scornful cock bird slinks from under their points, forcing them into an endless game of point, break, relocate, and point again, the flushing springer bores right in and pushes his running quarry into full flight.

And once the hapless ringneck is zeroed-in on by a well-trained springer, fly he must, or risk a rump-chomping by a pair of eager jaws. Permitting a pheasant to gamble on his best defense — making tracks like a racehorse — is a card the springer never deals; only in the air is the gaudy rooster vulnerable, and that's where the springer puts him, quickly and surely, with no wasted motion.

As a separate and truly distinct breed of gun dog, the English springer spaniel has been with us only a relatively short time. Two dates, 1812 and 1902, figure prominently in his purebred history. The earlier date marks what is generally accepted as the beginning of the first pure line of springers established, by the Boughey family of Aqualate, Stropshire, England. The later date is the year in which official separate classification was obtained for the breed in England.

Although numerous references to "spaniel-type" dogs have been found throughout recorded history from Roman times on, they provide no positive indication that the dogs described were spaniels as we know and accept them today.

The first written record detailing the spaniels' manner of hunting was set down by a French nobleman, Gaston de Foix, about 1387. A wealthy gentleman whose kennels frequently housed up to a thousand dogs, he wrote in his *Book of the Hunt* of the spaniels' method of quartering ground in front of the hunters, their water-working abilities, and their praiseworthiness at retrieving diving ducks.

Two centuries later, Dr. John Caius, an English dog authority, described the spaniels more fully and divided them into land and water varieties. Ultimately, the land spaniels were further divided into two types: springers, which flushed game for the sight-hounds

Whether the game is pheasant, grouse, woodcock, rabbit or waterfowl, the owner of a springer seldom goes home with an empty bag.

or hunting hawks, and setting spaniels, which pointed game for the nets. The latter, it is generally believed, were the forbears of what eventually, through judicious selection, became the breed we recognize today as the English setter.

The flushing type of land spaniels varied drastically in size and acquired different names after the game on which they specialized. Generally, the smaller specimens were used as "cocking spaniels" for hunting woodcock, thus becoming known as cockers or cocker spaniels. However, since bloodlines were intermingled so freely, with no attempts toward any form of selection or standardization, a young dog might begin life as a cocker and then grow into the springer classification as he matured.

Around the start of the twentieth century, after the first few spaniel field trials had been run in England, sportsmen began taking increasing note of the springer and his superior abilities. A clamor was set up for separate classification of the springer soon after these larger and speedier specimens exhibited consistent ability to win over the cockers and other types of spaniels. As mentioned earlier, this separate classification occurred in 1902 and marked the official beginning of the history of the modern springer spaniel.

Five years later, in 1907, purebred springers were first introduced in America. Since these imports were small in number, and the interest of American sportsmen so centered at the time on English setters and pointers, springers went practically unnoticed until the early 1920's. Then the efforts of a Canadian, Eudore Chevrier, in importing, training, and selling springers in great quantity, both in Canada and the United States, began to give the breed a foothold on this side of the Atlantic.

Freeman Lloyd, a well-known American sportsman, was responsible for extolling the merits of the breed and promoting it among a group of influential Easterners who, founding the English Springer Spaniel Field Trial Association in 1924, held the breed's first American field trial that year at Fisher's Island. Winner of that historic event was Aughrim Flash, who further distinguished himself by copping top laurels the following year, as well.

Notable springers of that era included Horsford Hetman, Tedwyn's Trex, Green Valley Punch, Fast Bozo's Bar Mate, Rufton Recorder, Flint of Avondale, Inveresk Chancellor and Inveresk Cocksure. These great dogs contributed mightily to the springer breed in North America, and their names can be found in the pedigrees of countless

American and Canadian springers today.

As a modern gun dog breed, the springer is perhaps the most versatile, hence practical, flushing breed available for the man whose main hunting interests are pheasants, ducks, and an occasional cottontail. An excellent retriever, the springer is extremely adept at marking the fallen bird, and his memory at marking multiple falls is on a par with many of the retrieving specialists.

If less spectacular than some of the retrievers in the water, and not up to withstanding the same severe water temperatures they endure, the springer nevertheless takes readily to a swim and acquits himself in a style guaranteed to please all but the most exacting duck hunter.

In his principal job of finding and flushing game for the gun, the springer wins over all similar working competitors, paws down. Despite being shorter in leg than either the Lab or golden, who are his only close rivals as upland flushing dogs, he travels faster on his "nose," which is superior to the water dogs, and consequently does a more efficient job, at consistently proper gun-range.

Quartering his ground, always within the range of his boss' scatter-gun, the springer continually tests the breeze for airborne bird scent. Once he catches a thin wisp of scent, he follows it right to its source, making game by excitedly wagging his stub tail as he closes in on his quarry. Then, when the bird is pinpointed, whether sitting or running, the dog charges in, pushes him into flight and instantly "hups," or sits, to await the shot. Sitting at flush and shot not only enables the dog to stay safely out of the gun's line of fire, but also lets him concentrate on marking the bird's fall.

After the fall, the springer waits for the command to fetch, and a minute or two later tenderly deposits the bird—usually a plump ringneck—in the outstretched hand of his owner. Properly executed by a well-trained springer, the entire sequence is a precision per-formance that cannot fail to thrill and impress the onlooker.

Unless discouraged from doing so, the springer will hunt rabbits as well, handling them in the same fashion he works birds. Of course, compared to the conventional rabbit hounds, the beagle and basset, the springer does not offer the thrills of a long chase to the accom-paniment of trail music. He is, after all, not a hound and, naturally, does not work like one. Were he to give full chase to a bunny, his speed would drive the rabbit to ground much too quickly to enable the gunner to get in a shot.

Bold, aggressive, and capable in the field, the English springer spaniel is an easygoing, affectionate companion at home. His longhaired coat of black and white or liver and white suits him for working in heavy cover and cold climates.

Yet, to some sportsmen, rabbit hunting with a springer stacks up as a much faster-paced, more challenging version of the sport than can be attained using hounds. What's more, unlike a beagle or basset, the springer will retrieve the downed cottontail on command.

To bird hunting purists, using a flushing breed on birds such as quail or woodcock which normally hold well to pointing dogs, is roughly akin to fishing dry-fly water with worms. Esthetically speaking, such men cannot be faulted. But esthetics must sometimes give way to expediency. And where practicality becomes foremost, the springer can be counted on to do a very serviceable job on woodcock and on bobwhites when they are restricted to small fields and pocket covers.

Even if he were much less talented as a gun dog the springer would still have much to recommend him. His affectionate, docile nature and deep devotion to the whole family of which he is made a viable part, places him near the top of the list of hunting breeds that double as house pets and hunting companions.

Few other gun dog breeds so bold, willing, and capable in the field are at the same time so naturally easygoing and companionable in the home.

Moreover, the springer is not a difficult dog to train for either role. Like most dogs who are given a sense of belonging, he exhibits a strong involvement with his "people." The result is a display of uncommon attentiveness to training that enables him not only to absorb his lessons quickly, but to retain much longer what he has been taught. Consequently, the owner of a springer seldom will be faced with the time-consuming task of the annual field training refresher course so often necessary for many other breeds of hunting dogs.

A medium-sized, comparatively heavy-boned dog weighing about fifty pounds, the springer stands from eighteen to twenty-two inches high at the withers. His coat, usually liver and white or black and white, is moderately long, flat or slightly wavy, and of fine texture. His tail is docked and, in general, his appearance suggests power, endurance, and agility.

Just to prove his breed's versatility, this plucky springer — Greenfair's Willing, owned by Carl W. Shattuck of Beva ns, N.J. — makes a tough retrieve of a Canada goose. **Photo by Gaines Dog Research Center.**

Sponsored in the United States by the National English Springer Spaniel Field Trial Association, a member club of the American Kennel Club, the springer of both bench and field varieties, is customarily registered with the A.K.C. As with most hunting breeds, care should be taken, when selecting your gun dog, to make certain he is from at least four generations of working field stock.

No matter what your predisposition in hunting breeds may be— with the notable exception of a hound—you should, if at all possible, try to see a good field-working springer perform before making up your mind. Even if your objectively-thought-out requirements militate against choosing him, you'll have given yourself a rare treat just seeing one of America's finest gun dogs in action.

Infused with more pep and bounce per square inch than any of the larger breeds, the energetic little cocker spaniel is a dynamo and a joy to watch afield. **Photo by Evelyn M. Shafer.**

THE COCKER SPANIEL

Breathtaking, thrilling, inspiring are a few of the many adjectives hunters use in attempting to communicate their impressions of gun dogs in action. Yet, how feeble is even the most vivid of these words when trying to recreate the imagery of that moment a hell-for-leather Labrador, legs outstretched in a flying leap, seems to hang suspended in mid-air before slapping the water? Or the time-stopping feeling that follows the sudden, screeching halt of a galloping pointer hitting a brick wall of bird scent that stacks him up like a study in cryogenics?

However inadequate in most situations, our language could not provide a word more perfect than "scintillating" to describe the sight of a merry little hunting dog busily plying his instinctive trade in the field. It captures the instant essence of the feeling conveyed when watching a diminutive gun dog who radiates animation in every step and sparkles with bouncy style and buoyant spirit.

Of our several small hunting dog breeds perhaps none more infectiously displays his animation than the field-bred cocker spaniel. Imbued with more pep per square inch than any of the larger breeds, this energetic little bird dog flits about, well within gun range, scouring every grass-patch and cover-tangle likely to conceal a sulking ringneck. Then, when he finds one, watch that stub-tail vibrate as he gets closer to the colorful rooster he'll push skyward in a second or two.

Even as the gun's roar subsides into the distant hills and the last irridescent feather rocks jauntily earthward, he'll bounce forward at the signal to fetch, and return—slowed somewhat by his burden— with a prize that seems almost as big as himself.

Such consistently dauntless performance has won for the working cocker not only bed and board but a security blanket woven of admiration, affection, and respect among a fair-sized contingent of sportsmen.

One of the oldest types of hunting dogs, the cocker stems from the spaniel family, a canine clan of ancient, if uncertain, origin, possibly dating back to the days of Nero. The earliest known written record describing the spaniel's hunting techniques was penned in 1387 by Gaston de Foix. About two hundred years later, the English anatomist, Dr. John Caius, wrote in more detail about the spaniels, dividing them into land and water varieties. He broke them down still further by subdividing the land spaniels into two different categories: those that "start the bird," and those that "simply point it out." The former type took the general name "springers," while the latter became known as "setting spaniels."

The flushing type of land spaniel, or springer, came in various sizes, each of which was loosely classified after his primary specialty. For example, the tiniest variety, weighing fourteen pounds or less, was known as the "comforter," or "lap spaniel." Slightly larger types that weighed between fifteen and twenty-eight pounds came to be designated as "cocking spaniels," or "cockers," by virtue of their favored use in hunting woodcock. The "springers" formed another category, named separately to distinguish both their hunting method and size, which topped the twenty-eight pound "cocker" limit and averaged around thirty-five pounds.

Freely interbred for years, the land spaniels were such a conglomerate of sizes and types that keeping them accurately sorted out was a near impossibility. With the advent of stud books and increased focus on selective breeding, such casual intermingling fell off sharply and bloodlines began to achieve logical separation according to fixed size and type.

The modern history and real beginning of the cocker spaniel as a breed, rather than just a type, traces back to 1879, the year a cocker called Obo was whelped in England. Considered the father of the modern cocker, Obo sired many descendants who made strong contributions to the breed both in England and America. Four years after Obo's birth, the cocker spaniel was accorded its own separate classification at dog shows in England. And within a decade, the breed won the privilege of separate registrations in the English Kennel Club's Stud Book.

Under the broad generic term, spaniels had been introduced into America long before the Civil War. But, with the migration westward, where vast, open terrain required faster, wider ranging dogs that would hold their birds on point, the flushing spaniels lost favor to the setter. Even the founding of the American Spaniel Club, in 1881, failed to revive more than token interest in the cocker or his springer cousin as gun dogs.

Not until the first championship field trial, held by the Cocker Spaniel Field Trial Club of America at Verbank, New York, in 1924, did the cocker's resurgence as a gun dog begin. From that date forward, under the intense and capable backing of such field dog stalwarts as Elias Vail, Ella Moffitt, H. S. Nielson, Ralph Craig and Leonard Buck, the breed experienced notable gains as a field trial competitor and gun dog. From the carefully blueprinted selective breeding programs initiated by their devoted supporters emerged a number of excellent field strains, including Elcova and Rowcliffe among others. For a few years things looked rosy; the cocker was slowly but inexorably becoming reestablished in his natural element —the field.

Then, in the mid-1930's, bench show interest in the cocker took a vigorous upswing, bringing with it increased public notice of the breed. The public's acceptance of the cocker rocketed the breed to unprecedented heights of popularity. In 1947, over 78,000 cockers were registered with the American Kennel Club that year alone. And in a mad scramble to cash in on the incredible demand for cockers, what could literally be termed "puppy factories" sprang up like skunk

Field champion English cocker retrieves a hen mallard for handler Jasper Briggs. Slightly larger than their American cousins, English cockers can be used for occasional waterfowl retrieving. **Photo by Evelyn M. Shafer.**

cabbage in the spring.

Fast-buck breeders with little or no experience bred every cocker they could lay hands on. Absolutely no thought was given to hunting instincts, but worse yet was the utter disregard of breeding for good disposition and temperament. The old, established breeders of cockers for the most part refused to breed inferior stock, but with so many others working against them, it was scarcely a contest.

Moreover, a generally poor situation was worsened by the bench breeders and exhibitors, who finally managed to change the old breed standard to accommodate their ideas of a cocker with coat so long and flowing that it fairly swept the ground.

Any breed escaping unscathed from such a ludicrous mishmash of circumstances could only have done so with the aid of a miracle. The cocker had none! A shy, nervous, snappy, ill-tempered cocker would once have been exceptional, but now these same traits—along with a chronic tendency to piddle at the drop of a hat—became fairly commonplace in the breed.

The war too had its effect. During the virtual moratorium on cocker field trials, from Pearl Harbor in 1941 to V-J Day in 1945, breeding activity in the field-proven strains suffered a severe slump, making good hunting cockers hard to find for some years. But the little knot of devoted field-cocker enthusiasts mentioned earlier still existed, and their ranks had added such worthies as Evelyn Monte, Henry Berol, Dr. Samuel Millbank and A. M. Lewis. They resumed both a repropagation of the hunting strain and a renewal of cocker field trials. Also helping to salvage the breed as a gun dog were the increased importations of the English cocker, recognized here as a separate breed but actually rooted in the same family origin as the American dogs. Developed along different lines, and having avoided the scourge of overpopularity which afflicted his Yankee cousin, the English cocker retained a high percentage of the necessary natural hunting instincts to qualify him for use in the field.

Where, then, does the cocker stand today? Can you still buy a cocker to fill the dual role of hunter and house pet? The answer is yes, but with qualifications. The casual purchase of an American cocker from just any source is certainly not recommended, the vast majority of them being heavy in bench show breeding. Yet, the buyer who takes the precaution to ascertain that his prospective pup comes from field-proven hunting stock for at least three or four generations can be pretty sure he's getting the type of cocker that should suit his needs.

For the field, or working type, American cocker, unlike so many of his bench-bred brethren, has retained in great measure the attributes of gentle, affectionate disposition and stable temperament that earned the breed favor in earlier days. These amiable traits, coupled with his handy size—about fifteen inches at the withers and around twenty-six to twenty-eight pounds in weight, make the average field cocker an ideal candidate for the home, as a trustworthy companion to family members of all ages.

In the field, too, his minuscule frame offers advantages that more than outweigh the debits usually associated with small size in a hunting dog. He can scamper underneath a good deal of the criss-crossing brush that a larger dog has to bull through, so he avoids the punishment and energy-sapping rigors that heavy cover inflicts on larger dogs. Moreover, the cocker is less subject to the speed-slackening effects of continual brush-bucking, which tends to negate some of the fleetness of the big breeds, and this advantage lets the bustling little gun dog compete on nearly equal terms.

A heritage of retrieving and water-oriented instincts is complemented by the cocker's naturally strong desire to seek and flush both furred and feathered game for the gun. No upland bird is beyond the

Although specializing in pheasants, the English (pictured here) and American cocker turn in good performances on grouse, woodcock, and rabbits.

plucky little cocker's working capacities, not even the ring-necked pheasant — a gargantuan bundle that strains his carrying ability right to the limit. Of course, big country that requires speed and extensive ranging to cover effectively is not the tiny spaniel's cup of tea. But, on woodcock — the bird for which he was named — ruffed grouse, or, for that matter, any game bird normally found or planted in moderate to heavy cover, the cocker is at his best.

Like his springer cousin, the cocker can be used to jump cottontails in front of the gun, handling them in the same way that he hunts birds: pushing them out of hiding; sitting at flush and shot; fetching tenderly to hand on command. And, although a big package to bring back, the occasional duck dropped in woodland pond in early fall, when the water's not too cold, will be eagerly, if laboriously, fetched up by the willing little cocker.

Though show stock comes in a variety of colors — solid black, red, gold, as well as black and tan, roan, and parti-colors (white with black or red markings) — a majority of field cockers' long-haired coats are of the latter coloration since they are easier to see in the hunting covers. Training, both afield and at home, is best accomplished with firm but gentle persuasion. Alert, intelligent, and highly anxious to please, the field cocker will respond most quickly to the patient, kindly approach and almost always reacts adversely to the harsh punishment inflicted by an owner's imprudent loss of temper.

Both the English and American cocker spaniels can be entered in the Field Dog Stud Book, but by far the lion's share are generally registered with the American Kennel Club. For that very reason, it is doubly important for you to make certain that the cocker pup, whether English or American, you plan to buy comes from field-proven and not bench show stock.

Properly trained, the cocker will contribute more than his share afield toward filling your game bag. At home, between hunts or between seasons, his merry, contagiously lovable personality will contribute the companionship, loyalty, and affectionate devotion that are so much a part of the truly well-rounded gun dog.

5

The Breeds That Fetch

THE LABRADOR RETRIEVER

AMONG THE VARIOUS types of sporting dogs in the United States, there is inevitably a single breed that, having early captured the public's fancy, tends to stand out as most traditional and most representative of his type, be it pointing or flush dog, sight or trail hound, or retriever.

Take retrievers, for example. Such fine retrievers as the Chesapeake Bay, the Golden, and the Irish water spaniel all have their steadfast supporters who, short of open brawling, would defend their chosen breed's honor to the last ditch. Only a handful of these devotees, however, would challenge the fact that it is not their candidate but rather the redoubtable Labrador that is most symbolic of all retrieverdom.

Virtually synonymous with the word "retriever," the Lab, as he is better known to scores of admirers, is easily the nation's most popular "fetch" dog. A rugged, highly proficient retriever on land as well as in the water, he has captured the hearts of American waterfowlers through a unique amalgam of natural ability, gentle disposition, winsome personality, keen intelligence and tractability. He is easily capable of amassing a substantial following on the basis of working skill alone, but he astutely extends his "fetching ways" beyond the

Virtually synonymous with the word "retriever," the Labrador is far and away the nation's most popular fetch dog. This one hits the water with the verve and spirit every hunter and field trailer loves to see.

confines of the duck blind to charm his master's wife and kids and secure an honored place for himself in the home (if not actually *in* the most comfortable easy chair, then, at least, right beside it).

Despite his name, the Labrador did not come from that island, but rather, according to all available records, from Newfoundland, springing from a breed known as the St. John's Newfoundland. The St. John's breed was distinguished from the ordinary Newfoundland by his smaller size, and shorter, smoother coat. Used to some extent to retrieve waterfowl, his principal forte was one of far more practical value to the fisherfolk of Newfoundland, who kept him mainly for the purpose of fetching ropes from ship to shore, and from one boat to another.

About the 1820's, the breed was brought to England at the instigation of the second Earl of Malmesbury. The Earl's social prominence undoubtably helped in spreading the word of the new breed's outstanding qualities as a peerless swimmer and efficient retriever. Such praise was quickly echoed by other members of the aristocracy and several noted sportsmen, among them the celebrated Colonel Hawker. He wrote of the breed: "This type is...extremely quick running, swimming and fighting. Their sense of smell is hardly to be credited: in finding wounded game there is not a living equal in the canine race."

In the ensuing years, during which the second Earl of Malmesbury and his successor, the third Earl, continued their breeding operations with the Labrador, the breed was kept comparatively pure. It is believed that other breeders were not so concerned with purity however, and may have crossed their Labs outside from time to time with popular contemporary retriever breeds. From the mid-1800's to the end of that century flat- and curly-coated retrievers became extremely popular in England, and there is little doubt that infusions of these breeds found their way into at least some of the English labrador bloodlines. Setter and pointer outcrosses also have been alluded to by later writers, but there is little or no evidence to support these allegations.

Pedigrees based on records from the stud book of the Duke of Buccleuch, who secured much of his Labrador stock from the Malmesbury Kennels, trace back to 1878 the ancestry of A. C. Butter's Peter of Faskally and Major Portal's Flapper, two dogs generally credited with being the founders of the modern Labrador breed. Accorded official recognition by the English Kennel Club in 1903, the Labrador soon secured his place in English field trials and bench shows, establishing notable wins in both categories.

Under the English system, no sporting dog can be awarded a bench championship until he has qualified in the field. Thus, in England, the Labrador's bench achievements have in no way been gained at the expense of his field prowess. This is a system which show fanciers of sporting breeds in America might do well to emulate, in order to prevent the further deteriorating effects of the double standard for sporting breeds that prevails here today.

In any case, the modern Lab took up residence in America shortly after the opening of the twentieth century, but it was not until about 1930 that his brethren appeared in worthwhile numbers. Soon, with the dedicated support of such fanciers and breeders as the late J. F. Carlisle (Wingan Kennels) and Averell Harriman (Arden Kennels), the Lab's winning ways asserted themselves in no uncertain terms.

From the very first licensed Labrador field trial, held in the United States, in the town of Chester, New York, in 1931, to the present, the Lab has cut a formidable swath for himself through American retriever trials, annexing more placements than all the other retriever breeds combined. The retriever trial greats, whose names will forever

A unique amalgum of natural ability, gentle disposition, winsome personality, and keen intelligence has helped the Labrador gain the respect and affection of a legion of followers.

evoke the pride of the Labrador fancy plus the esteem of the entire retriever fraternity, have been Dual Champion Shed of Arden, Nilo's King Buck, and Spirit Lake Duke, the only three multiple winners of the National Retriever Trial in its history.

There will be some retriever men quick to point out that the number of wins the Lab has accumulated is not a true barometer of his working superiority over other retriever breeds, because in total entry the Labrador far outnumbers his competitors in retriever trials. But, while such rationale may have some basis, the fact that so many more Labs compete in trials might also prompt the thought that the breed consistently produces a higher percentage of field-trial-qualified specimens.

The Labrador's popularity is irrefutable. For the waterfowl hunter he is ideal: a strong, natural swimmer with a passion for chasing down the often-difficult cripples that might elude a less capable dog and die a lingering, wasteful death.

No slouch on terra firma either, the Lab frequently finds favor in the uplands as a non-slip retriever (walking at heel until ordered to fetch a bird found by a pointing dog or spaniel and downed by the gun). In this capacity he devotes his entire attention to marking the fall, then, on command, going straight to it, making a crisp decisive pickup, prompt return, and soft-mouthed delivery.

The agile Lab has become increasingly popular in recent years as a pinch-hit flush dog for use on upland game birds. While not as fast or maneuverable as the springer spaniel, a Labrador who is properly trained for the uplands, and who is given suitable opportunities in them, can do a remarkably efficient job in any situation where flushing dog techniques are appropriate.

In the role of pinch-hit flushing dog, the Lab must learn to quarter his ground, to the front and sides of the gunner, at a pace and distance that keeps him working well within gun-range. If held under good voice and whistle control during the initial phase of his familiarization training in the uplands, he'll generally learn very quickly to adapt to the proper range and quartering pattern. Once he's found and had a few birds shot over him, to stimulate his hunting instincts, he'll become sufficiently encouraged to search actively for birds every time you take him afield.

Supplementing his primary specialty as a duck retriever by adapting him to upland hunting has unquestionably added a new and significant dimension to the Lab's overall appeal. During the years of

Increasingly popular in recent years as a pinch hit flush dog, the Lab deports himself efficiently on pheasants, as well as other upland game birds. Usually black, the Lab comes in yellow, like this one, and chocolate.

continually decreasing daily limits on waterfowl, the Lab, along with most other retriever breeds, experienced some slippage in popularity. Many hunters reasoned that training and keeping a retriever strictly for a two or three duck limit was a luxury they couldn't afford, and they understandably turned to buying other types and breeds that would provide them a wider range of hunting use.

Fortunately, the Labrador proved that his talents could be extended into the uplands and in so doing provided undreamed impetus to his popularity rating. Today, he's at the top of the heap among retriever breeds, and tomorrow, may even eclipse some of the upland specialist breeds.

Whether from land or water, the Lab takes to retrieving instinctively, with very little urging. His marvelously even temperament, intelligence, and ebullient eagerness make him a pupil of rare attentiveness and quick learning.

Despite his comparatively large size—dogs stand from 22½ to 24½ inches at shoulder and weigh between sixty and seventy-five pounds—he manages to deport himself sedately enough to merit house-pet status in any but the most cramped living quarters. And his smooth, short-haired coat of solid black, yellow, or chocolate is easily groomed to keep it free from excessive shedding and dirt.

Mild-mannered and affectionate, the Lab is an excellent companion to adults and children alike. In fact, his gentleness enables him to wrap the lady of the house right around his not-so-little paw. It doubtless accounts for his appeal to the male population as well. And any hunting dog that can please a man in the field and win total approval of the wife and kids at home just can't help but evoke the enthusiastic response that the Labrador has come to enjoy over the years.

The Labrador Retriever Club of America, a member breed club of the American Kennel Club, is the official sponsor of the Lab in the United States. The greatest majority of Labradors are registered in the A.K.C. Stud Book; some are entered in the American Field Publishing Company's Field Dog Stud Book and a small percentage are registered in both.

Probably the foremost indication of the Labrador retriever's high esteem among sportsmen was the tribute paid him in 1959. That year marked the first time a dog was pictured on the Federal Migratory Waterfowl Hunting Stamp, along with the legend: Retrievers Save Game. The dog selected to symbolize the legend was John M. Olin's two-time national champion, Nilo's King Buck—a Labrador retriever.

If handsome is as handsome does, then the Golden retriever qualifies on both counts. A strong swimmer and capable water worker, he is equally adept as a pinch-hit flushing dog in the uplands, and easily tops all retriever breeds in the good looks department.

THE GOLDEN RETRIEVER

Giving the lie to the adage that beauty is only skin deep, the golden retriever displays a warmly affectionate personality that perfectly matches his handsome exterior. Second only to the Labrador in popularity, the golden easily tops all retrievers in the good looks department and takes a back seat to none when it comes to helping his owner put game in the bag.

Whether the setting is an inland river blind, a sneak-boat in a coastal bay, a cornfield or a mixed stand of conifer and hardwood, the golden is never out of place; he is about as versatile as any retriever breed can be, equally capable of flushing small game in the uplands or fetching ducks and geese in the lowlands.

If dogs could read, one might suspect that the golden's eagerness to please is motivated by a desire to overcome the story of his origin. Accepted and put into print as gospel over long years, it was only recently that the tale of how the breed began was revealed as a yarn to rival even the wildest Paul Bunyan story. According to what we now might call "the great golden hoax," Lord Tweedmouth, a Briton of rare sporting instincts, became awestruck by a troup of large Russian dogs performing an intricate routine in a circus of Brighton, England, in 1860. Smitten by the dogs' beauty and obvious intelligence, Lord Tweedmouth, with a fistful of long green as bait, approached the Russian trainer and sought to purchase a pair of his magnificent dogs.

A resounding "Nyet" greeted the good Lord's first offer; selling just two of his dogs would ruin the act, the trainer contended. But, Tweedmouth, upholding the finest tradition of British tenacity, unhesitatingly countered with his trump card...and became the instant owner of all eight circus dogs.

Not content with an already colorful set of circumstances, the perpetrators of this whimsy proceeded to milk it further. The great circus dogs were given a name—Russian trackers—and a reputation as an old utility breed native to the mountain regions of Asiatic Russia. In their homeland, the yarn continued unabashedly, they served a variety of functions, most notably as herding dogs. They were reputed to care for entire flocks with consumate skill throughout the long arduous winters, while the native shepherds remained snug and warm at home in the villages until spring.

With dogs such as these Lord Tweedmouth was supposed to have created the breed of the present-day golden retriever. In truth, he did provide the original stock for the golden, but his dogs never saw, much less worked, in a circus.

Lord Tweedmouth actually began his experiments with a dog named Nous, a yellow-colored puppy from an otherwise all black litter of wavy-coated retrievers. Nous was later bred to Belle, a Tweed water spaniel, a pale liverish-hued breed common to the Tweed River region of lower Scotland where Tweedmouth lived. Progeny from this breeding was crossed back to the Tweed water spaniel and, subsequent linebreeding along with several outcrosses to wavy-coated, flat-coated and Labrador retrievers ultimately produced the uniform type and yellow coloration Tweedmouth desired.

For reasons not entirely clear, the golden did not achieve official recognition as a separate and distinct breed in England until some forty years later, in 1913, when it was accepted for registration by the Kennel Club of England.

Although the first goldens imported to North America reportedly were brought into Canada by former British army officers around

Considering the competition encountered from the traditionally favored Labs and Chessys, the Golden's climb to the number two popularity slot among retrievers is graphic testimony to the breed's abilities. **Photo by Evelyn M. Shafer.**

1900, none of the breed reached the United States until shortly before World War I. And since this was a relatively new breed whose popularity was slow in developing here, the golden was not accorded official status as a separate breed in the Canadian and American Kennel Clubs until 1927 and 1932 respectively.

The first golden retriever to win the title of Field Trial Champion in the United States was the fabulous Rip, owned and trained by Paul Bakewell III of St. Louis, Missouri. Rip annexed the title in 1939 and also copped for two successive years (1939 and 1940) the Field and Stream trophy for outstanding retriever of the year.

Thus Rip stands among, if not heading, the immortals of his breed, which include such names as Speedwell Pluto, Saffron Chipmonk, Chiltington Light, Wilderness Tangerine, Banty of Woodend, Stilrovin Rips Pride, Tonkahof Esther Belle and Stilrovin Nitro Express.

Rip represented the real turning point for the golden in this country. For his fantastic successes at the trials quickly focused public attention and interest upon the golden retriever, and the breed's popularity began a long-deserved upward swing, which in the years since has placed it among the top three retriever breeds in America.

Considering the stiff competition encountered among traditionally favored Labs and Chessies such a climb is an accomplishment of no small proportions, and a graphic testimonial to the golden's outstanding retrieving abilities.

To those who know him best, his most devoted fanciers, the golden is considered without peer for his all-around qualities of excellence in the blind, duck-boat, or uplands, as a close companion in the field and at home, and as a pupil whose remarkable intelligence makes him a naturally easy dog to train.

A very dear friend of the author's once owned a golden who was so smart he could spell. That is perhaps a slight exaggeration, for the dog could not really spell in the true sense of the word. But, simple commands such as sit, stay, here, and down were instantly obeyed by the dog when spelled out for him.

Ordinarily, the dog would not respond to spoken commands issued by anyone but the owner or his family. Yet, any stranger who knew the secret could exact unhesitating compliance by the dog simply by spelling out known commands. Why? I don't know, even the dog's owner was at a loss to explain. Perhaps the spelling lessons which were a bit more difficult to teach than the spoken words, were so indelibly impressed upon the dog's mind that it simply didn't matter who spelled them out for him. But the point is that with proper patience there is very little that cannot be taught to the golden retriever.

A strong and able swimmer, he's an eager, and extremely capable water worker, marking down ducks with uncanny accuracy and making his retrieves with the swift, business-like precision retriever men love to see. His thick undercoat, topped by a flat, or somewhat wavy, long-haired outer coat of rich golden color, provides him ample protection against all but the severest conditions of wind, weather, and water. And the rugged stamina inherent in his sturdy structure more than qualifies him for the task of frequent swims in pond, lake. and river waters when the duck shooting gets fast and furious.

The same reliable efficiency is exhibited in the golden's work ashore. In fact, his extra-sharp scenting powers provide him with precisely the sort of nose needed to untangle the puzzling trails left by crippled upland game birds. Few birds escape the accurate marking eyes of a golden; those that do, still have to reckon with his choke bore nose.

Undoubtedly due to his superior scenting abilities, the golden's role as a pinch-hit flush dog for upland game has steadily increased in recent years. In all fairness to the golden it must be admitted that in this task he certainly poses little threat to the specialized upland bird hunting breeds, but if he is given even a modicum of training for it, his performance will ordinarily satisfy the gunner whose interest in pheasant, grouse, and woodcock is secondary.

Standing twenty-three to twenty-four inches at the withers, most males tip the scales at approximately seventy pounds. Females average roughly ten pounds lighter and stand two to three inches shorter. Not exactly lap dogs! Yet, with the possible exception of size, which in some cases might constitute a disadvantage, the golden embodies all the requisite qualities of an ideal house pet.

A gentle nature and even temperament are characteristics that contribute heavily in his favor as a well-behaved and thoroughly trustworthy companion to the whole family. And, while seldom an openly aggressive dog, either toward other dogs or strangers, he knows no hesitation in protecting his loved ones or himself if the need arises. Though never flaunting it, his quiet courage, like his loyalty and devotion, lies deep within his heart—rarely seen but thoroughly indisputable.

The same efficiency he shows in the water is displayed in the Golden's work ashore. Extra-sharp scenting powers aid him in unravelling the trails of crippled game birds that might otherwise be left unfound.

Little more could reasonably be asked or expected of any breed, yet the golden goes right ahead and offers still another significant asset to his owner. An unusual degree of intelligence enables him to grasp quickly whatever is taught him. This, coupled with his ingrained urge to please, makes him an alert, responsive pupil, whose obedience training generally can be accomplished with a minimum of effort.

Naturally, these same desirable traits extend to his lessons in retrieving game for the gun, no small blessing for the average amateur trainer with limited time and experience. The fact that golden retriever pups need little coaxing to "get wet all over," plus their instinctive desire to fetch any and all thrown objects, makes even the greenest trainer's chore — if that is the right word — considerably more fun than work.

The Golden Retriever Club of America, founded in 1938, is the official sponsoring organization of the breed in the United States, and is recognized by the American Kennel Club. Goldens are usually registered with the A.K.C. but also are eligible for registry in the American Field Publishing Company's Field Dog Stud Book.

The sight of an enthusiastic retriever hitting the water, swimming strong and true to a crisp, decisive pick-up, flawless return, and delivery to hand of the season's first mallard will provide any golden's owner with his ultimate reward — a chest-swelling pride and sense of satisfaction that proves beyond a doubt at least in the golden retriever's case, that there really *is* something in a name!

Big, courageous, and independent, the Chessy can hardly be termed handsome. But he is as functional in the water as a fish. **Photo by Winston H. Moore.**

THE CHESAPEAKE BAY RETRIEVER

Truly great qualities in man or beast can inspire the imagination to some pretty wild heights. And if most folk legends strain at the truth, at least some come amazingly close to credibility simply by building upon a particular quality or characteristic already well known and impressive to people. Like the tale that prevailed for many years about a female Chesapeake Bay retriever type dog who, in mating with an otter, produced the original breeding stock for the Chesapeake in America.

That this sort of fantasy could be believed—and it was, in some superstitious quarters—serves as a tribute to the Chesapeake's fantastic prowess as a water dog. For anyone who has witnessed one of these magnificent animals performing under conditions of unimaginably foul, sub-zero weather, in seas that would sicken an old sailor, is tempted to believe such a story of his ancestry.

Certainly, the duck hunter doesn't exist who could ask or expect more of a retriever. And if one did, the Chesapeake would doubtless deliver—or go down trying, with never a whimper.

Whereas the majority of gun dog breeds in America stem from foreign origin, the Chesapeake is one of only two who can lay claim to having been conceived and developed exclusively on our shores. The stories of his beginning may vary somewhat, but they all agree on the major points.

A pair of Newfoundland puppies, aboard a ship sailing for England in 1807, were either shipwrecked along the coast of Maryland or taken on board another vessel bound for Baltimore. At any rate, Sailor, a dingy, red-colored male, and Canton, a black female, purportedly named after the Baltimore-bound vessel that rescued both dogs and crew members from disaster, found their way into Maryland. From that point the story has two versions.

The first recounts that Sailor was given, in gratitude for hospitality shown the crew, to John Mercer of West River, Maryland, and Canton, for similar reasons, to Dr. James Stuart of Sparrows Point, Maryland. The second account has both dogs becoming the property of a George

Beyond question the Chesapeake Bay retriever is the finest water worker in the world. For sheer ruggedness, power, endurance and capability under the most adverse conditions, no other fetch dog can match him. Chesonomas Louis, owned by a West Coast sportsman, exhibits true Chesapeake verve in his enthusiastic water entry.

Law, also of Maryland. Neither story provides clue to whether or not Sailor and Canton ever were mated to each other.

But according to written accounts by General Ferdinand Latrobe, Sailor and Canton were crossbred with the black-and-tan coonhound. Latrobe was a former mayor of Baltimore who for almost thirty years was associated with the Carroll's Island Club, an organization credited with exerting considerable influence in developing the Chesapeake breed. The black-and-tan, a favorite with Maryland and Virginia hunters of that period, was a hound of extraordinary scenting powers. It's contended that this infusion of hound blood vastly improved the Chesapeake's nose and stamina, provided the strong, heavy tail so important to superior swimming ability, produced the yellow eyes, and lightened the shade of the coat to its present typical dead-grass color.

Other breeds or strains were undoubtedly incorporated into the early Chesapeakes, but these never were authenticated or, in most cases, even recorded. It does seem likely, though, that such breeds as the curly-coated and the flat-coated retrievers and, perhaps, the Irish water spaniel or a similar type may have contributed to the Chesapeake's evolution.

Though the state of Maryland must be credited with originating the breed, development of the Chesapeake was not restricted to the Old Line State. Gunners in Minnesota, Wisconsin, and along the Mississippi flyway were employing the breed as a favored retriever even before the start of the twentieth century, and it is undisputed fact that they, too, were instrumental in its development as a superior water worker.

Despite the early formation of numerous localized clubs interested in the Chesapeake, the breed had no representation on a national level until the inception in 1918 of the American Chesapeake Club. Within a few years, interest in the club sagged badly because of its inability to provide trials for the breed, and it did not revive to any great extent until 1935, when Anthony Bliss became club president. During his tenure, field trials for the Chesapeake became a reality and did much to renew interest and spark competition within the ranks of supporters of this grand water specialist.

Renowned field trial winners of that period, to whom many of today's Chesapeakes can trace lineage, included Sodak's Gypsy Prince, Skipper Bob, Shagwong Gypsy, Gypsy Prince, Chesacroft Baron, Chesabob and Gunnar II.

The present day Chesapeake is beyond question the finest water working retriever in the world. For rugged power, endurance, and skill under the most trying conditions, no other water working retriever can hold a candle to him. His enthusiastic willingness to enter unhesitatingly, time after time, into punishingly frigid, wind-whipped waters after dead or crippled ducks has won him admiration in waterfowl hunting circles the world over.

His memory, enabling him to mark down as many as half a dozen ducks at a single fall, is as remarkable as the native intelligence he shows in his work merely as a matter of routine. Seemingly possessed with the power to reason, he will, in a multiple retrieve situation, seek out and deliver all crippled ducks first, before bothering with the dead ones. Similarly, should a fallen bird be carried out of sight on a strong river current, he will strike out, without slightest confusion or hesitation, in a downstream direction to recover the stray.

A remarkable memory enables the Chessy to mark down as many as half a dozen falls at one time. This dog, AFC Atom Bob, eyes a pair of incoming pintails as gunners prepare to score. **Photo by Winston H. Moore.**

A natural aptitude and instinctive love for the water, coupled with an ardent enthusiasm for retrieving, greatly simplify the task of training him. So pronounced is his love for the gun that, afforded even the barest amount of formal training, the average Chesapeake will turn in a serviceable performance from the duck blind.

Despite his natural supremacy in the water, the Chesapeake's popularity runs a poor third to the Labrador and golden retriever breeds. There are reasons for this — some of them justifiable. Probably one of the most significant is that he is not, in the usual sense, an ideal house pet. He is a big dog, averaging about sixty-five to seventy pounds and standing as tall as twenty-six inches at the shoulder. The oiliness of his dense, double thick coat, is decidedly an advantage in withstanding the rigors of swimming in icy waters, but it is regarded by some as objectionable in the home.

But even more significant than not being traditionally a hearthside companion has been the Chessy's inability to adapt to supplementary use as a flushing dog in the uplands. Not that he hasn't and cannot be used as such, but on average he simply falls short of showing the same real verve and efficiency on land that both the Lab and the golden possess.

Perhaps because he is so water-oriented, because his body structure and muscular development make him less maneuverable on land, because he is less amenable to or dependent upon directions, he does not particularly excel at spaniels' work. But, no matter what his capabilities might be on terra firma, they'd be bound to suffer by comparison with the phenomenal feats this great duck and goose dog performs in the water.

Although the Chesapeake's disposition generally reflects the qualities which make him such a standout performer in the water — courage, aggressiveness, confidence and independence — he can be made into a good companion. Hardly a dog to be fawned over, he is always loyal and dependable, but his feelings for his master are implied, or understood, rather than demonstrated through outward gushings of affection except in uncommon individual cases.

Ordinarily posing no problem to the one-dog owner who prefers keeping him outside in a kennel, the Chessy's rugged constitution and courageous spirit bear watching in instances where he is required to share space with one or more kennel mates. Conditions of "peaceful co-existence" usually can be maintained, however, through the exercise of proper training and reasonable supervision. Should he get involved in a fight, however, just don't put your money on the other dog.

In the looks department the Chesapeake could hardly be termed handsome. His coarse outer coat varies from several shades of chocolate brown to faded dead grass or tan, and his general conformation denotes power and endurance rather than sleek or graceful symmetry. Supporters of the breed have long and steadfastly resisted any movement to beautify him, on the theory that all such attempts, however well intended at first, might eventually place undue emphasis on eye appeal to the disregard of functional abilities.

And perhaps, they are to be admired in their dedicated stand. For, the old adage "Handsome is as handsome does" could not be more appropriate in calling attention to the talents of the greatest of all water dogs—the Chesapeake Bay retriever.

ANOTHER PAIR TO MARK WELL

The dog-buying public is a fickle fraternity. Ruled slavishly by a passion for what is currently fashionable, it sways hither and yon like a willow in the breeze, and depending on its fancy, a breed can sky-rocket to success or wither into obscurity. What is today's fashion often becomes passé by tomorrow, with a new fad quickly springing up in its place. Yet, when public tastes neglect a sporting breed of proven merit, then, surely, those tastes are open to question.

Two such practical retriever breeds as the Irish water spaniel and American water spaniel present a case in point. Why a pair of breeds with the versatility quotient possessed by these two should so often be overlooked by the average hunter today just doesn't make sense.

Surely, if you've ever owned or had a yen for a standard poodle, then the Irish water spaniel already has a good start in appealing to your visual preferences. At first glance, he could easily be mistaken for a poodle, with his chocolate-colored coat of tight little curls and his crowning topknot.

But, after a few minute's scrutiny, you'd begin to spot some distinctive differences, and if his bigger-than-standard-poodle size didn't give him away, then his full-length, practically bald tail would. Right after you'd decided that he wasn't a poodle, the thought might also strike you that he really didn't resemble a hunting dog either.

Yet beneath that somewhat comical exterior are a wealth of qualities that help fill a sportsman's game pocket. Chuckles at his looks inevitably give way to smiles of approval when he gets to work, unhesitatingly breaking skim-ice to fetch up a long fall on inland pond or displaying his smarts by making entry well downcurrent from a duck dumped into fast-flowing river or stream.

Intelligence, stamina, and willingness to work under the most rugged conditions characterize the Irish water spaniel, one of the most functional of retriever breeds. Although, technically, a member of the spaniel family—the largest member, in fact—he is generally classified with the breeds that specialize in retrieving waterfowl, a job he's performed for the past one hundred years in this country, and even longer in his native land.

The Irish water spaniel's origin, unlike so many of our hunting breeds, is readily traceable. Justin McCarthy, an avid sportsman and

Appearances can be misleading, as the Irish water spaniel proves. Despite his Poodle-like exterior, the Irishman is a hunter to the core. **Photo by IWS Club of America.**

gun dog enthusiast, originated and began developing the breed in southern Ireland in 1850. Perhaps motivated more by a whimsical sense of humor than the churlishness some attribute to him, McCarthy always managed to withhold the most significant details about the crosses he utilized to establish the breed. Of course, guesses have never been in short supply. Some of these express the belief that the breed resulted from crossing the poodle with the Irish setter; others have either or both of these breeds being crossbred with the old Spanish pointer.

Perhaps more credible is the theory that McCarthy created the breed from the South Country water spaniel, a curly-coated dog common to the South of Ireland, and the old Portugese water dog, which some authorities contend may have been one of the progenitors of the poodle.

Except for size, which has increased, the present-day Irisher is a carbon copy of the original McCarthy dogs. Innumerable writings of the pre- and post-Civil War period refer to the breed in the United

States, so it is apparent that fair numbers of Irish water spaniels were imported here very shortly after McCarthy originated the breed.

The first one officially registered in this country was listed in Volume I of the National American Kennel Club Stud Book, published in 1878. That same year twenty-two other Irish water spaniels were registered and, with the exception of a pair of Chesapeake Bay dogs, were the only retrievers recorded in the stud book that year.

The Irishman proved especially popular in the midwest with both sportsmen and market gunners. His ability to put in a full day's work under conditions ranging from rough, icy water to densely overgrown cover gained him the unstinted praise of the ordinarily stoic market hunter, a man whose bread and butter depended on his shooting eye and the work of a reliable dog, with little margin for error on either count.

The breed's popularity during those years spread outward from the central part of the country to both coasts, with Eastern and Western shore gunners extolling the dog's usefulness in equally enthusiastic terms. Within the next few years the Irish water spaniel increased in stature, literally as well as figuratively, as American shooters sought the additional serviceability provided by larger, longer-legged specimens. These proved even more efficient than their predecessors in negotiating the weedy covers so typical of the sloughs and tidal marshlands where they found their greatest use.

The Irishman's star continued to rise until well after the start of the twentieth century. More Irish water spaniels were registered in the Field Dog Stud Book in 1922 than any other breed of retriever, and their popularity remained high through the rest of that decade. Only after the introduction of the Labrador and Golden retrievers did the Irish "fetch" dog's numbers begin to dip. Among the explanations for this decline are several very logical ones. Both the Golden and the Labrador were far handsomer breeds than the Irish and that, coupled with their newness and the promotional efforts put behind their establishment here, took much of the play away from the tried and true veteran. Also to be reckoned with was the fact that the newcomers displayed more of the flash sought in field trial performers, a quality the Irish water spaniel has seldom shown in sufficient degree to win retriever trials consistently.

Since the founding of the Irish Water Spaniel Club of America, in 1937, the breed has managed to maintain a fairly even level of popularity, showing neither spectacular gains nor losses, despite the stiff

The Irish water spaniel is keenly intelligent, alert and thoroughly devoted to his family. Seldom demonstrative, he nonetheless has a pleasing and ebullient nature. **Photo by IWS Club of America.**

competition of the other retriever breeds.

Today's Irish water spaniel, like his earlier relatives, is most appreciated by the dyed-in-the-wool lowland gunner, whose sport takes in the shooting of ducks, geese, and such shore birds as sora and clapper rails. For these last two, the Irishman is without peer, his physical structure, highly water-resistant coat and endurance perfectly fitting him for the sloppy, energy-sapping task of making innumerable retrieves on these high-limit game birds in the formidable combination of water, muck, and dense vegetation that is their haunt.

An exceptionally strong swimmer, with a natural love of water, the Irish water spaniel works well out of all conventional duck hunting rigs, be they shore or water blinds, pits, or sneak-boats. His keen eye for marking a fall, coupled with typically sharp spaniel scenting powers, adds to his high success ratio at bringing back even the most lightly crippled birds. The skeptic who bets against the Irisher's returning with any given cripple he's sent after had better get pretty stiff odds if he doesn't want to lose his shirt, and his pants along with it.

Many of the breed's fanciers utilize their dogs for multi-purpose duty in the uplands, springing game birds and trailing rabbits in the

manner of their other spaniel cousins. Properly trained and experienced in such work they can turn in very serviceable performances
as flush dogs, and, they do an admirable job of retrieving shot game
for the bag.

The Irishman develops somewhat more slowly than other retrievers,
usually attaining physical and mental maturity at about two years of
age. His spaniel heritage is evidenced in the fact that rough, abusive
handling tactics are certain to bring only negative results. As with all
spaniel breeds, firm, gentle persuasion will produce the most satisfactory responses in the Irish water spaniel, whose keen intelligence
prompts quick learning and long retention of lessons properly taught.

Dogs generally stand about twenty-four inches at the shoulder and
tip the scales at an average sixty pounds, with bitches running slightly
shorter and a bit lighter. If his size seems a deterrent to housepet
status, his well behaved, often reserved, manner usually overrides
the common objections and earns him a permanent berth in the
family diggings. Seldom will he let down his dignity by slobbering
over strangers, yet, where his own people are concerned, he is a
devoted, though not overly demonstrative companion.

His tight curly coat comes in one color only—a solid, rich, dark
liver. His finely tapering tail sports two or three inches of thick curls
at the root, with the remainder covered with very short smooth hair.
The most common, if not very complimentary, expression used to
describe his unique appendage is "rattail," a term which I detest and
would like to see dropped for all time from the breed's official standard.

Another distinguishing characteristic of the Irish water spaniel is
his topknot, which consists of loose curls that grow down in a definite
peak between his eyes and contrast strikingly with the smooth short
hair on his face.

What he may lack in classical gun dog good looks, he more than
makes up for as a loyal companion, alert watchdog and functional
asset to the gun. And, if there is even a spark of truth to the adage that
"all the world loves a clown," then, certainly, the Irish water spaniel,
that affable "clown" of gun dogdom, must one day recapture the full
popularity he so richly deserves.

The American water spaniel, one of only three sporting breeds of
purely American origination and development, is the embodiment of
utility personified. Probably the single exception to the statement
made earlier in this book that the all-around hunting breed doesn't
exist, this little gun dog shows a penchant for hunting virtually any

small game species that swims, runs, hops, or flies.

If I exaggerate, it is only slightly; few, if any, American water spaniels hunt fox, bobcat, coon, or possum. But, trail hound duties form about the only blank spot in this tiny tyro's hunting repertoire. Pheasants, grouse, woodcock, rabbits, hares, all are handled in the uplands by the American water spaniel in the typical manner of the flush dog. In the lowlands, working as a very competent retriever, he is equal to almost any fetching task on ducks and all but the largest geese. And, just for good measure, again performing as a spaniel, he'll put up for the gun sora and clapper rails and those most tantalizing of all aerial targets, jacksnipe. Imbued with such extensive versatility, the American water spaniel's relatively low popularity rating becomes all the more enigmatic.

Although we have few records of the breed's origin it is considered probable that his ancestry stemmed from a combination of the old English water spaniel, the Irish water spaniel and the curly-coated retriever. All of these breeds had been imported to the United States by the 1880's, when it is believed the American water spaniel as we

Blessed with a penchant for hunting almost any small game, the American water spaniel is the embodiment of utility personified. He is affectionate and mild-mannered, and displays a spirited, cheerful personality. **Photo by Evelyn M. Shafer.**

know him today first began to make his appearance, so their contributions to his development seem logically well founded.

His principal strongholds were located in the midwest and northeast regions of the nation, where the needs for a real "meat-and-potatoes" gun dog fostered his development along distinctly utilitarian lines. No specialist to be sure, he was nevertheless a competent assistant, more than equal to holding up his end of the job of putting meat on the family table.

Despite the American's popularity in the field during the latter part of the nineteenth century and the early years of the twentieth, there was little formal promotion of the breed here on a national level. It was not until about 1935 that a club was even formed to represent the breed. Three years later, after diligent club efforts, the Field Dog Stud Book accepted the American water spaniel for registration as a purebred dog. Recognition by the American Kennel Club subsequently followed, in 1940.

A small-to-medium-sized dog, the American stands from fifteen to eighteen inches high at shoulder and weighs between twenty-five and forty pounds. His full-length tail is covered with curly hair. Although not too compactly built, his body being a bit long in comparison to his height, he is still handily proportioned for the gunner whose living quarters are somewhat restricted. Affectionate and mild-mannered, the American water spaniel manifests all the qualities normally sought in a house pet and family companion, along with an excellent predisposition to accept formal training.

Far more spaniel-like than his cousin the Irish water spaniel, the American has a cheerful temperament that always mirrors gay spirits and an overflowing desire to please. If dealt with kindly, he can be trained with a minimum of effort, but overly rough correction brings out his spaniel tendencies toward sulkiness. On the credit side of his spaniel ancestry, he easily retains what he's been taught, making it very seldom necessary to spend time reviewing the things he already knows.

His native swimming ability and fondness for the water provide him with the ingrained potentials of a good retriever, more than serviceable enough for the average waterfowler in these days of generally sparse duck limits. Then, too, as a flush dog for upland game birds, he is equal if not superior, by virtue of his smaller size, to a majority of retriever breeds. Technically not a retriever, but a spaniel, the American sports a dense wavy or curly coat of solid liver or dark chocolate color. For both land or water work it provides ample protection against the elements as well as the punishment of heavy cover.

Possibly only because he has never competed in field trials of any sort has the American water spaniel failed to reap the public attention that almost automatically goes with such competition. Were he a flashy trial contender — even though that is not his bent — he could not go unnoticed. Still, if that were the sole criterion for focussing a neglectful public eye on him, he would have to undergo drastic changes to accommodate competition standards. Then, of course, he'd sacrifice so many of the very qualities and characteristics that make him the fine, versatile hunter that he is.

Rather than change him, it can only be hoped that increasing numbers of practical hunters, in their search for suitably practical gun dogs, will discover and one day elevate the American water spaniel to the popularity level where he truly belongs.

6

The Breeds That Trail

THE BEAGLE

IF THE COTTONTAIL could talk, he'd surely scotch the idea that there's any special good luck powers in a rabbit's foot. As proof, he might cite the fact that even with four rabbit's feet his luck is seldom as good as that of a hunter who owns two pairs of beagle feet with beagle attached, of course. For once his trail is picked up by this keen-nosed and tenacious little hound, Mr. Cottontail is usually but a hop or two this side of the stewpot.

Since the cottontail rabbit is the most sought after of American small game, it logically follows that his principal nemesis, the beagle — scourge of the brush pile and brier patch — should be the nation's most popular hunting dog. One of the smallest of the innumerable hound breeds, the white, black, and tan beagle is a rabbit specialist supreme, one who takes to bunny chasing as naturally and eagerly as a cock grouse to a drumming log.

His bawling voice, drifting back across wooded hillside or open field on a frosty autumn morning has become as much a part of the rural American scene as Thanksgiving or apple pie. Without him, countless hunters would have less than sufficient incentive to go afield for a day's sport with scattergun or rifle. And boys, of all ages, for lack of a beagle named Dan, or Belle, or Champ, might grow into adults never knowing the solace of a canine crying towel whenever their world caved in, the snug security of a beagle blanket on the foot of the bed, or the tender persistence of a warm-tongued "alarm clock" when it's time to get up.

The beagle we know today differs a bit from his forebears, according to records that trace his ancestry back to sixteenth-century England during the reign of Henry VIII. The old writings, besides confirming the belief that the breed had even earlier origins, state that the dogs were taken to the field in the saddle baskets of the nobility, a fact that lends weight to the theory that those first beagles were miniatures of our modern breed.

While some historians think that the beagle derived from cross-breedings of the harrier and the South of England hound, no solid evidence supports their contention. What is generally conceded, however, is that the modern beagle stems from members of an exceptional pack of hounds gathered together in Essex by the Reverend Philip Honeywood about 1850. Importation of the first of these modern beagles to America, in the 1870's, is credited to General Richard Rowett of Carlinsville, Illinois.

In the 1800's, a scant decade after the first arrivals, considerable

Size, temperament, tractability, ease of training and a strong inborn love for the hunt all keep the Beagle on top of the heap as the most popular hunting breed in the nation.

Beagle pups from proven hunting stock ordinarily require little formal training, aside from the opportunity to work, to become good, serviceable rabbit dogs. **Photo by Evelyn M. Shafer.**

discord developed over the qualities that constituted the ideal beagle. As a means of ending the haggling and determining a suitable standard for the breed, the American-English Beagle Club was founded in 1884, and a committee was formed to work out and adopt a set of standards — standards which to this day have been little altered by the present National Beagle Club of America.

Among the noteworthy early beagles in the country, many of which were the pillars of today's stock, were such names as Warrior, Rosey, Dodge's Rattler, Lee, Triumph, Wanderer, Blue Cap, Chimer, Frank Forest, Sue Forest, Clyde, Sunday, Gypsy, Forest, and Trick.

Under the sponsorship of the National Beagle Club, the first field trials for the little hounds in America were conducted at Hyannis, Massachusetts, and Salem, New Hampshire, on November 4 and 7, 1890. Ever since that pioneering effort there has been a steadily mounting interest in beagle field trials here, one that has yet to reach its peak potential. But the average sportsman aspires neither to glory nor to silver cups and contents himself with enjoying his beagle as a combination house pet and hunting partner.

With so many hunting breeds to choose from, one naturally wonders what keeps the beagle on top of the heap, year after year. Aside from his unrivalled proficiency at rabbit hunting, which alone would seem reason enough, he manifests the qualities that sportsmen regard as the epitome of practicality in a hunting dog, and in exactly the right proportions. Size, temperament, tractability, ease of training—all vitally important factors in choosing any breed of hunting dog—are rarely combined so compatibly in a single package as they are in the beagle.

The casual observer might describe him simply as small; staunch supporters more aptly term him "handy-sized." Bench and field standards, being more precise, divide him into two classifications: fifteen inches at shoulder or under, and thirteen inches or under. In any case, the beagle can safely be called convenient-sized. He is easy to feed, to house, to transport.

While hardly a sensitive dog, to be handled with kid gloves or gushed over, he will, like most animals, readily respond to attention and affection from his owner. And his good-natured disposition enables him to meet with gentle patience the most overenthusiastic treatment doled out by the "sandbox set." If other breeds are better qualified for the role of family pet, few beagle owners will admit it.

Matching the beagle's affable nature is his willingness to please those he loves. Despite retaining a certain amount of hound-like independence, and the same tendency to roam, if permitted, he will eagerly accept all the lessons an attentive owner patiently teaches him.

As a hunter, the ideal beagle displays boundless determination, an innately unquenchable desire to hunt, the proper functional conformation to do so, a sharp sense of smell, a good voice, the willingness to work in all types of cover, a merry disposition, and tractability.

The sportsman who takes pains to select his beagle pup from ancestry embodying these characteristics in greatest measure will already have won half the battle of acquiring a first class rabbit hound. The other half, of course, depends on the kind and amount of training and field experience he is able to give the pup. But, certainly, none of the hunting breeds is any easier to train successfully for the field.

Even the barest amounts of formal training will help develop the average beagle from longtime field stock into a highly serviceable meat dog. Most beagle owners start training their young dogs merely by hunting them with an older, more experienced beagle. Normally,

A fresh snowfall, a brier patch and a Beagle, followed by a hunter of almost any age, are the classic ingredients of a memorable day outdoors. **Photo by Dave Moreton.**

little more than the good example set by the veteran is needed to thoroughly rouse the latent hunting instincts of any beagle youngster worth his chow.

Like most hounds, this little guy hunts strictly by scent, casting about for hot, or fresh, tracks and running the line, following every footstep left by a fleeing cottontail, and giving tongue all the way. His lack of speed, at least contrasted to the rabbit's, is the real secret of his success since, he seldom pushes the bunny hard enough to drive him to ground. Inclined as he is to circle back, rather than leave his home territory, the rabbit is certain to pass within gun range of the beagle owner who simply stands pat, waiting for his dog to bring the cottontail around.

Although most often thought of strictly as a rabbit dog, the beagle is frequently called upon to pinch-hit on pheasants. With the ringneck's running proclivities, this game bird leaves a good deal of foot scent, not unlike a typical bunny trail, making it fairly easy for a beagle to follow his line. Urged on by his boss, almost any beagle experienced on rabbits learns very quickly to adapt to trailing pheasants. And if his work can't be compared to the spaniel's, at least the ringneck-hunting beagle manages to get the job done well enough to give his owner an occasional change from rabbit stew.

Some beaglers use their dogs for infrequent forays into grouse and woodcock covers. And while they do sometimes pick up a bird or two, such success is generally accidental. For one thing, these game birds ordinarily don't leave the liberal supply of foot scent that the ringneck does; for another, they prefer to fly rather than run from imminent danger, lessening the little hound's opportunities to do much trailing of them. Third, and perhaps most significant is the fact that rabbits are too often jumped in these same covers, and no beagle could ever be expected to pass up hot bunny scent for anything wearing feathers.

More beagles are registered in the American Kennel Club than any other breed, but probably only a small percentage of these are used for hunting. Large numbers of beagles, of the strictly working variety, are entered in the stud book of the United Kennel Club of Kalamazoo, Michigan. But, only the Good Lord can keep track of what is doubtless an even greater number of unregistered beagles that earn their vittles hunting rabbits across the length and breadth of America.

Unquestionably, the diminutive little beagle's remarkable ability to develop into a top-notch rabbit dog on little more than his own basic inheritance constitutes one of the major advantages of the breed to the average practical sportsman. And, with so many other outstanding qualities, who possibly could—or would want to—dispute the beagle's right to the place he has won as the most popular hunting dog in the United States, today?

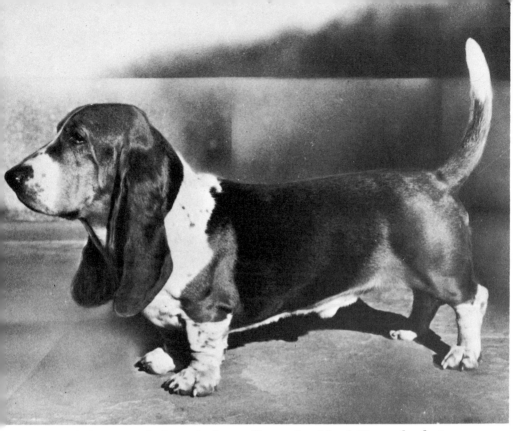

Gentle by nature, the basset is also good-humored and loyal. He may be short on leg, but he's always long on personality, and makes a good companion to the family.

THE BASSET HOUND

Sometimes it's difficult to account for the sudden rise to prominence of a particular breed of dog. Doubly so, if that breed has been hanging around the American scene for nearly a century without attracting much more than a relatively small following. But, there's not much to speculate about in the case of the basset hound, that sad-eyed member of the hound group whose exposure on a couple of national television series a few years back brought the breed to the attention of millions of Americans.

Doubtless, the TV tube was responsible for placing innumerable bassets in homes across the nation strictly as family pets, a role the breed is well qualified to fill. But, just as surely, it also resulted in getting substantial numbers of them into the field as efficient, companionable hunters, giving the breed a long overdue boost toward recognition. For despite a unique appearance suggesting he's too awkward to get out of his own way, the basset is one of the most proficient game trailers in the business. He has a nose that ranks second only to the bloodhound, and an insatiable love for the chase that's common to all members of the hound family.

As any veteran dog man can attest, there's always a practical reason for what may seem an odd or physically abnormal conformation in any breed. And there are good and valid reasons for both the basset's unusual structure and his superior scenting abilities. Of course, records and factual details available to canine historians are typically sketchy and too imprecise to trace the basset's exact origin without some degree of conjecture.

According to the universally accepted reconstruction of the breed's history, the basset descended from a cross of the old French bloodhound and the hounds of the Abbots of Saint Hubert, a monastic order that lived in Belgium several centuries ago.

This order of monks, named after the patron saint of hunters, bred rather short-legged, mostly white hounds that were used to trail game in very heavy cover. The shortness of leg found in the St. Hubert dogs gave them two distinctly practical working advantages over other more conventionally proportioned hounds: It permitted easier negotiation of dense covers, which they went under as often as through, and allowed the dogs to keep their noses naturally closer to the ground without slowing their normal running pace.

With the crossing of the French bloodhound and the hound of St. Hubert, the length of leg was reduced even further by careful selective breeding. Through what was undoubtedly a chance mutation, a strain with crooked forelegs later emerged from this cross. Since the crook in the front legs placed the dog still closer to the ground — where his nose virtually rubbed the scent trail left by game — this type of hound soon attained favor over the straight-legged basset.

A lack of dates in the early writings on the basset makes it difficult to trace the breed's dispersion into various parts of Europe. It is known, however, that bassets ultimately found their way into Germany, Spain, and Russia, and that several differing varieties, or types, existed during the eighteenth and nineteenth centuries.

Two major strains came to the fore in France about 1850. These were the Le Contealx and the Lane, each named after the man who developed them. They differed principally in the head and eye; the Le Contealx having a narrower head and less prominent eye than the Lane.

The Basset's short legs enable him to go under much of the tangled cover that a taller hound would have to plow through. **Photo by Basset Hound Club of America.**

The first bassets to reach England, a pair of the Le Contealx strain sent as a gift from the Comte de Tournow to Lord Galway, arrived in 1866. The following year Lord Galway bred the pair, named Basset and Belle and obtained a litter of undetermined number, which he sold some five years later to Lord Onslow. He supplemented this string with additional imports from the kennels of Le Contealx, but in 1882 he sold the lot to George Krehl and Sir Everett Millais. Millais initiated a bloodhound cross with his bassets to intensify a number of qualities he believed were gradually being weakened.

Descendants of the Krehl and Millais Bassets were imported to America around 1888 and are generally regarded as the foundation stock of the bulk of the breed in this country today. However, earlier importations, the exact dates of which are open to conjecture, are known to have been made from Russia. And there are some authorities who uphold the contention that the very first bassets probably came into America among the hound packs presented to George Washington by the Marquis de Lafayette at the close of the Revolu-

Puppies are all lovable, but Basset puppies — at least these three — are among the most lovable of all.

tionary War. In any case, it's a pretty safe bet that today's American basset is an admixture of French, Russian, and English types.

Until recently, the basset never attained truly popular status in America, possibly due to his almost comic appearance but more likely because of the overwhelming competition provided by the beagle. Since both breeds are in many ways similar — they're used on the same kinds of game and employed in much the same manner in hunting it — they have naturally been forced to vie for popular acceptance among the same group of hunters.

The beagle early captured a lion's share of this fancy, and for years the basset had to be content merely with holding his own. Now, however, with more hunters entering the field every year, the tides of fortune have helped swing a fair share of the new recruits into the basset camp.

Nor can such recruits regret having joined his team if rabbits are their major gunning interest, with perhaps an occasional foray for coon, possum, fox, squirrel, and pheasants thrown in. The basset will do a creditable job of tracking virtually any small game species that leaves a ground scent trail for him to follow, which makes the breed a practical choice for any sportsman who dabbles in hunting a little bit of everything.

Like the beagle, though, the basset is considered primarily a rabbit dog, casting about the woods and fields until he either jumps a bunny or strikes a hot line of fresh rabbit scent. Instantly bawling his rich baritone song on the trail, he eventually pushes Mr. Cottontail close enough for the waiting gunner to make a killing shot. His extremely short legs allow him to keep his ultra-sensitive nose close to the source of foot scent without interfering with his natural stride and pace, an advantage resulting in fewer time-wasting checks or back-tracking to pick up a lost line.

Admittedly, those short legs carry him at a somewhat slower pace than that of taller hounds; yet, he is by no means a piddling slow-poke. Many gunners consider the basset's an ideal pace to follow on foot and would even feel uncomfortable in back of a speedier hound. Moreover, as his devotees astutely point out, he trails at a speed that gently prods game to keep moving without panicking, so that game will generally travel in smaller circles around the gunner and, thereby, afford him much better opportunity for an effective shot.

The basset's sure-nosed trailing ability has also led to his increased usage as an efficient pheasant dog. Aside from his natural enthusiasm for the job, his low-slung frame enables him to negotiate brushy tangles almost as easily as a running ringneck and he's highly adept at rooting smart old cock birds out of rugged cover that might stymie or, at least, discourage many another breed.

Easily trained to trail and tree squirrels, the basset makes a competent assistant to take into the oak or hickory woods for an afternoon's change-of-pace sport with the little bushytails. And with a little experience, he can be taught to run coon and possum for the man who enjoys some hunting after dark. In this latter sport, the dog's deep, bawling voice, with its rich, resonant tone and long-carrying range, favors him as an excellent hound to follow at night, when the chase may often lead him several miles from the hunter.

While strong natural instincts and keen desire for the hunt are basset hallmarks, the breed, as a rule, is a later developer than the beagle. Consequently, the over-impatient owner who wants to transform his pup into a finished, veteran game-getter in the span of a single season, is bound to meet with frustration and disappointment if he selects a basset hound. Overnight successes are very definitely the exception with this breed. But the basset will learn his lessons well if he is given suitable opportunities and the necessary time to develop properly—important considerations with any breed of gun dog. And, once learned, they are generally *his* for life, eliminating the extensive retraining programs that owners of some other breeds face at the start of each new season.

Gentle and intelligent, the basset has much to recommend him as a companion dog. He is good-natured and loyal, so loyal, in fact, that he displays strong tendency to become a "one-man dog" if fed, trained and handled by a single individual most of the time. This predisposition can easily be overcome, though, by securing him as a young pup and encouraging each member of the family to participate in his regular care and training.

Bassets can vary considerably in size. In comparison to their height —nine to fifteen inches at the withers—they are good, solid dogs, long in body and ranging in weight from thirty-five to seventy pounds. They have pendulous ears and long tails and their basically white, short-haired coat is generally patched with black or tan or even both of these colors.

The American Kennel Club registers the majority of the nation's bassets, with by far the greatest number of these being pets and show stock. Working members of the breed often are registered in both the United Kennel Club and the A.K.C.

The average basset is far from a dull character. Short on leg, but certainly not on personality, his expressive looks need no words to translate their meaning. And an owner's stern moods are short-lived in the face of the basset's infectious good humor, jocular spirit, and comical antics. At home or afield, this knock-kneed, funny-looking but lovable hound just can't help endearing himself to any man who ever owns him.

Bold, aggressive and determined on the trail, the black-and-tan at home is an extremely friendly, affectionate fellow, with a gentle, sensitive nature.

THE BLACK-AND-TAN COONHOUND

Ask any ten hunters what breed of dog automatically comes to mind at the mention of rabbit hunting and, chances are, all ten answers would be the same. Mention bobwhite quail shooting, or sub-zero weather waterfowling, and once again unanimity would be likely. But bring up the subject of coon hunting and you can bet that no two answers would match. For every conceivable type of "coon dog" from farm shepherds and collies to registered hounds — including an infinite variety of crossbreeds — has been used to hunt Old Ringtail in practically every part of the United States, today.

It's easy to understand, then, that what the term "coon dog" conjures up in the mind of one man may mean something entirely different to another. Yet, if any sort of standard exists for meaningful discussion of the "coon dog," it must certainly be found within the hound group. Of this group, which includes redbone, bluetick, treeing Walker, Plott, and black-and-tan, only the last one has achieved official recognition as a separate and distinct breed of coonhound by the largest organization registering purebred dogs in the country, the American Kennel Club.

All other coonhounds, though they may well be purebred for many generations, are usually classified as types, strains, or varieties rather than true breeds. Thus, the black-and-tan, by virtue of his officially recognized standing in the A.K.C., has become for many the sole symbol of standardization of the coon dog in America, today.

Somewhat bloodhound-like in appearance, and often misidentified as such by the novice, the black-and-tan coonhound has a history and origin which, like so many of our hunting breeds, is veiled in uncertainty and conjecture.

The general concensus holds that the black-and-tan evolved from the Talbot hound, an ancient breed, now extinct, that was brought from England into Virginia by some of that state's first settlers. Among the various strains and types of hounds that sprang from Talbot stock was a variety predominantly black and tan in color. Dubbed "Virginia black-and-tans," these dogs achieved eminence as a favorite local strain, highly prized for fox hunting.

Exactly how, or when, the Virginia black-and-tan foxhounds made the switch to tracking coon and possum is a matter of pure guesswork. Some devotees of the breed believe that culls from the kennels of wealthy Virginia gentry were occasionally foisted on folks from the back country who supposedly didn't know the difference between a first-class hound and a poor one. These dogs, purportedly being inferior fox hounds, readily took to running trail on all sorts of game, including raccoons and opossum. In becoming top-notch "meat dogs," they actually proved themselves invaluable investments for the backwoods boys who were theoretically being "taken" by the so-phisticated foxhound breeders.

Eventually acquiring substantial numbers of these potentially poor foxhounds, the back-country folks began their own breeding program, selecting only those black-and-tans that displayed the "treeing" instinct in marked degree for breeding to others of the same quality. Soon, with their fame as treeing dogs preceding them, the strain grew in popularity and gradually moved westward across the country.

A strong infusion of bloodhound was introduced into the black-and-tan — just when, nobody can say — further improving the qualities already strengthened through selective breeding practices.

By the early 1900's, the black-and-tan was firmly established as a coonhound strain with a national reputation. Largely due to the promotional efforts and careful breeding records kept by dedicated fanciers of the strain, the black-and-tan finally was accorded official recognition as a separate and distinct breed of coonhound in 1945, by the American Kennel Club. Since then there has been some small discord, as inevitably seems to arise, between field and show factions of the breed. The former argue principally against the impracticality of the pendulous thirty-inch ear spread so zealously promoted by show enthusiasts of the black-and-tan. Some regard this as a minor point of contention compared to the almost diametrically opposite viewpoints separating field and show factions of certain of the other hunting breeds.

Raccoon dog supreme, the black and tan coonhound provides a symphony of hound music that thrills any true coon hunter. The big hound's fetching tree signal is a chopping bark that means business.

Some day, though it may be too much to hope for, we just might learn our lesson over here and adopt the sensible system long ago devised in England to avert the whole nonsensical business of clinging to two separate standards for the same breed. The English system, predicating that a field dog is a field dog first and a show dog second, provides that all members of the hunting breeds prove their basic worth at the work for which they were originated before being allowed to campaign as show dogs.

Obviously, under such a practical system only one standard can exist, thus enabling both field and show people to work together in harmony improving the hunting breeds, instead of pulling in opposite directions, to the detriment of the breed in question.

As previously mentioned, there are many types of dogs which with diligent training and a fair amount of luck can convert into good and even excellent coon dogs. But, the black-and-tan has a basic advantage over most of them. Backed by many generations of purposeful breeding, with emphasis on meticulous selection for ability to trail successfully to tree, he is nearly always a natural, instinctive coon hunter that breeds true and passes along this inheritance to succeeding generations.

His is a real choke-bore nose, the kind needed to pick out the thin, ambling trails, often hours old, left by a raccoon on the feed since early evening. With surprising swiftness, nose low to the ground, he follows the pad scent of his quarry, bawling, in the sheer pleasure of his work, that thrilling symphony of hound music that keeps the night hunter apprised of both the dog's progress and whereabouts.

Certainly, if not the richest, the voice of the black-and-tan is among the most booming, best carrying of any of the trail hounds. And its sudden change from bawl to steady chop cannot fail to put wings on the feet of even the most stolid coon hunter, impelling him to heed the "tree" signal as a fetching cry to hurry...hurry...hurry.

Determination to put his quarry to tree, a quality that not only adds extra zest and enthusiasm to his work on the trail but also assures a greater percentage of coons in the bag, is one of his most outstanding traits. Moreover, the natural desire and instinctive abilities for the hunt that make him an easy dog to train place the black-and-tan very near the top of the popularity list of avid coon hunters all over the nation.

Since the raccoon is essentially a nocturnal animal, doing the greatest part of his wandering in search of food after dark, the black-and-tan

Although his specialty is obvious in his name, the black and tan can be used successfully on a wide variety of game from squirrels and bobcats to bear and boar.

has necessarily become an adept night worker. At first glance this would seem to present a rather challenging training problem. Trying to start and keep track of a young dog while stumbling around in the dark is a lot for a man to attempt and still keep both his sanity and sweet disposition. Fortunately, there are a number of ways to circumvent the problem and accomplish the bulk of the black-and-tan pup's initial training during daylight hours.

One of these is the "drag" method, in which, by means of one of the commercially manufactured game scent compounds, a comparatively simple trail is laid for the pup to follow directly to tree.

Another practical technique — one which can pay double dividends during the open shooting season — is simply to take the pup squirrel hunting. This is made-to-order schooling for the young coonhound, providing him with excellent and almost unlimited opportunities to trail and tree. And later, since squirrels seldom are abroad during the hours that coons are sought, such training will not interfere with his sticking strictly to the business at hand.

Though his speciality is obvious in his name, the black-and-tan coonhound has chalked up noteworthy success on other kinds of game, too. Probably as many possums have met an early end as have coons at the hands of hunters running black-and-tans. And certainly, no one would even try estimating the number of mountain lions, bobcats, lynx, bear, deer, boar and various other big game species successfully brought to bag with this fine hound.

A handsome fellow, with a sleek, glossy black blanket contrasting pleasingly with the rich tan coloring of his feet, legs and underparts, the black-and-tan wears a smooth, short-haired coat of sufficient density to provide him good insulation from extremes of both hot and cold weather. Standing from twenty-four to twenty-six inches at the withers, males weigh between fifty and sixty pounds. Females may stand an inch or so shorter and weigh as much as sixty pounds or as little as forty pounds.

The black-and-tan's ears — a point of contention previously mentioned between field and show folk — are fairly long, by either standard. The bench show addicts seek an ear spread (measured from tip to tip) of thirty inches, while field devotees prefer a maximum spread roughly equivalent to the dog's height at shoulder.

In overall appearance the black-and-tan suggests strength, agility, and great staying power. Though he is bold, aggressive, and shows independence and determination in his work on the trail, the sad, kindly expression in his eyes belies these qualities and gives clue to his gentle, sensitive nature. He is an extremely friendly, affectionate dog, which makes all the more unfortunate the hard fact that he is just too large a pet for a cramped household.

Yet, for those good souls who disagree, because their hearts are infinitely more spacious than their hearths, let it be said that if ever a tight squeeze were worthwhile, it could not be made for a finer, more deserving hound than this big, lovable old fella.

SOME JUST PLAIN HOUND DOGS

When a fellow says he keeps a hound, he's actually telling you a great deal about himself. From this single fact, anyone who has fooled with hounds at all will immediately understand much about the character of the man in question.

For hounds, and the men who *run* them (one can never be said to *own* a hound in the true sense of the word) are a very distinctive lot; as diverse in some ways as the leaves in the forest, yet as peculiarly similar in others as peas in a pod. Whether his preference centers on cottontails or coons, bobcats or boars, panthers or possums, every man who follows a hound shares a common bond with each of his fellow hound men. That common denominator is the ecstatically thrilling primeval sound—the trail music—emanating from a dog in a life-and-death pursuit of his quarry.

That sound, and all it connotes, is utterly and absolutely infectious to some men; even the tyro becomes enthralled with it if he's really potential hound-man material. The spell can seldom be cultivated—like a taste for oysters or caviar—in those initially lukewarm people who do not sense its joy immediately and unequivocally.

There is much to be said for hunting with hounds, probably not the least of which is the tremendous variety of game they successfully track. Hounds can be and have been employed for hunting such widely divergent wildlife as upland game birds, almost all the valuable fur-bearing game animals of the world, the principal varmints, the main big-game food staples, and the dangerous predators that threaten man or his livestock.

Innately, every hound is as versatile as his master and the geographical limits of his home grounds permit. Still, specialization has today become more the rule than the exception for most of the hound breeds, types, strains, and varieties. Thus, though almost any scent hound could be used to hunt virtually any kind of game, certain types will be found to excel, by virtue of years of breeding and specialization, on one or two specific game species.

The most popular small game animal hunted in America today is, of course, the cottontail rabbit. Any sportsman dedicated exclusively to the sport of cottontailing can choose either of two hound breeds—the beagle and the basset—that defy all other competitors in their specialized domain.

Admittedly, neither beagle nor basset tangles with the sort of dangerous quarry that, when brought to bay, provides the heart-pounding suspense experienced by those who hunt big game hounds. Missing, too, is the often grueling, hours-long chase so familiar to devotees of the predator-hunting hounds.

Yet, even the ubiquitous cottontail offers the beagle or basset owner a sport embracing the major ingredients that make up the basic appeal of running hounds: the pick-up of the cold trail; the rising excitement as the scent grows hotter; the strike that puts the quarry on the run; and the chance for a kill. Yes, and even the "music" is there.

Although cottontailing with the little hounds is a distinct sport in itself, it often serves as the stepping-stone to other forms of hunting with hounds. And when the beagle or basset owner succumbs to the lure of the bigger hounds, he enters a whole new phase of excitement, pleasure and, invariably, dedication of the highest order.

The kind of hound he selects will be determined largely by the game he prefers to hunt. And, although the different breeds, strains, types and varieties of hounds are almost as profuse as the game species possible to hunt, the average sportsman will undoubtedly make his choice from among the five best-known hounds in the country: the black-and-tan (described previously), the treeing Walker, redbone, bluetick and Plott.

The treeing Walker, like the black-and-tan, is a coon hunting specialist. He's said to be nothing more than a strain of the original Walker type of foxhound. The only discernible difference between the two types is the former's strong, natural instinct to trail and "tree," rather than run game "to ground." Predominantly white, the treeing Walker's short-haired coat carries secondary black and tan markings. He is muscular but gracefully streamlined for his weight (fifty to seventy-five pounds) and height (twenty-three to twenty-six inches at shoulders).

His clear bugle notes on a cold trail switch to a crisp chop as the scent grows more intense, and eventually change to a deep, throaty chop that, unmistakably, announces: "He's treed, Boss." He is one of the fleetest of trail hounds and has been used extensively on various big game as well as predators.

The redbone today might be claimed by the coon hunter, the bear hunter, or even those sports who fancy chasing the cougar. True trailing and treeing instincts are possessed in no greater degree by

A Walker-type hound (foreground) waits for his chance to get in his licks as hound pack keeps wild boar at bay in Tellico area of Tennessee. **Photo by Tenn. Fish & Game Dept.**

The Redbone hound, a gentle-dispositioned dog, has a passion for hunting. His trailing and treeing instincts are possessed in no greater degree by any other hound, and his voice has a honeyed quality. This one is owned by Bill Wilbur of Bartlett, N.H. **Photo by Dave Moreton.**

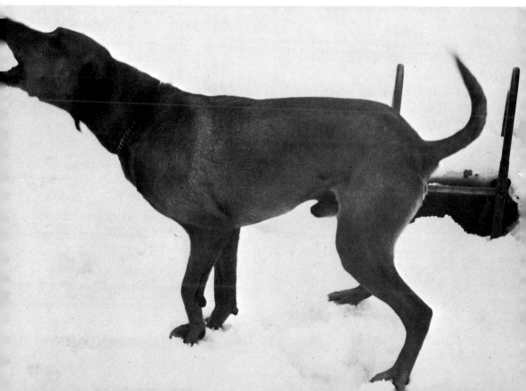

The Bluetick, though offering the least definition in size, type, voice, and overall performance, can tackle anything in fur. This Bluetick's wearing an electronic shock collar. **Photo by Lee Supply Co.**

any hound. Nor are any of the five major American hound varieties likely to produce specimens as uniformly similar to a fixed standard as the redbone. A gentle-dispositioned dog, he has a passion for hunting that belies his medium-large frame (forty-five to sixty pounds and twenty-two to twenty-six inches at shoulder). The redbone's voice might best be described as mellifluous—a bawl less voluminous than other varieties, and a bit more clipped, yet honeyed, in tone on the trail.

His preferred coloration is solid red but small touches of white on his blanket and feet are permissible, according to the United Kennel Club standard.

Of all five hound varieties the bluetick offers the least uniformity in size, type, voice, and overall performance. Despite this liability, the individual bluetick can be "one helluva hound" on virtually anything in fur.

Roughly, the ideal bluetick measures from twenty-three to twenty-six inches at shoulder and, in good running condition, weighs between sixty and seventy-five pounds. He is most often basically white with heavy flecks or tickings of bluish-black marbled into his short-haired coat. Some specimens sport a bit of tan along with their black and white markings, and others, less frequently encountered, are white-and-red ticked.

Vocally, the bluetick should "sing" with a moderate bawl on strike of hot trail; switch to rhythmic chop while running, and break into a tough excited chop when his quarry is at bay, tree, or goes to ground.

The Plott hound, though most often thought of as a boar and bear dog, has distinguished himself in practically all fields of hound endeavor. On coon and possum he's a whiz; on cougar, bobcats, and deer he ranks with the best. Lacking nothing that a first class trail hound should have, he adds tenacity and fighting courage and, just for good measure, displays early development in his job.

Perhaps less uniform in type and size than the black-and-tan, or the redbone, the Plott ranges between forty-five and sixty pounds in weight and twenty-one to twenty-five inches in height at shoulder. Brindle, or brindle with black saddle, is the color of his coat, which is short and fine-textured but sufficiently profuse to provide adequate

The Plott hound, primarily a boar and bear dog, distinguishes himself on virtually any game a hound can trail. This prize bear dog is shown with owner Bill Wilbur of Bartlett, N. H. **Photo by Dave Moreton.**

protection against most climates. His clear bugle bawl carries well on trail and his staccato chopping notes are equally audible at the tree.

There are, as has been mentioned, numerous other types, strains, and varieties of hounds being bred and hunted in America today. All sorts of crosses and mixtures, including some non-scent hounds, can be found to do the work and bidding of the hunter, no matter what the special or peculiar demands. Many of these crosses produce individuals that perform brilliantly, but seldom can these exceptional specimens reproduce themselves in kind. Without time-consuming careful selective breeding, the complex structure of genes refuses to pattern exactly the same way twice.

For this reason, the average hunter would do well to stick with those hounds that through the years have demonstrated their ability to reproduce reasonably true to type. Most such hounds are registered with the United Kennel Club of Kalamazoo, Michigan, a registry that records pedigrees of working hounds and encourages the goal of producing hounds that meet uniform standards. Other American hound registries include the Full Cry Kennel Club, Sedalia, Missouri, and the Chase Publishing Co., Lexington, Kentucky.

Part III

Purchasing the Prospect

7

Picking a Puppy

EVENTUALLY THE TIME will come when you make up your mind about what you want in a gun dog. You will have taken into account all preliminary considerations; checked out the various breeds and their specialties (see Part II of this book) and made a decision; settled the matter of keeping your dog indoors or out; and determined which sex you prefer. You'll be thinking now of how, when, and where to buy your dog; the answers to these questions depend on whether you've determined to raise a puppy or invest in a trained dog.

Ordinarily, there's not much reason to delay acquiring a gun dog pup once you know what you want. Aside from making all the necessary provisions well in advance of the day you bring him—or her—home, putting off your purchase can only waste valuable time that could be spent more profitably with your prospective puppy at home.

However, as with any commodity, there is a best and a worst season for puppy buying. The months of April, May, and June are ideal, while September and October stack up as the poorest time to purchase a young puppy of one of the hunting breeds.

Puppy shopping just before or during the hunting season has all the disadvantages of buying a car late in the model year, with none of the latter's bargain prices. Like the dilatory car buyer, the last-minute puppy shopper always faces the prospect of getting whatever's left. Just as with the auto dealer's surplus inventory, litters of pups are sure to have been pretty well picked over late in the year. And, because these pups are several months old and in short supply, they'll generally command the higher prices that go with the increased overhead paid by the breeder.

Most amateur and professional breeders strive to breed their bitches so as to whelp spring litters; the warmer months being less problematical in the rearing of puppies. Also, pups whelped in March, April, and early May will range from five to seven months of age by October, the time much of the nation's public hunting seasons begin. Such early or mid-spring born pups can be introduced to preliminary field work at an ideal age during that fall's open seasons.

Thus, with late fall and winter the conventionally preferred breeding time, and early spring the whelping period, the months of April, May, and June constitute what economists term a "buyer's market," or what in the vernacular of the dog world is better known as "puppy pickin' time."

Lining up a source of supply of the breed of your choice is the first step in buying a gun dog puppy. Buying from spring-weaned litters, such as this bunch of English setters, gives you more pups to choose among.

During this period the customer has the advantage not only of choosing from full, or near-full litters at a given kennel, but also of a lower price tag on puppies when the supply usually exceeds the demand.

The question of how to go about buying a gun dog puppy inevitably breaks down into several parts: (1) how to find the best source of supply? (2) how old a pup to choose? and (3) how to select the "best" puppy in a litter?

Unless the breed of your choice happens to be a comparatively rare variety, probably the simplest and most conventional procedure for locating a source of supply is a check of the various publications most likely to carry for-sale advertisements of the desired breed. These would include any number of rod and gun magazines, specialized journals devoted to a specific breed, and the classified sections of daily or weekly local newspapers.

Additionally, there is word of mouth—a conversation with your neighborhood sporting goods dealer, your area game warden, the owner of a nearby shooting preserve, the fishing and hunting editor of your local newspaper or of the newspaper in the nearest large city. And should all these prove fruitless, you have another alternative: writing to the Secretary or President of the national club representing the breed of your choice, to request a current list of local or regional kennels specializing in that particular breed.

Once you've uncovered several potential suppliers, how do you choose among them? Here, a great many factors can influence your decision. Breeder X may offer just the bloodlines you'd prefer in your pup, but his kennels may be too far from your home to allow a personal visit. Breeder Y's kennels may be much more conveniently located; still, his puppies may not carry the ancestry you had your heart set on. Or, maybe, Tom Jones, who lives right in town, has a litter of pups, out of his own shooting bitch, for sale. What to do?

Generally, unless a buyer has had many years of experience he would do well to restrict his looking to reputable commercial breeders and steer clear of "home-grown" puppies offered by private individuals. Too often, such "home-bred" litters are the result of accidental unions or, at best, matings of convenience, with little or no objective assessment of the merits of both the parents and their forebears.

Not every private individual offering a litter of pups for sale is a rank amateur, nor for that matter is he insincere and out to palm off

A personal visit to a kennel close to home enables you to observe all the pups for sale. All but one of these English setter pups seem eager to explore the world outside their kennel run.

pups of inferior breeding on an unsuspecting buyer. But the uninitiated buyer should keep in mind that the law of averages overwhelmingly favors buying from the professional commercial breeder. His knowledge and experience in breeding top-quality dogs is usually far superior to the private individual's, and, since he makes his livelihood strictly on a proven reputation, he simply cannot afford dissatisfied customers.

Assuming your list of sources has narrowed down to several kennels, your next consideration is generally one of distance. Puppies and trained gun dogs are very often bought from kennels in opposite ends of the nation, with written descriptions (and sometimes pictures) providing the only idea of what kind of dog the buyer is purchasing. Customarily, dogs purchased by mail are sold on a trial basis, giving the buyer a chance to change his mind within a few days time if the animal is not satisfactory or has been misrepresented. If you are dealing with reputable breeders there is nothing wrong with this method, but it is obviously an impersonal system.

Far better is a personal visit to a kennel nearer home, where the buyer may inspect all the puppies available for sale and make his own selection. At the same time he may also see one, or possibly both, parents, and get a pretty fair idea of what the pup he chooses will look like at maturity.

In the process of lining up a source of supply, the prospective buyer should also have given some thought to the age of the puppy he wants. Probably, there are as many diverse opinions on what constitutes the ideal age at which to secure a puppy as there are breeds to choose from. Some favor the older puppy of six to ten months, on the basis that one can tell a great deal more about its ultimate coloration, conformation, personality, intelligence, and potential abilities. Others swear by the middle ground: puppies of three to four-and-a-half months of age, who provide sufficient clues to later looks yet allow the new owner a bit more time to mould and develop a still-pliable personality through training and environment.

At the other extreme is the faction advocating procurement of the puppy as soon after weaning as possible, meaning at from five to seven weeks of age. This premise is based upon the theory that earliest environment plays the key role in formulating the rudimentary attitude and response patterns upon which all subsequent personality is shaped and developed.

As can easily be seen, each philosophy has its strong points, but equally apparent are some weak ones. In choosing the six-to-ten-month-old pup, for example, one runs the risk of what is commonly called "kennel-shyness," an insecurity often manifested in extreme timidity by a puppy who, prior to your visit, has seldom or never set foot outside his kennel run. This is usually a temporary condition, but it creates a problem since it is difficult, if not impossible, to differentiate between ordinary "kennel-shyness" and shyness of a chronic nature.

By the same token, taking the youngest pup, virtually from its mother's breast, is not without certain risks. Infinitely more scrupulous care and almost constant supervision must be given the five-to-seven-week-old puppy to see him through the highest mortality risk period still facing him. Then, too, there are the added expenses of feeding him for a longer time, as well as additional veterinary treatment in the form of extra wormings and protective inoculations. These are considerably more expensive for the private owner than for the large-scale commercial breeder.

The middle ground—pups from three to four-and-a-half months of age—offers a combination of some of the advantages and disadvantages of both the other schools of thought. All things considered, it is probably the most judicious compromise for a majority of persons.

Picking the "best" puppy in a litter is a highly misleading expression which might better be abandoned by the dog fancy. For there is not always a "best" puppy, in the sense that one individual far outshines all his litter-mates in every respect. The "best" of a given litter will only be determined when full maturity is reached, on the basis of a well-rounded amalgamation of such factors as color, conformation, temperament, nose, game-sense, intelligence and over-all performance of his job in the field. And even then, the "best" is still subject to being judged and rated under differing standards and divergent opinions as to what constitutes quality.

Instead of worrying needlessly over whether or not you're going to pick the "best," you would do well to concentrate on choosing a good, sound puppy, with no major flaws, most representative of the breed. Avoiding both the largest and the smallest pups in favor of the two, three, four, or more which are of most uniform size, you should carefully observe these puppies' reactions to strangers, noises, movements, and to each other. As you observe, you'll automatically be narrowing your selection, discounting the overly timid, the dull, listless, or sickly pups.

Before reaching a tentative final decision, you should ask to see each of your two or three top candidates out in the yard, one at a time, away from his kennel run and litter-mates. When he's alone in unfamiliar surroundings, the pup's behavior will generally reveal a good deal about his true nature. The pup you want will be the one who shows a more venturesome spirit than his brothers and sisters, a boldness and curiosity. He will be the one who, if backed off by something never before encountered, at once returns to it, sniffing investigatingly until his curiosity is satisfied, and the search for something new and different takes him off again on another tack.

Once you've zeroed in on this kind of puppy, all that remains are the details. You'll need to check with the breeder on the pup's health record—what immunization shots he's been given; when, if at all, was he wormed; what type and brand of food he's used to, and how often he's fed—and to obtain his registration papers and, if available, a copy of his pedigree.

Many buyers insist—and they can't really be faulted for doing so—on obtaining a guarantee in writing that the pup's parents have been certified free of hip dysplasia. This is an inherited disability that, in varying degree, can affect a dog's ability to get around. It seldom manifests itself in young puppies, but it is easily detectible in older dogs by means of a radiograph. Thus, if the breeder has had his stock x-rayed, it's a simple procedure for him to obtain dysplasia-free certification by the Orthopedic Foundation for Animals, a non-profit service organization at the University of Missouri's Columbia School of Veterinary Medicine, 817 Virginia Ave., Columbia, Missouri.

Once your arrangements for purchase have been concluded and you've made certain to obtain all possible information about the pup's routine feeding and care, you'll be ready to begin the trip home with your new puppy. If he's a very young one—under eight or nine weeks—he can make the trip safely and most conveniently in an ordinary corrugated box, lined with newspapers and, of course, open at the top.

However, an older pup, of say three-and-a-half-months, should be transported in a wire shipping or car crate, where he'll be safe and comfortable and can't possibly mess up your car. Thus, with your new pup securely aboard, you can head for home with the wheels barely touching the road, confident in the fact that you've made a wise choice and thoroughly convinced that "puppy pickin' time" is one of the happiest adventures in any sportsman's life.

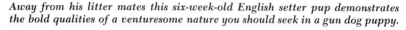

Away from his litter mates this six-week-old English setter pup demonstrates the bold qualities of a venturesome nature you should seek in a gun dog puppy.

8

Buying a Trained Dog— Direct or Mail-Order

YOU'VE THOUGHT IT over very carefully and have come to the only logical decision possible. Puppies are just great, there's no doubt about it, but not right now, not for you. Too much to do...too little free time...it just wouldn't be fair to get a pup and then wrestle with your conscience about not giving him the time and opportunities to develop the way he should.

Naw, it's got to be a trained gun dog for you, a dog that knows the ropes, one you don't have to bring along from scratch, one you can pop into the car and take off with to the woods for a day's shooting, whenever you get the chance.

Okay, you know what you want. But, now, just how do you go about it?

Pretty much the same way you'd buy a puppy; that is, you'll first have to line up some sources of supply. Since these should preferably be local sources, you'll check newspapers, and local and regional periodicals devoted to hunting, shooting, and dogs. You'll also want to look into any information that your local newspaper outdoors editor can furnish; also chat with a couple of nearby sporting goods dealers and shooting preserve operators. You won't overlook the national rod and gun magazines either, for advertisements placed by kennels in your vicinity.

If you're fortunate, you'll locate a couple of kennels within driving distance of home that can offer you the breed of trained gun dog you're after. Then all it takes are a couple of phone calls to check prices and other specific details before making a personal visit to see the dogs you're interested in work out in the field.

But, suppose your search for sources near home draws a blank? Are you out of luck? Do you dare risk the chance of buying a trained hunting dog from a breeder a thousand miles away? How can you be sure you'll get what you want and what you pay for, when you order a gun dog by mail?

These and probably dozens of other questions are bound to plague any sportsman contemplating purchase of his first mail-order gun dog. But in spite of the understandable anxieties involved, it's a very common and fairly uncomplicated process which usually works out to the mutual satisfaction of many thousands of buyers and sellers

Making sure that the breeder, kennel owner or individual you're going to deal with is thoroughly reputable will be your first consideration. And since he knows you don't know him, he won't be insulted if you ask for references when you correspond with him. If he doesn't willingly supply references, forget him.

But, we're a bit ahead of ourselves. You'll first have to uncover several likely prospects to write to, informing each in explicit detail about what you want in a trained dog. Sending several inquiries at a time will assure you of some choice in potential candidates, prices, and terms offered. And you'll save a lot of follow-up letter writing if you spell out in your first letter all the specifics the breeder-trainer will have to know, and ask all the questions you need answered.

In other words, tell him the breed, sex, age range, color preference — with second and even third choices, if you're that flexible — as well as the degree of training, the range and pace and even the size of the dog you want. If you're looking for specific bloodlines, tell him that, too. And, if, depending on the particular breed involved, you're seeking certain additional training refinements, such as a pointing dog that's steady to wing and shot, or one that retrieves, make certain to include mention of these.

Among the answers you'll need from him besides price quotes and a written description of each particular dog he may offer, are the length of the trial period, the shipping methods, and any specific terms and conditions of the sale. Be sure to request that he supply you with photos — snapshots will do — of each of the dogs he's trying to sell you. And make sure all the candidates are either already registered or eligible for registration.

As soon as the answers to your letters arrive, you can start narrowing your possible choices. But, aside from simply selecting the most appealing dog offered, you should carefully scrutinize the terms and conditions of the sale. Be wary of a trial period that's too short, or a breeder who wants your money in advance.

A three-day trial is as meaningless to the buyer as to the seller. If through a subsequent letter, you can't get the period extended to at least seven days, no matter how good the dog in question may be, you'd better forget him. The week-long trial period is far more meaningful, and ten days is even better, and closer to the norm. Any trial longer than two weeks usually works to the psychological advantage of the seller since, the longer the prospective buyer keeps a dog, the stronger his personal attachment to him becomes.

As for the financial arrangements, no money should ever be re-quested by or paid to the seller in advance. The usual procedure is to pay the full purchase price to the shipping agent, who holds it in escrow until the trial period has ended. In the event that you have to return the dog prior to the trial deadline, you can obtain a refund directly from the shipping agent. You should expect to pay shipping charges—both ways if the dog proves unsatisfactory and you decide to return him.

When you are able to select a dog that meets all your requirements, on paper and in a photo at least, you'll have to get another letter off to the breeder to advise him of your decision and to let him know the details he needs to make shipment. Air freight, although a bit more costly than surface transportation, is generally the quickest and most advisable method of shipment. To ease the suspense and anxiety, it's a good idea to request that the breeder confirm by phone or telegram the shipment time and schedule of stopovers, if any, as well as estimated time of arrival at your local airport.

Finally, though it will seem an eternity, the dog will arrive. Chances are it will be over a weekend, and since you'll be off from work, you'll be tempted to take the dog right out to the nearest cover to see how he measures up. Don't. Expecting a new dog to step from his shipping crate right into the field is asking a bit much. It would be a gross disservice to the dog, to the seller and to you, the buyer, to attempt evaluation of a dog's hunting abilities and field perfor-mance the minute he arrives on your doorstep.

Expecting the mail order dog to step right from his crate into the hunting field is asking a bit much. Make sure you give him a day or two to readjust before trying him out.

After all, he's just been uprooted from all his old familiar surroundings, shoved into a crate, and transported many miles in a noisy darkened baggage compartment. If there were stopovers, he's received food and water, and maybe a brief walk—all at the hands of strangers—before being relegated to his crate once more. He's been subjected to a lot of curious sounds and smells, and, finally, he is released from his crate again in a new home filled with people and objects entirely strange to him. If he's a trifle unnerved by the whole experience, who can blame him?

For all these reasons, he should be allowed at least a day or two of grace to become acclimated and adjusted to his new surroundings. During this period, far from wasting valuable trial time, you are getting to know the dog—and he you—observing his general temperament, personality, and reactions to the new situations that confront him.

Given a fair chance to demonstrate their abilities, most mail order hunting dogs, like this Weimaraner, will measure up to claims made by a reputable seller. **Photo by Lewis D. Roberts.**

Is he bold or timid? Flexible or defensive? Submissive or hard-headed? Does he seem to know his name and the basic commands of "Here," "Sit," "Down," "Stay," "No," and "Heel"? These are the things you should watch for and note objectively while trying to gain the dog's friendship and trust before even thinking of trying him out in the field.

On his initial tryout much will depend on his breed, age, degree of training and the circumstances under which you work him. If you expect him to strike game, then you must take him to a suitable area where the type of game he specializes in can be found in reasonable quantity. Naturally, you should check your local game laws to make certain you will not be in violation of them by running a dog before the official hunting season opens.

With the notable exceptions of hounds bought for fox, coon, pos-sum, bear, or other big game hunting, most breeds of hunting dogs

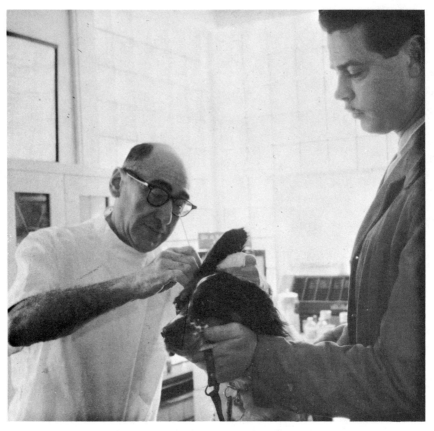

A thorough examination by your veterinarian is always wise procedure before finalizing your purchase.

can be tried out very advantageously on commercial shooting preserves. Since the majority of pay-as-you-go preserves begin their shooting seasons in September, such places afford the opportunity not only of trying out a dog on game but also of shooting that game.

This last is important in evaluating a dog of almost any hunting breed which may be required to retrieve. It also completes the full cycle of his work and your sport, and provides the necessary answer about how he reacts to the sound of gunfire.

But the commercial shooting preserve offers still another big advantage. The manager of such an establishment invariably knows gun dogs pretty well; in fact, he may even be a professional dog trainer and handler. For a small fee, or perhaps no charge at all, his services in helping you evaluate the dog's abilities and performance can usually be obtained. His impartial and thoroughly objective opinion can often mean the difference between your keeping the dog or sending him back before your trial period deadline.

In the case of a fully trained bird dog or retriever, where the purchase price can well involve several hundred dollars, it is only common sense to solicit the appraisal of a professional trainer who specializes in the breed or type of dog in question. Even the most experienced dog men generally prefer to seek more than one qualified outside opinion before purchasing a fairly expensive gun dog.

In all fairness, don't be too quick to judge the dog's performance after just one field workout, either. Make sure you give him every reasonable chance to measure up to the claims made for him by the seller. For if you do reject the dog, you will most certainly have to bear the expense of shipping him back, since that is stipulated in almost all mail order contracts.

Once you're satisfied that the dog does fill the bill, one more precaution should be taken before closing the deal. Have your local veterinarian check him over thoroughly to make certain he's physically sound and in good health. If the dog comes from one of the southern states, where heartworm is prevalent, insist that the vet run a blood test on him. In fact, this should be standard procedure no matter what part of the nation the dog comes from, for heartworm, a seriously debilitating and often fatal disease, is not strictly limited to the warmer climes.

If you've chosen and dealt with an honest, reputable supplier, stated your wants clearly, and been absolutely fair in evaluating the dog sent to you, you will be about 95 percent certain to wind up with a satisfactory gun dog—one you can enjoy at home as well as afield for years to come.

The chart below is designed to provide you with a guide to the approximate prices you might expect to pay for any of the various types and breeds of well-started, partially trained and fully trained hunting dogs offered for sale in the United States.

POINTERS & SETTERS (Well-started, 9–14 months, $250–$450)
(Partly trained, 16–22 months, $400–$600)
(Fully trained, 30 months & up, $600–$1,200)

CONTINENTAL BREEDS
Brittanies, Shorthairs (Well-started, 8–13 months, $300–$475)
Weimaraners, (Partly trained, 15–22 months, $475–$600)
German wirehaired (Fully trained, 26 months & up, $600–$1,000)
pointers, Vizslas,
W.P. Griffons

SPRINGERS & COCKERS   (Well-started, 10–16 months, $350–$475)
(Partly trained, 18–24 months, $500–$700)
(Fully trained, 30 months & up, $750–$1,300)

RETRIEVERS
Labradors, Goldens,   (Well-started, 8–15 months, $450–$675
Chesapeakes, Irish &   (Partly trained, 17–28 months, $700–$950
American water   (Fully trained, 36 months & up, $1,500–
spaniels $2,500)

HOUNDS (Registered)
Beagles, Bassets,   (Well-started, 7–12 months, $175–$300)
Black and Tans, and   (Partly trained, 14–20 months, $300–$475)
most others   (Fully trained, 24 months & up, $475–$650)

Part IV

Training and Performance

9

Preliminary Training

GUN DOG TRAINING techniques and the philosophies that spawned them haven't changed much since Hector was a pup. But some of the accessories used in the field education of Hector's modern-day descendants have come a long way toward making the trainer's job far simpler than it used to be.

True, a great many traditional tools are still essential to providing the field dog with a practical education. After all, what could replace the whistle, the leash, the check-cord, the retrieving dummy, or numerous other time-tested training paraphernalia? So, before considering the more recently developed devices, let's become acquainted with those old standbys, the fundamental implements that dog trainers — professional and amateur alike — still find irreplaceable. Since many of these tools are more or less specialized, some will have no application to one particular type or breed and yet prove essential to training and handling others. For the sake of clarity, let's first look at those basic items of universal importance to every dog trainer and handler, and then go on to the somewhat more specialized tools.

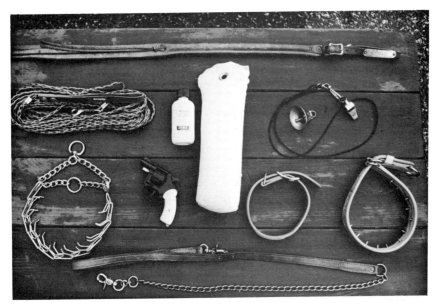

The basic tools needed by almost any dog trainer include (from left to right, starting at the top): flushing whip; 50-foot check cord with leather handle loop; commercial training scent; canvas training dummy; dog bell; whistle and lanyard; chain choke collar with metal prongs; .22 cal. blank cartridge revolver; leather collar with I.D. plate; J.A.S.A. leather training collar with spikes, and leather and chain combination leash. **Photo by Dave Petzal.**

The Leash

A good quality leash of substantial strength is a must for controlling your dog during regular walks at home, for yard-training and for any occasion that requires his being restrained for convenience and safety. The ideal "all-around" leash should be six feet long and have a sturdy metal snap that attaches to the D-ring in the dog's collar. It should also be equipped with a wide hand-loop for comfortable, secure grip. An all-chain leash will do, but is the least desirable type. The all-leather variety is light and flexible, but is easily weakened if subjected to chewing by the dog during extended use. Far better than either of these two is the combination leash, chain in the lower part and leather in the upper portion.

The Collar

A collar should always be worn by your dog when he is outdoors. Not only does it enable you to control him with or without leash, but it also serves as insurance should he stray—assuming you have attached to it a metal identification tag that lists your name, address and telephone number. There are three basic collar types; round leather, flat leather and chain link. For heavy-coated retrievers or longhaired breeds the round leather collar is normally preferred. Flat leather collars are generally chosen for pointers, beagles, bassets and other shorthaired dogs, while the chain link type, which is actually a choke collar, can be used on all breeds during yard-training. Since the chain type gets too readily caught up in fences and brush, though, it is not recommended for hunting or field-training use.

The Whistle

One of the most important training and handling implements, the whistle is used to signal, call, stop and direct your gun dog in the field. Specific whistle signals and their uses will be covered in a later chapter, so we won't describe them here. Although there are several kinds of whistles available, the ordinary police-type, containing a pea-sized cork that enables you to effect a variety of trills, is preferred. Plastic or bakelite is best, since metal can "freeze" to the skin in very cold weather. Silent whistles—the kind that are pitched beyond human hearing—are not suitable for field use, because of the very fact that the user himself can't hear them, therefore can't perfect the variety of signals needed. For wide-ranging dogs, or under unusually windy conditions, the long-distance police-type whistle made by the National Scent Company of Garden Grove, Calif., is most practical.

The Blank Cartridge Gun

An ordinary .22 caliber blank cartridge gun is a necessity for all gun dog trainers. It is used in any breed's early field training to accustom the dog to sudden loud noises similar to the sound of gunfire, when he makes contact with game. Revolvers holding six to eight blanks in the cylinder are generally favored over automatics.

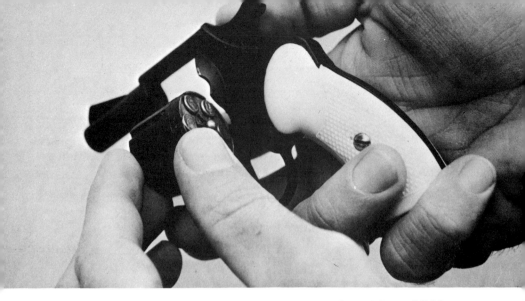

An ordinary .22 caliber blank cartridge gun is a necessity for training and field trial use. **Photo by Dave Petzal.**

The Dog Bell

Strictly speaking, the dog bell isn't a training device, but it does help the trainer, just as it does the hunter, keep track of his dog when working in heavy cover. Pointing breed owners find it especially useful; when they hear the bell stop, they know their dog is on point. High-tech, battery-operated electronic tracking devices, serving much like a dog bell, also have come into use in recent years. Small hounds, such as beagles and bassets, that aren't readily visible in thick brush, often are belled as a safety precaution against accidental shooting by other rabbit hunters.

The dog bell helps the trainer and the hunter keep track of a dog in heavy cover. **Photo by Dave Petzal.**

Training Scents

Commercially manufactured compounds that duplicate a wide variety of game bird and animal scents find common use for training all breeds and types of hunting dogs. Especially valuable for teaching hounds to follow ground trails laid by scent-drags, these compounds prove equally effective for training dogs "off" specific animals. Such "breaking-scents" can cure dogs of the deer-chasing habit, discourage a coon hound from trailing possum or a rabbit dog from tracking hot fox scent.

The Training Dummy

A tool no fetch-dog owner should ever be without, the training dummy, which resembles an ordinary boat-fender, is the standard implement used in training all dogs to retrieve. Available in various sizes and types, the most popular variety consists of heavy duty canvas filled with kapok. Sufficiently buoyant in water, it's also rugged enough to withstand long use on land. Its canvas covering absorbs and retains commercial scent compounds well. It's heavy enough to be thrown some distance, yet light enough for a dog to retrieve easily.

The Training Collar

Three kinds of training collars can be used in obedience, yard and field training of all breeds. The regular chain link choke collar, which tightens with pressure on the leash, ordinarily is sufficient for obedience and yard training dogs of average temperament. More stubborn cases may require use of a chain link choker equipped with two sets of blunted metal prongs around the inside. These prongs pinch but do not injure the dog when pressure is applied. Still a third type of collar, called the J.A.S.A. model, is used on very hard cases, as well as for staunching and steadying pointing breeds on birds. This collar is made of wide leather, lined on the inside with two staggered rows of semi-blunted prongs. It disciplines the dog only when pressure is applied.

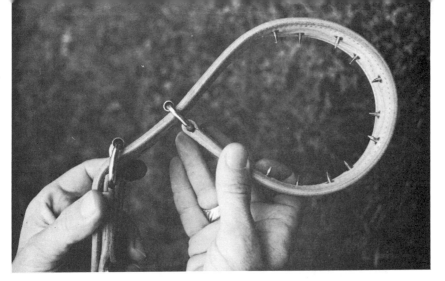

The J.A.S.A. Spike collar is very effective for recalcitrants. If spikes are too sharp, they should be blunted with a file. **Photo by Dave Petzal.**

The Check-Cord

As its name implies, the check-cord is used to check or restrain a dog in the field. It's invaluable for staunching or steadying pointing dogs, especially in combination with one of the three training collars described above. It can also prove effective for controlling the range of pointing dogs, spaniels or retrievers doing pinch-hit flushing work in the uplands. Generally, check-cords are made of thin, strong nylon which slips through grass and brush easily. The most popular lengths are 25, 50, 75 and 100 feet.

Teaching a pointing dog to remain steady to wing and shot requires a good stout check cord. Here Falk flushes quail and fires .22 blank while helper holds check cord. As pointer charges after bird, helper will haul back on check cord, upending dog as Falk issues "Whoa" command. **Photo by Dave Petzal.**

The Flushing Whip

Used by trainers and field trialers of pointing breeds, the flushing whip is an implement originated for the sole purpose of flushing close-lying birds in heavy grass. About thirty inches long, the standard flushing whip is constructed of bridle, harness or latigo leather encasing a flexible spring that provides body through about two-thirds of its length. The remaining portion of the leather is left unsewed to form two or more strap-like appendages for flailing the brush. The whip's handle usually has a leash-type snap that attaches to one's trouser belt for easy carrying. Because the flushing whip has other utility besides its original purpose, it has become a standard item for almost all hunting breed trainers and handlers. Not only does it find its most obvious use as a disciplinary tool, but it also doubles as a short, handy field leash.

Modern Devices

Among the more recent innovations of modern technology designed to provide easier and more effective training of dogs in the field is the remote-control shock collar. A contribution of the science of electronics, this relatively new training aid is magnificently simple and direct. Its sole object is to deliver a harmless but startling electric shock to a dog—even at considerable distance—at the precise instant the trainer wishes to exert his authority.

The shock collar consists of a hand-held, battery-operated transmitter unit and a leather collar to which a small receiver containing the shocking coil is attached. Pressing a button on the transmitter directs a radio signal to the receiver on the dog's collar, tripping a switch that activates the coil and delivers an instantaneous electric shock to the dog. Although harmless to him, the shock—roughly equivalent to that of an electrified cattle fence—is sufficiently jolting to stop him from whatever he's doing at the time.

The practical uses of such an instrument are almost limitless. Virtually any situation requiring immediate sharp correction, such as preventing a hound from chasing deer or other undesirable game, or discouraging a hard-headed pointing dog from breaking wing and shot to chase flushed birds, is potential shock-collar treatment material. And outside of the hunting field its uses are equally practical

A Labrador retriever wears an electronic shock collar, an effective training device when properly used. **Photo by Lee Supply Co.**

for such problems as excessive barking, fighting and car-chasing.

Providing a form of correction otherwise impossible on a free-running dog, the shock collar enables you to deliver preventive punishment at a distance, when it is most needed and will prove most effective. Psychologically, the instrument is perfection itself since the dog, rather than blaming his owner for the unpleasant shock, associates his punishment directly with the misdeed. Thus, if every time your rabbit hound takes off to chase a deer he gets a juicy jolt, it won't be long before he'll begin associating physical discomfort with the scent of deer, and judiciously avoid it in the future.

Valuable as the shock collar can be, however, it should not be considered a cure-all, to be used carelessly or indiscriminately. Many trainers, pros and amateurs as well, regard it as a last resort, to be employed on problem dogs only after exhausting all other conventional training tools and procedures. Caution, of course, is never a bad policy when training a gun dog; *his* mistakes can usually be corrected, but *yours* are not always so easily undone.

Another electronic training device—this one designed strictly with pointing dogs in mind—is the remote-controlled bird releaser. This rather ingenious contrivance, of box-like construction, securely holds a single quail, pigeon or pheasant until the moment the trainer wishes to release it skyward, simply by pushing a button on a portable, battery-operated transmitter unit.

For more advanced training work, an alternate method of ejecting

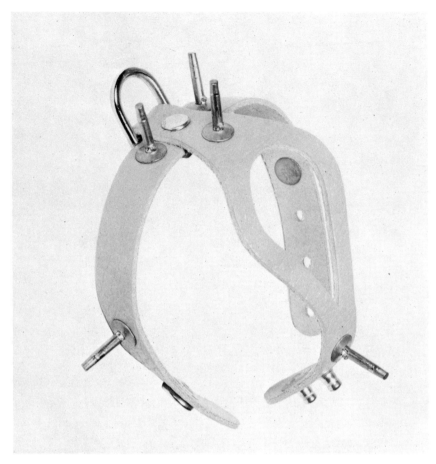

Le Captive, a simple harness that can be fitted around a Bobwhite quail, keeps the bird alive and unharmed for repeated use in training bird dogs. Spikes prevent dog from injuring quail if mouthed.

the bird can be employed by using a special collar-transmitter worn by the dog. A small adjustable antenna on the collar unit enables the trainer to preset the distance at which the device will automatically trip the release…and eject the bird. Use of the collar transmitter teaches the dog a more cautious approach on his bird. If he attempts to move in too close before he points, the bird will "flush," just as it would in the wilds.

The remote-controlled bird releaser proves especially practical in the early stages of a pointing dog's work on birds. Allowing maximum control over both dog and bird during each of the most critical steps in the natural sequence of a pointing dog's training, the electronic releaser is not only easy to use, but is also compatible with limited size training areas.

First, the releaser is loaded with a live bird and concealed, with a few sprigs of natural cover, in a suitably birdy spot. Then the dog is worked upwind, on a check-cord, toward the hidden releaser, which has wide side vents to effect a free flow of bird scent. Once the dog locates the scent source and snaps into a point, the check-cord will restrain him long enough for you to move in and staunch or style him up.

When you're ready to flush the bird, you simply press the button on the transmitter unit. At the same time as you flush the bird, you can teach, or reinforce, steadiness to wing and shot by "whoaing" the dog with the check-cord as you fire your .22 blank cartridge pistol. Nothing could be simpler...or more effective.

For the intermediate and advanced training of retrievers, there's another implement that's worth three times its weight in gold. Called the "Retriev-R-Trainer," it resembles and works on the same principles as the beer-can launcher familiar to target shooters. It consists of a straight hand-grip topped by a hollowed-out circular metal disc that serves as both chamber for a .22 caliber blank cartridge charge and seat for a pliable plastic training dummy. A metal rod, pulled straight back from the bottom of the handle, acts as the trigger, firing the cartridge and launching the training dummy up to a distance of 250 feet. Regular and heavy-duty charge cartridges plus the angle of trajectory determine the distance the dummies are thrown. The device accustoms the dog to the sound of gunfire and aids in training him to mark distant falls.

The shock collar, electronic bird releaser and training dummy launcher are only three of innumerable training implements introduced in recent years to simplify the field education of today's gun dog. In the proliferating parade of such products—many of which are, unfortunately, little more than gadgets—these three have proven to be of genuinely outstanding usefulness to the trainer. In combination with the traditional accessories, these new tools give today's trainer a practical edge over the gun dog handler of yesteryear.

Even if this young dog has never heard gun fire, he's so intent on chasing this bobwhite that the sound of the shot won't bother him.

DON'T GAMBLE ON GUN-SHYNESS

Despite each man's understandable tendency toward wishful thinking, no hunting dog is ever perfect. However minor, some flaw in performance, some imperfection in structure, some frailty in temperament or quirk in personality invariably shows up to keep every dog just out of reach of the ultimate ideal. And so it should be, for without the ideal to strive toward, dog breeding, training and even ownership would soon become much less interesting and absorbing.

Yet, of all possible canine faults, congenital or acquired, none is at once so pitiable and unpardonable in a sporting breed as fear of the gun. Gun-shyness, that abhorrent affliction that transforms an otherwise vigorously outgoing, promise-filled young specimen into a quaking, belly-slithering bundle of nerves, becomes all the more detestable with the knowledge that it leaves a gun dog as useless for his job as a dead horse in harness.

Equally appalling is the certainty that the gun-shy dog did not enter this world that way; he has simply fallen victim to someone's bumbling or headstrong methods of introducing him to the gun. Unfortunately, the belief that gun-shyness is inherited still persists among some people, though the evidence of years overwhelmingly refutes such fact. Of course, just as there are degrees of gun-shyness, there are also some dogs that manifest greater susceptibility to the problem. It is, however, only in this sense that heredity plays a part.

Puppies of a timid, retiring nature probably have the greatest potential for gun-shyness. Common sense dictates that pups of this sort should be avoided by the purchaser in the first place, or at least handled far more carefully with respect to virtually every phase of their training.

On the other hand bold, friendly pups who exude curiosity and tend to investigate everything new around them, are naturally least susceptible to problems caused by the noise of the gun. Yet, even these ideal-tempered pups are not immune to becoming gun-shy if an owner introduces them to the gun imprudently and then continues to compound his mistake.

The degree of susceptibility to gun-shyness is therefore something that can be measured inversely from the norm—the "norm" being based on an average or slightly above average pup, whose initial exposure to the gun is conducted without flagrant or repeated mistakes. To put it another way, no dog is guaranteed gun-shy proof—the bolder type of puppy merely offers a bit more tolerance to the inexperienced trainer's potential mistakes, whereas the very timid prospect is likely to succumb at the least provocation.

In discussing gun-shyness, it's astonishing how many novice owners are initially interested in how it can be cured, when, in fact, they should be most concerned with how it can be avoided. Curing gun-shyness is a tough task, one better left to professionals who get results or accept no payment for the attempt. Avoiding gun-shyness, however, is far easier; any beginner can do it.

The basic pitfall for most novice owners is their natural impatience, hypoed to some extent by the training literature they read. Any book on gun dog training can be read far more rapidly than the lessons it outlines can be applied. Yet, because the step-by-step progress of the hypothetical pupil in the manual flows so quickly from page to page and chapter to chapter, the reader sometimes tries to push his own dog's education at similar pace. Unfortunately, this leads the inexperienced trainer into the idea that something—anything—must be happening to his dog whenever the opportunity arises, in order to advance his progress at a faster rate. Thus, the apprehensive amateur unconsciously ends up devoting far more time and energy to obtaining a specific result than is required.

Many authorities advocate getting a dog accustomed to the sound of a gun on a gradual, sustained basis. Some recommend firing a cap pistol just prior to feeding time, discharging the toy gun about fifty feet from the pup at the start and reducing the distance to a few feet over a three-week period. If no ill effects result, the routine begins anew with a .22 caliber blank being substituted for the cap gun. The .22 blank eventually gives way to a .410 shotgun, which is carried over for a time to the pup's first few field excursions, before progressing to the higher noise level of a 20 gauge.

We have even seen the suggestion advanced in print that, as a supplementary gun-conditioning procedure, the young dog accompany his owner to trap and skeet shoots and be brought gradually closer to the ceaseless barrage to reinforce his immunity to the noise of gunfire. If a young dog manages to survive this, there can, of course, be no doubt that he's either stone deaf or not gun-shy.

Although the gradual, sustained method of introducing a young dog to the gun has much to recommend it in the case of a pup who is or may be timid, it also has some distinct drawbacks. Unless you live in the country, it's not likely that neighbors will long endure, or local ordinances permit, the daily discharge of .22 blanks, let alone a .410 shotgun in your backyard. Thus, the average owner is limited to the use of a cap pistol to accustom his pup to the noise of a gun. Properly followed, the cap-pistol-at-feeding-time routine can be an effective beginning to the introduction of the gun. It has been employed for years by countless amateur and professional dog trainers across the country.

Personally, though, except under kennel conditions where keeping a large number of pups precludes individual attention, I view the use of the cap pistol as an extraneous step that can prove a needless hazard in the training procedure. Why? Simply because the routine, practiced over an extensive period, may lead to careless or over-confident use of the tool. For example, without thinking, you might carry the food pan over to the doghouse, fire the gun and startle your pup out of a sound sleep. Sure, the pup has heard the cap pistol before. So have you. But, if someone woke you with the sound of a cap gun going off four or five feet from your bed, what would your reaction be?

Then, with the pup showing obvious signs of nervousness, the fear that your pupil may be backsliding tempts you to put him to the test again. You fire another shot—probably even closer to the pup, so you can carefully observe his reaction—and succeed only in reinforcing in his mind the idea that that same loud noise really *is* unpleasant. Mistakes like this can undo weeks of successful progress and may even sow the seeds of gun-shyness when no such problem would otherwise have existed.

Okay, if the cap pistol routine is not only unnecessary, but hazardous, how should you accustom your young dog to the sound of a gun? There's only one reason why a dog should ever hear a gun go off before he's become thoroughly accustomed to the sound. That reason is the sight of game at which the hunter is shooting in the field. A young dog who's really caught up in the exhilarating excitement of pursuit, intent on chasing a just-flushed bird or rabbit, will seldom show that he's even heard the gun go off. This is generally true whether or not he's ever heard the sound of a gun before.

What this means is that if the gun is prudently introduced in the *hunting field*, where its report can properly—and, at first, subconsciously—be associated with the stimulating sight and scent of game, any dog's acceptance of it should come quite naturally. Of course, reasonable care must be exercised the first few times you shoot. Wait for just the right moment, when the pup is some distance from you and engrossed in chasing bird or bunny, before discharging the gun into the air.

If the noise should disturb him, you'll do better to ignore him entirely, nonchalantly continuing the hunt. Permitting the next contact or two with game to draw no fire should return the pup's zest and enthusiasm to fever pitch once more. Then, at the next opportunity, firing should be delayed until the pup is chasing his game at greater distance from the gun.

If he shows no visible reaction to the noise, all well and good. Following a similar pattern on two or three subsequent field outings

Gun-shyness is seldom a problem if the sound of the gun has been introduced in the field, where it can be associated with the exciting sight and scent of game. This English springer spaniel knows the gun is a natural part of bringing game to hand, in this case a plump cock ringneck.

should find him sufficiently accustomed to the gun to insure against any future problem with gun-shyness. On the other hand, if he exhibits more than mild and momentary concern for the gun's noise, further shooting should be withheld for the rest of the outing. In such event, the only sensible course is for you to proceed slowly with his future gun training, perhaps even limiting yourself to one shot per field trip until the pup's apprehension completely disappears.

Sticking to this in-the-field technique will generally prove far more practical and effective—and certainly less risky—than any other method. Gun-shyness should seldom be a problem with a well-bred hunting dog, of normal temperament. If you worry yourself into making a complicated, contrived project out of introducing your pup to the gun, then nine chances out of ten any problem that does arise will be one of your own creation.

THE DOG'S WORKING VOCABULARY

How much of our language can a dog understand? The question can have nearly as many answers as there are dogs, for the extent of the canine vocabulary varies considerably according to age, environment and native intelligence.

The average gun dog will acquire a working vocabulary of approximately two dozen different words during the first four to six years of his life. Add in phrases containing up to three key words and this total can easily reach a high of about thirty-five—a pretty impressive lexicon.

Yet, it must be said that a large vocabulary contributes little to the gun dog's success in life. In fact, as far as the man who trains him is concerned, the more the dog's vocabulary can be trimmed, the better. Paradoxical? Hardly.

Although clear and meaningful to us, our spoken words are merely sounds to the dog. When first heard, they convey just about as much to him as Swahili would to us. He must be shown, by demonstration, and made to understand, through constant repetition, what each word means to him, in terms of expected behavior or reaction.

Some trainers liken the process to the one by which a child learns. Up to a point, this analogy may hold true, but there is very little legitimate basis for comparison. Certainly, a parent often uses phrases and even complete sentences to express ideas and meaning to a baby. Yet, the baby must learn not only the meaning of words but also the more complex process of duplicating their sounds in eventual speech. Thus, for the child, the patterns of speech sounds—for imitation— quickly assume almost equal importance with the knowledge of their meaning.

The dog has neither the intelligence potential of the human nor his need or ability to speak. Phrases and complete sentences, therefore, serve no useful purpose toward advancing the dog's training and functional value. In fact, at least in the early and intermediate phases of his education, they can actually confuse him and hinder his ability to absorb training and perform at top efficiency.

Ordinarily, a new owner displays a natural human tendency to clutter up his dog's lessons with excess verbiage. "Atta boy, Joe, now come on in here, like a nice fella, we've got a good biscuit for you, if you behave yourself and don't run away again," is hardly a suitable

Short, crisp commands are easier for the dog to add to his working vocabulary than are phrases or sentences. Here, the "Whoa" order, reinforced with check cord and spike collar, elicits instant response. **Photo by Dave Petzal.**

command by which to effect an errant young dog's return. (Without rereading it, can you repeat it? Of course not. Well, how can you expect a dog to respond to something you can't even remember yourself?)

Still because speech patterns, endlessly repeated, vocally and in print, seem so natural to the amateur trainer, he unconsciously resorts to their use in trying to teach a dog. When his dog, out of pure confusion, fails to comply or responds inconsistently, the command inevitably becomes even more cluttered—with the addition of a few choice oaths—and only further compounds the animal's confusion.

It is not impossible, of course, to train a gun dog by such methods; the hunting breeds are amazingly flexible and, in time, will catch on to even the most complex commands. Old dogs, thoroughly familiar with the moods, whims and routines of their masters, seem to respond almost by telepathy. But, the point here is to speed up the training task by using the simplest, most effective system of commands to teach the young dog what is required of him.

Long before any breed of hunting dog is taken to the field for anything more serious than familiarization, he must become what we might best call "civilized." In the process, he should learn a few simple basic commands that will be important preliminaries to all future training; his name, "No," "Here," "Sit," "Stay" and "Kennel." With this vocabulary alone, any pup can become acceptably "civilized" in a matter of a few weeks.

A short, crisp, distinctive name, one that sounds nothing like any of the commands to be used now or later, should be chosen. It serves two purposes: 1) to give the pup identity, and 2) to gain his attention for further orders.

"No," is the simplest negative; it substitutes adequately for several otherwise extraneous commands such as "Get Down," "Shame on You," "Quiet," "Dirty" (for housebreaking errors) or "Bad Dog."

"Here," of course, is the single-word recall order that makes the pup come to his owner. It is obviously more terse and effective than "Come on in here," or "Get in here," and avoids confusion with possible later commands similar in sound but different in meaning.

"Sit" and/or "Stay" are the short commands that establish both the owner's authority and the pup's attention. "Kennel," again, is a short, crisp order that saves the need for additional words that would otherwise have to be introduced later. It means, as far as the dog is concerned, "Get in your box (or bed)" "Get in your kennel run," "Get in your doghouse," "get in the car," or "Get in the crate in the car," depending on the circumstances of the moment.

How much more effective and time-saving such single-word commands are, especially when carefully chosen so as to accomplish more than one desired act in the gun dog. Sure, his vocabulary has been trimmed, but certainly not his understanding of, or adherence to, your orders.

Later, his yard-training, which will utilize and reinforce most of the above commands, can expand his vocabulary to include the new orders of "Heel," "Whoa" and "Down." With the possible exception of the last, there should be no cause for confusion with other commands. However, having used "No" to discourage various undesirable acts, such as teaching the dog not to jump on people, one may now use the word "Down" to indicate only one thing to the dog: lie down.

Eventually, in the field, he will have to learn still more commands. Once again, these should be selected on the basis of crispness, simplicity and whenever possible, pertinence to a variety of situa-

The single word "Fetch," suffices to make this German wirehaired pointer "hunt close" for a "dead bird," then "bring it here" and "sit" when delivering it to his mistress. **Photo by Jerome J. Knap.**

tions. For example, "Whoa," the meaning of which has already been taught, stops the dog in his tracks; it makes him wait for you to catch up before entering a particularly gamey piece of cover; it literally puts him on point to avoid accidentally flushing a bird you've seen running but which he's unaware of; it makes him honor another dog's point; it prevents him from starting out before you're ready.

Another instance: many hunters use the order "Hunt Close," to pull their dogs in for close range work. But by using a combination of "Whoa" and "Here," the dog can be made to hunt close without having to learn a completely new command.

Among the new words he'll have to be taught are those that order him to range out and hunt; to proceed without so much caution or fussing; to search diligently for a downed bird; and to retrieve. As many as four different commands are used by some hunters to have their dogs accomplish these four actions: (1) "Get Ahead," (2) "All right," (3) "Dead Bird" and (4) "Fetch,"

But the truth is that only two different commands are needed. "Go On" will suffice for the first two, and "Fetch" will do for the others.

Why waste time and effort trying to teach a dog twice as many new words as are necessary?

Though some of the actual commands may differ, depending on the type of dog as well as his particular job and hunting technique in the field, the basic philosphy of a trim vocabulary holds true for all gun dogs. The use of the fewest and shortest commands possible cannot fail to make your job of training and the dog's job of learning much faster and easier.

Unless you happen to have one of those very rare "talking" canines we've all heard about but have never seen, there's just no point in overloading your dog's vocabulary. Keep it as lean as you keep his physique and you'll both be in better shape for field work.

FIELD SIGNALS: THE LUNG SAVERS

Strong hardy, red-blooded outdoorsmen are not known for letting minor ailments, like colds or sore throats, keep them from their appointed weekend rounds afield with dog and gun. Jack was a strong, hardy, red-blooded outdoorsman: he had a cold, a sore throat and...a Saturday quail hunting date. Naturally, he kept it.

Despite his admirable display of guts, he was in miserable shape. It simply was not to be his day. But, then, neither was it to be his dog's. A big, rangy English pointer, his dog covered ground faster than a Texas rain squall. But, with Jack's vocal chords reduced to the decibel level of a stringless guitar, it fast became evident that his dog sorely missed the generous coaching help he was obviously accustomed to getting from his handler.

Every time Jack wanted to stop his dog, either to turn him when we changed direction or to keep him in closer, he'd open his mouth to yell, but nothing above a hoarse whisper ever came out. Watching his frustration mount, I decided to offer some help. "Wanna borrow my whistle, Jack?"

"Naw," he croaked, "it wouldn't help, I've never bothered with a whistle...figured if I couldn't handle my dog with voice he was ranging too far out anyway. Guess I just never figured on laryngitis."

The details of the rest of the day are not too important, except to

One short, sharp whistle blast has put this young Lab in the sitting position, attentively awaiting additional directions from his handler.

report that Jack finally asked me to handle the dog by relaying his whispers into audible orders. At first, because my voice was unfamiliar to the dog, it was touch-and-go. Eventually, though, he seemed to understand the situation and responded well enough for us to get into some bobwhites. The fact that I, too, became hoarse in the process was incidental.

All of this points up the advantages to the hunter and his dog of having a system of communication other than the spoken command. Whistle signals, for example, are invaluable for a number of reasons: they can be heard more readily over a distance; they are once thoroughly learned, more intelligible; they are usually more sharply compelling; they save undue wear and tear on a handler's lungs and larynx.

Hand signals, too, have functional value in the successful teamwork needed between man and dog in the field. For many of the same reasons that whistle signals prove practical, visual instructions are often more easily transmitted and obeyed than are verbal orders.

And, by combining both whistle and hand signals, the hunter and his dog can work together with almost clocklike precision under virtually any set of circumstances ever encountered in the field.

Of all the gun dog breeds and types that are worked with signals, the retrievers probably stand out as the most prominent examples and beneficiaries of the system. It would be difficult to imagine any of the fetch breeds performing at anything approaching their peak efficiency over an extended period without the benefit of a signal system between themselves and their handlers.

On blind (unmarked) falls, for instance, even the best retriever would be up against almost hopeless odds were it not for signals from his owner. Without being given a "line," or starting direction in which to proceed, then a "stop" and a "right," "left," "forward" or "back," to put him on an unmarked bird, the fetch dog would have to cover all four points of the compass, in ever-widening circles, to pick up his bird. And if the unseen bird turns out to be a cripple, the time wasted in searching in three possible wrong directions could cost the loss of the bird to the hunter's bag.

Similar problems and motivations face the spaniel owner. The flushing breeds are neck-and-neck with the retrievers as both beneficiaries and dependants of the signal system. Moreover, with a spaniel the

Audio-visual directions swing your dog in the direction you want to go. For better visibility, use the whole arm in giving signals.

system takes on an expanded role when considered in conjunction with his customary live-bird flushing duties.

Although used to a lesser extent with the pointing breeds, whistle and hand signals play a highly practical part in handling bird dogs smoothly and efficiently. In fact, probably the only type of hunting dogs that work without some sort of formalized signal system are the hounds. And yet, even these breeds are generally taught to respond to the hunter's recall horn.

Fundamentally, whistle signals for handling any kind of gun dog break down into three types: 1) to stop, or whoa the dog, causing him to fix his attention on his handler for further orders; 2) to send the dog on; 3) to call the dog in.

Hand signals, reduced to their simplest form for use in the field, merely indicate the direction in which the handler desires his dog to go: left, right, forward or back. There is also another hand signal—arm extended and palm out, in traffic cop style—that's commonly used to whoa a dog at close range. Ordinarily, this signal is employed only to caution or reinforce a dog already in the stopped position.

How can a dog be taught to respond properly to basic whistle and hand signals? Very easily. Although the teaching is not complex, it must, like most other forms of dog training, be progressive and repetitive.

Begin with the easiest of the three whistle signals, "Go on." Each time you turn the dog loose to run or hunt, command him to "Go On," then blow two quick, short blasts on the whistle as you release his collar. After he's doing this without hesitation—and since he's so eager to be turned loose, he'll learn the lesson rapidly—you can eliminate the spoken command and use only the whistle.

Teaching him to come in to the whistle may prove a bit more difficult, but no more so than calling him in by voice. A long check cord attached to his collar will simplify as well as enforce compliance. Call the dog in to you with your usual command and immediately follow it with a long tootling blow on the whistle as he starts toward you. Soon, he should respond to the whistle alone, on or off the check cord.

Stopping a dog to the whistle is unquestionably the most exacting of the three basic signals to be taught. Essentially, it's an extension of the "Whoa" command used for pointing dogs, the "Sit" order for retrievers and the "Hup" directive for spaniels. The latter two commands are more easily taught than the first, which has almost as many suggested variational techniques as there are pointing dogs.

Substituting the whistle for the vocal order in the "Sit" or "Hup" commands can best be achieved by starting the dog on leash. Assuming he has already been taught to obey the order to sit or hup, the leash will serve strictly as a supplementary tool to make the job easier. First, start with the dog walking at heel on a loosely held lead. Stop and give the order to sit or hup, and quickly follow up with one short whistle blast, pull the leash straight up, simultaneously exerting downward pressure on his rump with your left hand.

Gradually decrease the vocal command as you increase the use of the whistle, until the single sharp toot produces the response you want automatically. Extending the lesson from leash to check cord, and ultimately eliminating both, you should have the dog sitting the instant the whistle is sounded.

Having progressed to the point where you can stop, hup or whoa your dog at any time in the field, it is just one extra step to teach him directional hand signals. With his attention riveted on you, extend your arm straight up and then swing it in the direction you want him to go. At the same time, take a step or two in that direction and blow the two short blasts that signal him, "Go on."

Left: *Hand signals like whistle signals, are easily taught in the yard. Author demonstrates the signal he uses to make dog sit—palm outstretched and extended downward, like waving goodbye.* **Right:** *Getting the dog to lie down is just as easy with a hand signal. Using a choke collar reinforces a dog's compliance.* **Photos by Dave Petzal.**

For better visibility, and to avoid confusion, always use the entire arm to give directional signals, the left arm to send him that way, the right one to send him in that direction. The gesture used to direct the dog to go back is similar to the other hand signals, except that the motion of your raised arm is toward the dog and is accompanied by the command, "Back," just before blowing the whistle.

Various aids may be used to make the job of signal training easier. These can range from tidbits used in the backyard to live birds or retrieving dummies in the field, all strategically planted or tossed to the left, right or behind the dog. In each instance, the association of a reward gained through obeying his handler's directions will help the dog learn his lessons more quickly and enthusiastically.

Through perseverance you can teach your dog to obey hand and whistle signals. And, after employing them faithfully for a season or two, you'll both enjoy a richer, fuller bond of communication that can only result in the greater dividends that practical teamwork in the field provides.

YOUR PUP'S FIRST SEASON

What kind of performer will he be, that new gun dog pup you'll be taking out for his first season in the field this fall? Will he turn into the stylish kind of hunter you can be proud of in any company, every time out? Will he become the type of dog that would rather hunt than eat, the kind that sets your pulse racing at the sight of his game-handling capabilities? Or will he turn out to be a crashing dud, the sort of dog you'd almost rather leave home?

If it's not in his inheritance to begin with, of course, it matters little what you do. But if the potential *is* there, what happens to it during his first full season afield is strictly up to you. For solely upon an owner's awareness of the first season's vital importance to a young dog's development can the promise of a pup's full potential ever be realized. Any young dog's initial experiences establish the basic working foundation for all the rest of the careful training needed to mold him into the sort of performer you want. And nothing worthwhile was ever built on a poor or weak foundation.

A young dog should build enthusiasm and self-confidence during his first season afield. Here, young setter rears up on hind legs in his eagerness to watch flight of wild-flushing woodcock.

Despite the fundamentalness of a dog's first season afield, it should be one of the most relaxed and pleasant periods for the owner who understands its few primary objectives. Regardless of breed, hunting technique or game sought, a dog's inaugural season in the field should be essentially a time of awakening. It should be an opportunity for him to excite to the keenest degree his natural instinct for the hunt, through the stimulation provided by frequent contact with game. Generally, the fewer complicating factors introduced, the greater the likelihood that he'll attain the fullest measure of his inherited potential.

Unfortunately, between the start of the dog's first season and the attainment of its ideal goal lurk numerous pitfalls for the owner who isn't alert to them.

A common pernicious tendency is to race the clock, attempting to transform the raw yearling into a flawless game-getter virtually overnight. Especially if his pup seems more precocious than average, the novice trainer finds it an irresistible temptation to push just as hard as he can. Such accelerated training, with its accompanying over-disciplining, doesn't always ruin a dog by the end of his first season, but it does produce a scared, confused, mechanical worker, totally lacking in style or the initiative to seek and find game without a constant flow of directions from his handler. There's not much pleasure, and little satisfaction, in watching or hunting over a dog like this. And what's even more pitiful is the probability that, allowed to progress normally, developing his instincts naturally, through a love of hunting, the precocious pup might well have turned into an outstanding performer, one who'd have given his owner all the thrills of stylish work and greater dividends in game as well.

By keeping discipline to a reasonable minimum — that is, issuing as few commands as possible during your pup's preliminary field excursions — you'll be encouraging him to develop the self-confidence he needs to range out and hunt. Self-confidence will in turn lead to the independence all hounds and bird dogs — and for that matter retrievers used as flushing dogs — must gain in order to seek out and find game effectively.

Trying to rush the young dog's education can lead to overdisciplining and too harsh treatment of a pupil before he's sufficiently developed. **Photo by Dave Petzal.**

Once your pup demonstrates his enthusiasm for hunting, he's ready for some serious training. Now you can begin gradually to establish the control and discipline factors that will channel his hunting capabilities into serving the gun. The aggressive, investigative pup will generally develop more rapidly — depending on how frequently you get him afield — and exhibit his readiness to accept formal training in progressively larger doses. If your pup is timid and slow to show his spirited interest in hunting, however, you'll have to withhold strict discipline, substituting instead patient perseverance designed to stimulate his self-confidence. Often the pup who seems painfully slow to develop will, if patiently handled, all at once catch fire and display faster progress from then on than his bolder counterparts.

Other forms of impatience can create problems during the first season, too. For example, there is the sort that denies a young dog opportunities to gain sufficient experience in seeking and finding game. This occurs most often with the hunter who puts too much emphasis on filling an empty game pocket. Unless the hunter can get off a killing shot at every creature the dog turns up, this type of hunter usually regards working the pup as a waste of time, returns him to the car and hunts without him for the rest of the day.

Yet, it's not always the owner's preoccupation with killing game that restricts his dog's opportunities to gain needed hunting exposure. A hunter's gunning companions can exert considerable influence in this respect. The worst offenders are usually those with little or no experience hunting with dogs, who simply haven't the faintest idea of what the dog's owner is trying to accomplish. Their sole interest is putting game in the bag, and if a young dog provides too little help or, worse yet, occasionally messes up a shot, they're seldom slow in registering their complaints. The end result, if an owner wants to keep his friends happy, is that young Spot is stuck in the back of the car for the remainder of the trip.

Occasionally, an owner's distorted sense of courtesy cuts into the length and frequency of his pup's field work, too. Though the hunter's companions may be willing to take their chances with a novice pooch, they may have failed to express themselves in so many words. Yet, thinking they are just too polite to raise objections, a sensitive owner may well limit his young dog to a very brief outing, before relegating him to his crate in the car.

Certainly, none of the above situations is helpful in easing the normal course of a young dog's early education in the field. But, in overall effect, they are far less formidable than the problem posed by a trigger-happy acquaintance. This type will seldom object to having a pup out front. As far as "Old Itchy Finger" is concerned, everything the dog jumps within sight or sound becomes a fair target at which to empty his unplugged autoloader. A couple of his five-shot barrages would be sufficient to make even the most stoic old hunting dog quit cold; the effect on a yearling gun dog is likely to be infinitely worse, and a lot longer lasting.

Group, or "gang," hunts carry the same threat of too much shooting, shouting and confusion, and should be scrupulously avoided during the initial season afield.

Awareness of the fact that your companions can comprise the single greatest potential hazard to the proper development of the blossoming gun dog is half your battle. The other half consists of taking reasonable care to avoid the type of "friends" that could complicate your pup's early education.

If you must have company along on your pup's first-season outings, your buddies should be selected with extreme care, and limited to no more than one or two on any occasion. And "dog men" or not, they should be well briefed in advance on what you're attempting to de-

Hunting your pup alone during his inaugural season avoids most of the pitfalls that can slow his progress. Uninitiated companions can cause problems.

velop in your pup, as well as what you want or don't want done in the pup's presence. No friends could take offense at such precautions, and no owner should feel any embarrassment in exercising his prerogatives.

In the final analysis, however, it's a wise owner who'll arrange to make the lion's share of his pup's inaugural season experiences strictly solo affairs. Only by hunting his pup alone can a man devote his undivided attention to the dog, providing encouragement where indicated, observing and evaluating strong as well as weak points and noting for future reference those idiosyncrasies that make every dog a true individual.

Make no mistake about it, your dog's first full season afield is the most formatively important time in his life. Get him off on the right foot, give him the opportunities to develop those latent instincts to full potential. Then, later on, with proper formal training, chances are he'll more than measure up to the kind of performer you've always wanted...the kind that puts pride in your heart, and game in your bag.

HOW MUCH, HOW SOON?

When should you begin training a new pup to become the kind of hunting dog you've always dreamed about owning? What sort of schooling, and how much of it should he get to start him toward your goal?

Even if you're still only toying with the idea of buying a pup, the answers to these questions will some day prove mighty important to you. But if, right now, there's a frisky little bundle of canine energy tugging at your shoelaces, your need for the right answers is vital and immediate.

With the whole future of that lively little package resting entirely in your hands, you can't afford to dawdle over the decisions concerning what kind of education he should receive and when it should start. Neither can you afford to make any snap judgments that might seriously impair your pup's chances to measure up to all his potentials afield.

If you're like a majority of owners of new hunting breed pups, you'll probably be torn between two opposite schools of thought about training a field dog. One advocates beginning the pup's training the minute he's weaned, while the other suggests delaying formal training until the pup is well past a year of age. On the face of it, with even the so-called experts poles apart, novice owners can hardly be blamed for not knowing what to do.

The truth is that fundamentally, at least in the early stages of a pup's education, neither training philosophy is really as far removed from the other as it would first appear.

In fact, much of the apparently incompatible discrepancy between the two systems stems from the variable interpretations of a single word: "training." Too many of us are guilty of using the term loosely, so that it doesn't always imply exactly what we mean. Used in its broadest sense, training is merely a synonym for general education, the process of learning something, though not necessarily by means of a formal lesson. Conversely, in proper usage, the term does connote systematic instruction or drill; in other words, a lesson designed to teach a specific point.

Unfortunately, especially where hunting dogs are involved, the inexperienced owner is certain to interpret the word training in its latter sense, assuming it always implies something a dog must be taught in a mechanical, regimented—and deadly serious—manner. Actually, neither of the opposing schools of thought proposes educating your pup entirely that way.

For example, the "begin-when-they're weaned" proponents advocate "training" your pup to be clean in the house; to know his name; to

At eleven weeks of age, this setter pup is all mischief and inattention. Most of what he learns will come by "osmosis," not formal lessons.

come when called; to wear a collar; to walk on lead; to obey the "No," "Sit," and "Stay" commands – all by the time he's three-and-a-half to four months old. The opposite, or "take-it-easy," school subscribes to the pup's learning most if not all of these same simple aspects of becoming civilized by roughly the same age; but this school reserves use of the word training for later and more formalized lessons. Basically, there's little difference in the results sought or obtained; only the terminology and, to some small extent, the psychology differ between the two systems of educating a young puppy.

Certainly, extremes do exist within both factions; but these are the exceptions, more about which we'll delve into later.

Up to the age of about four months your pup should receive his basic education largely by exposure to all the new things around him and gentle but consistent direction from you. Like the process of osmosis, much of what he learns will merely be absorbed, rather than taught or drummed into him. Aside from the occasional mild reprimand with folded newspaper or displeased tone of voice, force and punishment should be withheld and replaced with encouragement and reward for proper behavior.

During this time, of course, you'll have to give your pup some instruction in order to convey to him the meaning of such simple commands as "No," "Sit," "Stay," and "Down." Even though he can hardly be expected to demonstrate instant or perfect obedience at such a tender age, the more attention you give him, the better he'll begin to understand what you want. Later on, when you start adding discipline to reinforce your orders, he should respond much more readily, since he'll be familiar with the meaning of your commands and know why he's chastised if he doesn't comply.

Essentially, all you should be trying to accomplish during the first several months of your pup's primary education is to gain his trust and affection, to familiarize him with his surroundings and the routine of your household, and to civilize him as much as possible. Up to this point the two schools of thought for training a field dog are fundamentally in agreement. Both concur that such preliminary groundwork is necessary to prepare a young dog properly for all of the future education he'll receive in the field.

Only when the pup reaches the age of four-and-a-half or five months do proponents of either system really part company. And, in this split can be found the sharpest division of opinion over what constitutes the proper age, pace, and procedure for starting, developing, and

Most Labradors can be encouraged to fetch dummies or other objects at an early age. Serious training, however, must wait until the gun dog is more mature, physically as well as mentally.

finishing a dog in the field.

Extremists on both sides of the fence are so far apart in their beliefs that, for all intents and purposes, they actually form two new schools of thought, one within each of their separate camps. At the "start-'em-early" end of the spectrum are those who advocate accelerating the young dog's training—and here we use the term in its strictest sense—at a pace designed to produce a practical, reliably working field dog by the time he's six months old.

At the opposite pole are those who firmly contend that a dog's freedom from almost all forms of regimentation and disciplined direction in the field should be withheld for at least sixteen to eighteen months.

To dismiss these extremist views without knowing why is a mistake, so let's examine their contentions to see where they lead and what, if any, validity they contain.

The folks who favor the fast-push philosophy cite new scientific knowledge indicating that a dog's mental development progresses at a much more rapid rate than has heretofore been realized.

On this basic premise an entire training program has been structured, stressing the idea that a puppy's greater mental capacities must be taken advantage of by accelerating the pace, amount and complexity of his schooling both at home and afield. Much of the rationale on which the fast-push philosophy is predicated seems logical; there are indeed many things a young dog can learn or be taught earlier than most trainers have thought.

There are two glaring flaws in the system as it applies to field dogs. The first is a failure to take into account the five- or six-month-old dog's physical immaturity, which, regardless of how rapidly his brain develops, restricts his ability to perform effectively. The child prodigy may well memorize every note of a Tchaikovsky piano concerto, but if he can't reach the keys or the pedals, he can hardly be expected to play it very well.

A five- or six-month-old pup—no matter what his breed—is, at best, little more than half-grown. He is physically incapable of certain tasks. Still in the awkward stage, he lacks adult size, coordination, speed, and stamina, all fundamental to a hunting dog's performance in the field.

The system's second flaw, while a bit less obvious, concerns the underrating of the importance of a hunting dog's instincts. Unlike the admirable but nonetheless mechanical range of work taught to seeing-

Your dog should develop at his own natural pace, without being rushed. This English pointer shows all the self-confidence and intensity that makes hunting over him a pleasure.

eye dogs—with which the rapid early training system has undeniably produced excellent results—the hunting dog's effectiveness hinges in large measure on his instincts.

These instincts—the inbred urge to range and hunt, to seek out quarry and trail, flush, or point—must be sparked, stimulated, and crystallized before they can be channelled, through training and discipline, into practical utility for the gun. No matter what scientific procedures are employed, instincts simply cannot be taught, and it is these instincts, after all, that set hunting dogs apart from all other breeds.

Thus, this combination of physical immaturity and not-yet-developed hunting instincts mitigates against the fast-push system's goal of producing a practical, functional hunting dog by the age of six months.

At the other end of the spectrum are the old hands who embrace the idea that a hunting dog, like good cheese, is best if ripened slowly. These purists place a premium on a dog's attaining the highest degree of natural development and inspired performance. There is nothing to fault the ideals of such men, and often enough their patient methods produce dogs of championship caliber.

Their system precludes any serious attempts to restrict a dog's freedom afield much before he reaches his sixteenth or eighteenth month. Then, all their efforts are carefully tailored to their dogs' individual personalities. Pressure and discipline are applied gingerly and increased or retracted accordingly. Occasionally, greatness results; sometimes, undisciplined outlaws are produced. Either way, a couple of years go by, far too long for the average hunting dog owner to wait before even beginning to collect any tangible dividends in the field.

What conclusions can be drawn, then, from the two most extreme philosophies advocated for schooling a hunting dog? Simply that each has some merit; each has drawbacks. On the one hand, pushing a young dog too fast and demanding too much, too soon, may ruin him or, at least, retard his full potential. On the other, waiting too long, doing and expecting too little can, at worst, have equally disastrous results—even for the veteran trainer—or, at best, unduly delay the dog's practical value to the hunter.

Obviously, somewhere in the middle ground, between the extremes, lies the best compromise for the average sportsman who seeks neither an automaton nor a field trial champion, but strictly a functional hunting dog he can enjoy and be proud to own. But, don't for a minute get the idea that this middle ground is just a convenient form of fence-straddling. The road, some sage once observed, has the most room in the middle. The same can be said of the area between extremes in field dog training. The wide latitude that enables you to adjust the timing, pace, and procedures of training to conform with your own dog's temperament, mental and physical development, and natural progress in the field also leaves room for making mistakes.

Despite all this leeway, though, there are still a number of general guidelines that should prove helpful to you and your pup. Let's go back momentarily to that point in your pup's basic schooling when the two training philosophies begin to differ. The split occurs after your pup's about five months old and has become familiar with his and your everyday routine and a few essential commands.

Is now the time to start his education in the field? Remember, he's still at the awkward stage and needs only encouragement to investigate the sights, smells, and sounds of what amounts to a whole strange new environment.

The less you say or attempt to do to direct him during these preliminary outings, the faster he'll acquire the natural confidence he needs to build up in himself. Your only role in these early field trips should be that of a trusted friend, someone the pup knows and enjoys being with. If you let him fend for himself in solving the myriad little dilemmas of negotiating brush, brambles, ditches, fences, and what-have-you, he'll eventually become accustomed to the big new world of the outdoors. Once he begins developing the confidence and independence he needs, his hunting instincts will start asserting themselves.

With every sparrow, chipmunk, rabbit, or squirrel he trails and chases, those instincts will be stimulated, finally blossoming into a feverish desire to get out ahead of you and hunt. Until this natural urge surfaces and has a reasonable chance to solidify itself, any attempts to force discipline or control on your pup in the field will be premature.

How long should you give him his head before beginning serious field training? No one can provide a definitive answer that would cover all hunting breeds. Even within a single breed there are so many individual circumstances to be considered that a general rule often won't apply.

The best advice is to let your dog tell you when he's ready. And, although lacking the powers of speech, he will tell you just as surely by his behavior and attitude in the field. His enthusiasm, the way he runs, his zest and spirit and overall eagerness will signal his readiness.

If he's a bold character, aggressive and thoroughly investigative of everything around him, the chances are good that he'll be exhibiting sufficient hunting desire and independence to begin accepting formal training by the time he's nine or ten months old. But, of course, this will depend on how frequently you've been able to get him afield. If your outings together have been limited to one or two a month, you can't expect the same rate of progress that three or four weekly trips would produce.

On the other hand, if your pup proves to be somewhat timid or slow to demonstrate his interest in hunting, you should withhold any forceful attempts to push training on him. Instead, concentrate on giving him every possible opportunity to stimulate his self-confidence. Such a situation is not distressing. Oftentimes, the pup who comes along slowly will, if nurtured patiently, suddenly catch fire and exhibit more stability than the one that seems an early-blooming natural.

Once you've decided your pup has "told" you he's ready, don't hesitate to launch his real training for the field job his breed is expected to do. Follow the tried-and-true procedures and step-by-step techniques recommended in a good book devoted to his specific type or breed of hunting dog. And don't be afraid to modify or improvise with common sense the lessons contained therein. Above all, remember that every dog, no matter what his breed, is an individual and that your dog is the particular individual you alone know best.

EDUCATION CAN BE A FAMILY AFFAIR

No matter what his breed, any normal gun dog puppy not only needs, but will actually thrive on a reasonable amount of playful diversion. In fact, without it he cannot fully develop the well-rounded temperament and adaptability so necessary to accepting more serious training later on in life. The "all work and no play..." adage is no less applicable to the attainment of a well-adjusted puppy than it is to little Jack.

Whether the pup's lighter moments are provided exclusively by the owner or partially by the younger members of the family makes little difference to the dog. The fact that they *are* provided is the important thing, and the owner whose children can augment and share in a pup's development should count himself fortunate.

All puppies thrive on playful diversion and the love that a youngster provides. This Brittany spaniel will be all the better for his association with an obviously adoring young lad. **Photo by Steber.**

Obviously, a child's participation shouldn't be haphazard and unguided when the dog's well-being and progressive development are at stake. But a parent who takes care to instruct his youngster in what, and what not to do, and how to behave with a dog will recoup his investment tenfold.

No better time exists for initiating youngsters into proper association with the pup that's slated to become Dad's gun dog than during the summer vacation months. With school out, a "care and training" project can do much to help fill a kid's spare time. The extra hours of daylight can, without interfering with Pop's work schedule, enable him to devote the few minutes that are necessary each day to instruction and demonstration of the proper care and training techniques his children should know.

Naturally, a child's age must be considered in light of just how much and what sort of responsibility can be reasonably entrusted to him. But, coupled with a parent's common sense, some judicious observation of the youngster's general behavior around the dog should soon provide the basic guidelines for what can be expected of him. Some children of five or six demonstrate far more natural ability to understand and get along with a dog than do youngsters several years older. By the same token, no matter what his age, a child with a short temper, a willfully mean or sadistic streak, shouldn't be trusted with a puppy at all, except under supervision. Such are the criteria on which each parent must make his own judgment.

By and large, though, there's scant reason why an average, normally intelligent seven-to-ten-year-old can't take charge of quite a number of dog care functions. For example, a three- or four-month-old puppy needs frequent exercise throughout the day. If he lives indoors, these regular outings are doubly essential toward his becoming and remaining housebroken. Certainly, the youngster can help out here, by taking the pup outdoors at scheduled intervals and praising him for each "good deed" done in the proper spot.

The older youngster can prove to be a valuable assistant in helping train a gun dog. This teenager gives a German shorthaired pointer a lesson in "heeling." **Photo by Dave Petzal.**

Even if the puppy is quartered in a backyard kennel, he should be taken out for several daily romps, preferably on a long rope that will preclude his getting away or beyond control. These exercise periods will prove beneficial to the pup, not only in terms of his physical needs but also in the companionable association with humans that they provide him.

Grooming the dog is another aspect the average youngster can handle. Obviously, the young boy or girl should not be expected or permitted to clip the dog's nails, to strip or trim his coat or clean out his ears. Such things are better left to the man or woman of the house. But a ten-minute grooming session with comb and brush is a good and necessary routine with which virtually any youngster can be entrusted.

And if ten minutes of daily grooming seems unnecessarily prolonged, just consider that there is more to be gained from it than simply a clean, glossy coat. For, once the pup becomes accustomed to the routine — another accomplishment in itself — the grooming process produces both a calming effect and, through physical handling, a closer bond of trust and affection.

A host of additional responsibilites, such as keeping the pup's quarters and feed pan clean, providing fresh water and measuring out and preparing rations, can be delegated to an ambitious youngster. His sincerity of interest in helping with family gun-dog-to-be will soon be reflected in the manner and regularity with which these chores are performed. If he goofs, he'll have no one but himself to blame for his folks' disappointment and possible reluctance to let him share in the larger responsibilities of the pup's later yard training and work in the field.

In most instances, the early association of youngster and pup will not, and should not, entail any serious formalized training. Remember, we're talking about a very young puppy, purchased and brought home at, perhaps, two-and-a-half or three months of age. At such tender age, any training should be limited strictly to those things the pup can absorb through constant routine, with none but the very mildest correction attempted.

It is during this period that the puppy will be making his biggest adjustment, forming his attachments and becoming "civilized." He needs play and exercise, care and companionship, all of which essentials, as already discussed, can be ideally supplemented by the youngsters.

Once the pup is fairly well acclimated and begins to attain some age and growth—usually in about his fifth month—progressive formal training can be started. He can be taught to sit and stay, to lie down, to heel, to whoa and can be expected to obey with increasing alacrity as his lessons progress. Although, obviously, this training will be initiated by "The Boss," the younger members of the family can eventually assist by learning precisely what commands Dad uses and how to enforce obedience to them. Since the enforcement aspect is the tricky part, Junior will have to be carefully instructed, and each technique demonstrated for him, to make certain he understands and can exercise its application.

As the youngster reflects his comprehension and capability, he can be permitted to augment Dad's training sessions with a brief daily review of the commands with which the pup is familiar. If the pup backslides, Pop can take corrective measures and, at the same time, find out if the youngster has gone awry in his technique.

The real culmination of making your dog's education a family affair comes with enjoying the fruits of your mutual labors. What happier moment could any father ask than to share an autumn day with his son, his Labrador, and a pair of ducks for the table.

Even if most fathers were not prone to taking great pride in their offsprings' notable accomplishments, mere practicality itself would make worthwhile the youngsters' active participation in the schooling of a gun dog pup. For, instead of becoming spoiled by indifference, the dog who lives in the house is far more apt to be kept better disciplined through the interested efforts of a youngster who, properly instructed, can share in the dog's training. By the same token, the kennel dog cannot fail to benefit from Junior's active interest. Rather than being shut up alone in his run between training sessions, the pup can look forward to additional exercise, training and, most important, the extra companionship an enthusiastic youngster can provide.

With proper planning, appropriate instruction and intelligent supervision, the care, raising and training of your new gun dog pup can become an enjoyable experience for the entire household. Why not make it—a family affair?

THE QUESTION OF PROFESSIONAL TRAINING

There's always a certain percentage of sporting breed puppy buyers who, despite their best laid plans, seem to run into snags in their training programs. Unforeseen changes in their personal lives, a new job, a promotion or a special project at the office can bite deeply into their spare time and drastically alter a routine that normally would easily have accommodated training a gun dog pup from start to finish.

Then, suddenly faced with a lack of time, such hapless owners are forced to abandon their pups' field training—often, as luck would have it—at a crucial stage, just when progress is at hand.

Even barring circumstantial factors, it's inevitable for some sportsmen to encounter training problems that they can't handle but which must be overcome in order to advance their dogs' field education. In these cases the services of a professional gun dog trainer become a real necessity. One that, in fact, may well be the only means of fulfilling their fondest hopes of owning a useful field dog instead of a loveable but inept fugitive from the family playroom.

Contrary to the barbs frequently hurled by envious acquaintances, enlisting the services of a professional trainer hardly constitutes an automatic cop-out on owner responsibilities. Rather, what it represents is an objective recognition of the advantages a pro can provide—time, ideal facilities and a ready supply of game—when your situation most requires them.

The pro's opportunities to work a dog day in and day out, over prime territory abounding with natural or stocked game, obviously give him a significant training edge. And, of course, the professional's experience enables him to spot a dog's present or potential faults and to correct or prevent them.

Suppose, then, for whatever reasons, you decide you'd like to have some professional training for your dog. How do you go about finding a good professional trainer? How long will you have to leave your dog with him? When is the best time to patronize a professional? How much will you have to spend? The answers are likely to vary accordingly with the age and breed of your dog, as well as with the trainer you select. So, the first and most important step is to locate a suitable pro.

The advertising columns of various journals devoted to sporting dogs in general, or to specific types of breeds, are an excellent place to start your search. Publications such as *American Field, Retriever News, Hounds and Hunting,* and *Full Cry* are typical of the specialized hunting dog periodicals that carry ads placed by professional trainers. "Where to Buy, Board, or Train a Dog," a free booklet available from Gaines Professional Services, P.O. Box 877, Young America, MN 55399, provides still another good reference for locating a trainer within reasonable distance of home.

Choosing a reputable trainer is a simple but important matter. Usually, a few casual questions asked of your local sporting goods dealer, the breeder from whom you purchased your dog or the owner of the shooting preserve you frequent can give you a pretty good line on any trainer operating within a couple hundred miles of home. Then, assuming the reports are favorable, a letter or phone call to the man himself can probably provide the name of a couple of local sportsmen whose dogs he has trained in the past. Further checking should reveal just what the references think of his work.

The next step is a personal visit to the trainer's grounds, accompanied by your dog so that the man can see just what he has got to work with. Normally, it won't take him very long to size up the dog's present capabilities and evaluate his future potentialities. Then, depending on the dog's age, breed and temperament, as well as the extent of any

Daily work in the field, which the professional trainer provides, can speed a young dog's education at the time when progress depends on frequent and productive outings. **Photo by Dave Petzal.**

specific faults or problems involved, he should be able to give you a tentative estimate of the length of the training period he'll require to accomplish the goals you want.

Some trainers accept dogs on the stipulation that if the dog shows no appreciable progress within a reasonable period, the owner will be notified and advised to come pick him up. Others will take a dog only for a specified minimum period ranging from one to three months, depending upon what sort of training job is involved. In any case, leaving a dog with a professional for a period of less than one month seldom affords very worthwhile results. Few good trainers ever encourage an owner to buy their services for less than a month or two, except on a trial basis.

If that seems a long time, just stop and consider that the dog must first become acclimated to a change of surroundings before his new handler can even begin to make friends with him. Still more time passes while the trainer gains the dog's confidence and respect prior to starting actual field work. Since it won't do to rush these important preliminaries, a week or ten days may go by before any serious sessions are begun. Once underway, however, they become progressively more intensive, and it's generally only the most backward pupil who fails to show the beneficial results before the month is out.

Ordinarily, disappointments stemming from misunderstandings are the exception rather than the rule; most professionals make it quite clear to owners just how much they believe they can accomplish with any dog within a specified period.

When is the best time of year to place a dog with a professional? Aside from young dogs just being started, the best time will be dictated principally by the type of hunting for which the dog is used. Hounds, for example, are best trained during open seasons on native game; for most parts of the nation, that means October through February. Bird dogs—both pointing and flushing varieties—which can be worked on released as well as native game birds, can be trained during all but the two or three months of worst winter weather. Retrievers, on the other hand, can be worked and trained throughout the year, needing only a small amount of open water to swim in. When being schooled in pinch-hit flushing work, of course, they'll be restricted to the same conditions that weather imposes on training bird dogs.

The cost of professional training for your gun dog is subject to such wide variation that it's impossible to generalize prices here. It can vary from as little as $85 to as much as $250 per month on average, and go even higher in exceptional instances. This includes board in practically all cases, though, which means that you're effecting a savings of what it normally costs to feed your dog.

Naturally, if you select a trainer in a distant state, you'll have to add in the cost of round-trip shipping charges. Under these circumstances, it hardly pays to send a dog off for less than three or four months.

Whatever you pay, within the limits of good sense and your own pocketbook, it will be money well spent if you've chosen a good trainer of reliable reputation. Using the services of a professional trainer should carry no stigma. Far from being a sign of weakness, it's more often a reflection of an owner who genuinely cares enough to make sure his dog receives the opportunities he might otherwise be denied by the vagaries of circumstances beyond his owner's control.

10

To the Field and Home Again

YOUR DOG ON WHEELS

THE SIGNIFICANT RELATIONSHIP between the gun dog and the automobile is, for some unaccountable reason, one of the last things the novice owner ever thinks of when planning his training routine. Perhaps it's because this basic form of transportation is taken so much for granted. But, whatever the explanation, the owner who fails to recognize and plan early for the role that the family car will play in his gun dog's future leaves himself open to major headaches.

In addition to serving as the means by which the gun dog is transported to and from the field, the car also doubles as the dog's sleeping quarters on weekend and overnight trips. In effect, then, the car becomes a sort of mobile kennel, one in which the dog must quickly learn to acclimate himself with a minimum of fuss.

Car-breaking the young hunting dog is not a difficult procedure. Ideally, it should be accomplished by introducing him to the vehicle in easy stages, at the earliest possible opportunity after he's become accustomed to his new home and master. Unless he's a very young pup who would have difficulty negotiating it by himself, he should be encouraged to enter the car completely on his own. Generally, this can be accomplished very easily by getting into the front seat, leaving the door open and urging your pup to climb in beside you.

Helping him a bit, once he's clearly shown that he's trying to join

Left: *Loose in the car, the gun dog who suddenly decides to show how much he loves his boss can be a definite hazard.* **Right:** *A sudden swerve, a sharp turn, and this canine passenger could end up in the highway. Even if he makes it safely to his destination, dust, dirt, and gas fumes can irritate and injure his eyes and nose.* **Photos by Dave Petzal.**

you, is permissible; but forcing him into the car against his will should be avoided until all other methods have been exhausted. Once he enters the car freely and without signs of nervousness, you should close the door quietly and remain with him for gradually longer periods. Talking in normal tones and playing gently with him will soon convince him that the car is a pleasant place to be. With a bit of encouragement, he'll soon begin nosing around, first the front seat, then the back, eventually familiarizing himself with the entire car.

Repeating this little exercise a couple of times daily, for a week or so, will put him completely at ease in your parked automobile. Now, you can begin the second phase, which will condition him to the sound of the motor and the sensation of the car in motion. In this phase, the secret of success is short but frequent rides.

Begin with a drive around the block, two or three times daily, for the first few days. Subsequent rides should be gradually prolonged until he shows decreasing nervousness and fewer signs of nausea. When he does become ill, as he probably will, don't be alarmed; car-sickness is a perfectly harmless, natural reaction that's bound to occur during the early stages of his conditioning. Though there's no way to predict how long it will last in any given dog, it's usually overcome in relatively short time. For the comparatively few dogs who don't soon conquer it, there is always one of the preventive medicines available through your vet.

The most important thing to remember in car-breaking your dog is to do it through short, frequent rides. Initially, no opportunity should be passed up. If you're only driving down to the corner store, take your dog along. The more time he spends in the car, the sooner your job will be successfully concluded.

Some sportsmen, in traveling back and forth to the field, permit their dogs complete freedom of the car. While on the face of it, this may seem the most considerate thing to do, the many drawbacks involved make it highly impractical. Without a safe, comfortable place of confinement in your car, a hunting dog can be both potential cause and victim to numberless mishaps.

Left loose in a moving automobile, a dog constitutes not only a nuisance but very likely a hazard. How many times have you seen a dog, in a sudden display of playful affection, jump up and plant his paws on a driver's shoulders, or around his neck? A serious accident could easily result. Is such a momentary demonstration of your dog's affection worth risking your life and the lives of others? Hardly.

Moreover, there's always the chance that your dog may be injured in the normal course of traveling the highways. A sudden stop can jolt him off the front seat and send him crashing into the dashboard or onto the floor. Taking a turn or sharp curve a bit too fast can fling

The station wagon barrier allows the gun dog lots of room, but restricts him to the rear compartment. Most barriers, like this popular Barrie-Aire, cost between $50 and $75 and are easily installed in almost any station wagon.

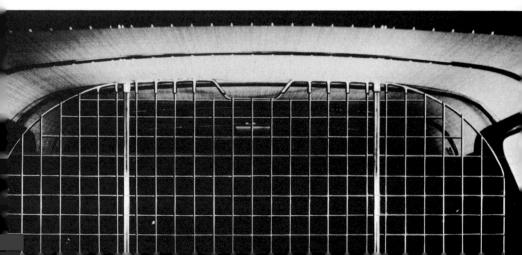

him against a door handle or, worse yet, right out an open window. Quick stops and sharp turns have been known to result in a dog's being clobbered by unsecured baggage in a heavily laden vehicle, too.

Even leaving him loose in the car overnight presents its share of problems. None but the seasoned canine traveler ever settles down quietly and gracefully accepts the fact that you've deserted him for the night. When his howling fails to accomplish his release, his frustrations are sure to turn to more vigorous pursuits, namely, trying to dig himself out of solitary confinement. Very little in the way of upholstery and paneling is likely to be spared his determined "re-decorating" efforts, and in the morning your disbelief that one other-wise gentle and loving gun dog could create such a shambles will perhaps be exceeded only by the warmly understanding reaction your spouse will have when you arrive home.

Sparing yourself and your dog such problems is an easy solution that precludes learning a lesson the hard way. The best thing you can do is provide your dog with some suitable means of confinement wherein he'll be able to travel to the field and be quartered overnight in safe, secure comfort. For the station wagon, van, or truck owner there are several practical options: the rear compartment barrier, the carrying crate and the tethering device. Any of the three will do the job, but, obviously, there is a difference in design and efficiency among them.

Least preferable but simplest and cheapest of the three is the tether. In effect, little more than a sturdy leash anchored to the rear compart-ment floor or wall, the device is generally made of chain link or wire, wrapped with a leather or plastic casing. On either end is a rugged snap, one to attach to the anchor-point — usually the ring section of a hasp — and the other to attach to the dog's collar.

The ideal tether should be just long enough — about three-and-a-half feet for medium-large breeds — to permit the dog to sit, stand and lie down, facing in any direction comfortably. Too long a tether will enable the dog to wrap it around himself or other items of baggage stored in the rear compartment. Conversely, one that's too short will prove uncomfortably confining.

The station wagon barrier that's become increasingly popular in the past few years is infinitely more comfortable and efficient than any tethering device. Constructed of lightweight wire mesh, it separates the rear compartment and the back seat, effectively isolating the dog from driver and passengers. Most barriers are quickly and easily

Carrying crates are available in a wide variety of sizes, styles and materials, and are the most practical means of safely transporting one or more hunting dogs. These crates, by Kennel-Aire, are typical of the wire-mesh types.

installed, since permanent fittings are seldom required, they can be removed just as simply.

Priced from about $50 to $75, the barrier's single greatest advantage stems from the generous amount of freedom of movement it allows the dog. This is fine, if you don't mind allocating the entire rear compartment exclusively to your gun dog. But it can prove disadvantageous if you're hauling a couple of passengers and a heavy load of baggage and equipment. By the same token, if one of your buddies wants to bring his dog along, you may have some problems, since the barrier offers no provision for keeping dogs separated.

Third and best of the three choices is the carrying crate. Available in a wide variety of sizes and styles, in wood, aluminum and light-gauge wire mesh, these portable kennels offer the most practical means of transporting and kenneling the gun dog ever devised. Not only do they provide maximum security and comfort to the dog while en route to the field, but they also serve as compact overnight quarters, keeping him snug, safe and out of any sort of mischief.

There are many grades of carrying crates; as you might imagine, the better quality jobs carry an appropriately fancy price tag. A first-class custom-crafted wooden model can go for as much as $185 in single-unit size. Dual units, for handling two dogs, in separate compartments, will run almost twice as much. The all-metal single-unit carrier, usually constructed of aluminum for sturdiness and portability, ranges from approximately $150 to $225, with double units going for about $295.

For the cost-conscious sportsman, there can be little question that the wire mesh crates deliver the most value for his money. Depending upon size and manufacturer, these types are priced between $39 and $89 and can handle any hunting breed from beagles, in the smaller sizes, to over-large Chesapeakes, in the biggest.

Among their distinctive advantages are their light weight and fold-up characteristics, which make them easy to store in a flat, compact package when not in use. Since they're of wide-space mesh design, they afford the driver good rear-view visibility and permit a canine occupant to see in all directions. Numerous accessories are available too — food and water bowls that can be clamped inside the crates; disposable floor trays that contain any spillage of food, water or the effects of car-sickness or "accidents"; foam-filled bedding pads; and, last but not least, canvas covers to help retain Rover's body heat in cold weather.

The sportsman who drives a sedan while not quite so well off as the station wagon owner, can nevertheless resort to one of a couple of solutions. Using one of the small-to-medium size wire mesh crates that will fit lengthwise on the back seat will prove a workable, if not precisely ideal, setup. Of course, some means of anchoring the crate securely will have to be devised. We've seen it done effectively, though not attractively, by passing a rope or light chain around the crate and tying each end to a window crank on opposite sides of the car.

Many sportsmen carry their dogs to and from the field in the trunk and seldom give it a second thought. They may get away with it for years without mishap, especially if their trips are short ones. But, unless the trunk is properly ventilated, it can be a real death-trap to a dog on a long ride.

Even the devices that permit the trunk to be locked in a partially open position do not necessarily solve the problem of proper air circulation. Wind conditions and even the styling design of the modern automobile can set up a flow of air currents that pull in noxious exhaust fumes at incredible rate. Over a long haul, breathing these fumes can make a dog sick and, in some instances, can prove fatal.

You can use your trunk safely, however, if you cut through the shelf under the rear window and install a ventilator that circulates the air inside the car into the trunk. Not only will the air thus circulated be free of exhaust fumes, but it will also carry the warmth of your car's heater directly into the trunk.

Getting that gun dog of yours to the field and home again safely is just as vital a part of your responsibilities as any other aspect of his care and training.

AFTER THE HUNT

It's all over for the day, the hunt that began early that morning. Now, it's full dark as you pull into the driveway, mentally admitting that you're thoroughly bushed. A lumberjack-sized dinner to satisfy the inner man, a steaming hot shower and, then, easing those tired old bones into the sack won't be at all hard to take. Yes, sir, it's a good feeling, the end of a satisfying day in the field.

But hang on a minute. That trio of woodcock and the pair of grouse... did you get them all by yourself? Or, could it be that the old fella back there in the dog crate helped some? Unless there isn't any dog crate

Hunting dogs burn up lots of energy during a full day afield. Before you start the day, give your dog about a quarter of his normal working ration to keep him sharp and energetic. **Photo by Dave Petzal**.

back there, or any old fella in it, your day hasn't quite ended yet.

Tired as you may be, you owe your dog a little something extra in the way of consideration after the hunt. It's not enough merely to transfer him from car to kennel, toss in a full feed pan and some fresh water and let it go at that.

Owners who so lightly dismiss their obligations on the basis that "Huntin' dogs don't have to be babied," are simply making a feeble effort to cloak their own laziness in he-man-sounding bravado. Far from being overly sentimental, the owner who adopts a sensible routine of after-the-hunt care for his dog displays a knowledge and awareness that such effort is practical insurance for continued first-rate canine service in the future.

What should you do for your dog after the hunt? In essence, the routine need not be complicated and the order in which you execute it is highly flexible. Aside from feeding, after-the-hunt care consists of a brief but thorough check of your dog, administering minor first-aid where needed, performing a bit of grooming and seeing to his general well-being and comfort.

Ordinarily, feeding and watering the dog would come last on the after-the-hunt agenda. However, we bring it up here first for several reasons. After long hours in the field the working dog requires greater amounts of nourishment to compensate for the extra energy his body burns. By and large, the average gun dog should receive about one-third more food per working day than his usual ration.

But giving him an increased volume of food at day's end is not the most logical method. Generally, a hunting dog having become over-tired, will eat less than his normal meal after the hunt. Consequently, it is a good idea to feed him about one-quarter of his dinner before the hunt begins. This assures that he will have sufficient nourishment even if he does not finish all of the food put before him later. More-over, the morning feeding gives him some extra calories to burn at the very time his body needs them most—while he's using up energy in the field.

Naturally, if the dog displays tendencies toward car sickness, it's best to wait until you arrive at your hunting grounds before feeding him. Give him a few minutes to rest after eating, then turn him loose. The relatively small quantity of food he's had will not make him logy or interfere with his ability to hunt.

As soon as you've quit hunting for the day, it's time to give the dog a quick check prior to starting your long drive home. Of course, if you're staying at a near-by lodge, or have been hunting close to home, this can wait until you get there.

On arrival, take him out of his crate to a quiet, well-lighted spot where you can inspect him thoroughly. Since he's apt to be wet or, at least, damp, the first thing to do is rub him dry. This makes him feel more comfortable, prevents his catching cold and lets you handle and inspect him more easily.

The order of inspection, although variable, usually follows a fairly logical pattern, based on the individual hunter's previous experience. Some hunters start by checking the dog's body; others, his legs. But, the oldtimers invariably begin with the gun dog's two most vulnerable spots — his feet and eyes.

No other part of a hunting dog's anatomy is as fundamentally important as his feet. All his other assets depend upon those feet. The keen nose that scents the quarry; the experienced eyes that spot the game-holding coverts or mark the fall; the attentive ears that listen for helpful commands — all would be utterly valueless without the assistance of those four good, sound feet.

In checking your dog's feet, scrutinize those areas between his toes, the folds that separate the pads. These are the places where otherwise unnoticed thorns or splinters work themselves in and fester. Any that you spot can easily be removed with a pair of fine tweezers.

At the same time as you're looking for imbedded thorns or splinters, you can watch for other trouble signs — cuts, abrasions, split and broken nails and, worst of all, torn pads. When split or broken nails are encountered, trim off damaged ends cautiously, taking care not to cut too deeply into the quick. Minor cuts, tears or abrasions of the skin should be cleansed with a solution of hydrogen peroxide to reduce the possibility of infection.

A mixture of pine tar and fuller's earth offers a useful soothing and healing agent for sore, tender feet. Both ingredients can be bought at any drugstore and mixed as needed into a thick paste. Other commercially made products, such as "Pad-Kote" and "Tuf-Foot," are also available for use both before and after the hunt.

Next, check your dog's eyes and the areas immediately surrounding them. Weed seeds, tiny thorns and even bits of twig often gather in the corners of the eyes and work themselves under the lids, there to cause discomfort and, possibly, eventual damage. Thorns, partially lodged in the outer skin of the lids, frequently result in serious damage to the eyeball if pushed further in by the dog's own efforts to dislodge them.

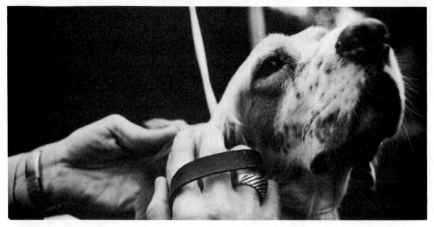

After a thorough inspection of your dog, a couple of minutes with comb and brush will clean up his coat and prove as refreshing to him as a shower will to you. **Photo by Dave Petzal.**

Remove such thorns with your fingernails, or, if necessary, a pair of tweezers. A piece of cotton saturated in ordinary boric acid can be used to bathe the eyes and wash away any accumulation of foreign matter from beneath the lids. A daub or two of yellow oxide of mercury (two percent strength) will aid in soothing irritations and preventing infection.

The ears of most hunting breeds are pretty well protected; still, they bear inspecting after the dog has put in a tough day in heavy cover. Check for minor external cuts, tears or scratches, which can be treated with a mild antiseptic. After removing any thorns or burrs from the outside of the ears, inspect the ear openings for foreign matter.

Aside from a few brier scratches there isn't much to look for in the way of problems with your dog's nose. Since anything you might apply in treating superficial nose injuries would be licked off as fast as it was administered, there's not much point of fussing there.

For those hunting breeds with full-length tails, split ends can sometimes present a problem. Such end-of-tail damage is easy to spot. The hair around the last joint or two will usually be caked with blood. Cleansing with mild antiseptic, such as hydrogen peroxide, alleviates any chance of immediate infection and is normally the only first aid required for minor split ends.

In cases of chronic tail splitters, veterinary attention is the wisest procedure. Taping the end of the tail occasionally permits complete healing, but if the dog is hunted regularly, even taping does little good. Invariably, the only real cure for the chronic tail-splitter is an operation to remove that portion of the appendage that continues to open every time the dog is run in cover.

The final part of the after-the-hunt examination concentrates on the dog's body. Since any major wounds or serious injuries doubtless would have been noticeable in the field, what you'll be looking for here are secondary cuts, deeply imbedded thorns or splinters and ticks.

If your dog is one of the longhaired breeds, you will almost certainly have a job of de-burring to do. It's best to remove all large concentrations of burrs by hand first, then to get rid of the minor tangles of matted hair with a stripping comb and finally to attempt any required first aid.

Once the necessary grooming has been completed, you can begin your final once-over. Check thoroughly for ticks, paying particular attention to the dog's ears, muzzle and underside, especially where the inside of the leg joins the body. Ticks can be removed by grasping them firmly between your fingernails and giving a straight, steady, outward pull. If you've no stomach for this, simply douse each one with a commercial tick-killer. They will fall out by themselves within twenty-four hours.

All that remains for you to do now is to provide the dog with fresh drinking water and the other three-quarters of his dinner. Your own dinner will be waiting for you, perhaps preceded by a taste of "good cheer" — if you've properly trained your loving spouse how to care for you — after the hunt.

Proper after-the-hunt care of your dog is both considerate and smart. This well-cared-for German wirehaired pointer shows the tangible benefits — in the form of a ruffed grouse tenderly retrieved — that accrue to a considerate owner. **Photo by Jerome J. Knap.**

11

When Trouble Brews

FIRST AID AFIELD

IT'S ONE OF those gorgeous, golden days in late October. The panoply of vivid crimsons and vibrant yellows has begun ever so slightly to fade. You marvel at the magnificence of the autumn foliage and silently acknowledge the emotional inspiration that has sparked so many poetic descriptions of it.

A rare privilege, you think, to be out on such a day, hunting behind a good and faithful bird dog, that just happens to be your own. Tucked comfortably in the crook of your arm, the little 20-bore over-and-under that never fails to speak with authority—well, most of the time—has already accounted for the modest but satisfying weight in your game vest of a solitary grouse that bumps warmly against your left kidney with each step you take. What, possibly, could mar the perfection of a day like this?

But, then, suddenly, up ahead, your dog slips on a moist, mossy rock and, tumbling end over end down a steep embankment, lands at the bottom whining in pain and comes limping back to you on three legs. What do you do? How do you help him?

Some people seem to know exactly what to do when accidents occur. But that knowledge didn't just materialize out of thin air. First aid is a learned skill. It must be studied formally or self-taught from written materials.

Obviously, all hunting dog owners should take the time to learn or at least familiarize themselves with basic first-aid procedures for the treatment of the most commonly encountered canine emergencies in the field. And even after learning what to do, it's important to remain prepared to handle such exigencies, and that means keeping handy on all gunning excursions a pocket-sized first-aid manual and a pair of first-aid kits. Along with the manual in your pocket goes a small, rudimentary kit to help handle emergencies on the spot. The second kit, far more comprehensive, stays back in the car, which probably is never more than ten minutes or so from the cover you're hunting.

We'll discuss what the first-aid kits should contain a bit later. First, let's consider a few of the fundamentals that are preliminary to virtually any first-aid care.

Depending on the extent of your dog's injury, he may not be "your" dog, so to speak, while he's frightened, in pain and, possibly, in a state of shock. Initially, in order to protect yourself, as well as make it easier for you to administer to him, he'll have to be restrained with an muzzle. Gauze from your pocket kit is normally the most readily available material for the purpose, but a short length of rope, cloth, or even a soft leather leash can also be used.

Loop the material around your dog's snout a few inches behind his nose, making sure his lower jaw is encompassed within the loop, and

Affixing an emergency muzzle of gauze around the snout is a wise safety precaution before administering first aid to your gun dog in the field. **Photo courtesy of Dr. Jill Endler Hanson.**

snug it up securely with a half-hitch. Then, take an extra couple of turns around his muzzle and, bringing each end under his ears, tie the gauze in a bow knot behind his head. It's important that you speak calmly and reassuringly to your dog as you apply the muzzle.

After restraint, the next thing to do is to try to assess the nature and extent of his injury. If he has sustained multiple injuries, then the most serious or life-threatening ones should be tended first. In general, your dog should be kept warm and as quiet and calm as possible while you examine him. After these few necessary preliminaries, you can safely begin administering first aid to him in the field.

Let's take a look at some of the mishaps most frequently suffered by gun dogs at work in the field and the recommended first-aid procedures with which to treat them prior to obtaining proper veterinary treatment.

Shock

Following any severe fright or injury, your gun dog could very likely go into a state of shock. Shock is a failure of the circulatory system to do its job properly and can be a life-threatening condition.

Symptoms are extreme nervousness or prostration; rapid, weak pulse and shallow breathing; eyes generally become glassy and gums pale.

In treating for shock, try to keep your dog quiet and maintain his body heat by covering him with your hunting coat. If he can be kept reclining without difficulty—and that means not having to wrestle him into submission—talk reassuringly to him and gently massage his legs to help re-establish circulation.

Broken Bones

Symptoms are obvious severe pain and inability to stand on or use the leg or legs; localized swelling and a distinct difference in the leg's length, size, and configuration; compound fractures are recognizable by bone protruding through the skin.

Never try to set your dog's broken leg, but simply keep it in position as well as possible and immobilize it by means of a temporary splint. In the field, about the only material suitable and available to you for making an improvised splint will be sticks of wood or saplings. Two

An injured dog should be kept as calm and quiet as possible while being examined. If the injury is a sprain, dislocation, or broken bone, a temporary splint is the safest first aid before getting the dog to a veterinarian. Photo courtesy of Dr. Jill Endler Hanson.

lengths, one for the outside and one for the inside of the leg, should be used to immobilize the affected leg.

Sprains and Dislocations

Symptoms are swelling and pain upon touching or moving the joint affected; signs are similar to and often difficult to distinguish from those of broken bones.

A minor foot or leg injury can be treated in the field with antiseptic and bandaged, if necessary, before resuming the hunt.

As with a broken leg, a dislocation should never be "corrected" except by a veterinarian. Since sprains and dislocations are so similar and difficult for the layman to diagnose, it's best to place a temporary splint on the dog's leg and get him to an animal hospital as soon as possible.

Heatstroke

Symptoms can vary from excessive panting and extremely labored breathing to collapse.

As in most first-aid measures, speed is essential in counteracting the effects of heatstroke. Your dog's body temperature must be reduced immediately or his very life is in danger. Get him into a brook, stream, or pond if one is close by; otherwise, douse his body with cool water from a canteen and get him to a shady spot right away. If he's able to drink, give him small quantities of cool water at frequent intervals, while fanning him with your cap or a leafy bough. Once he's cooled down, get him to the nearest veterinarian post haste.

Open Wounds

Symptom of a severed artery is an irregular flow of bright red blood; a cut vein will be recognized by an even flow of dark red blood.

In treating any serious open wound, the most important thing to do is try to control and stop the bleeding. Put a sterile gauze pad over the wound and, with the palm of your hand, apply firm, even pressure for five to ten minutes. Clotting will generally occur within this period and the bleeding will stop. Bandage the gauze pad to hold it securely in place.

A pressure bandage is greatly preferred over a tourniquet to stop bleeding since the latter, in the hands of the inexperienced, can prove dangerous; its use is recommended strictly as a life-saving device in the gravest of circumstances. Once the bleeding has been stopped or controlled, don't attempt to cleanse a serious open wound with antiseptic. In fact, don't even remove the original pressure bandage; leave it in place and treat your dog for shock.

Specialized Wounds

Symptoms of specialized wounds in which foreign objects become lodged are normally obvious on close inspection.

Metal, wood, or glass slivers left in wounds they've caused should be removed, if possible without excessive probing, to reduce continuing irritation and further damage, as well as infection. Use a sterilized pair of tweezers or needle and apply a pressure bandage.

In cases where your dog has been impaled on a branch or stick or any sizable foreign object still lodged in the wound, *don't* attempt to remove the object, unless it can be withdrawn very, very easily. Keep your dog as quiet as possible until you can get veterinary help in town.

Internal Bleeding

Symptoms may be relatively unapparent in some cases; in others there may be bleeding from nose, ears, mouth, eyes, or rectum; weakness and dizziness; plus pale gums.

Consider any signs of internal bleeding or injury to be of the most serious consequence. Keep your dog as tranquil as possible, treat for shock, and make tracks for the nearest veterinary hospital.

Seizures (Convulsions)

Symptoms are an onrush of extreme nervous restlessness, whining, and slight muscle twitching, followed by collapse, loss of consciousness, and muscle spasms.

Seizures can be caused by a wide variety of problems, and they can range from simple convulsions to those of longer, more serious duration. The type most often encountered in a hunting dog at work is brief and mild and usually considered to be caused by low blood sugar (hypoglycemia).

Should your dog go into such a convulsion in the field, wait until he falls to the ground, then cover him quickly with your jacket and, being careful not to get your hands near his mouth, snap your lead on him. Your jacket will help restrain him and the lead will prevent his running off when he regains consciousness.

As in treating for shock, keep him quiet and warm. When he returns to normal—usually in about 20 to 30 minutes—he can be given a few swigs of a special mixture of equal parts of brandy and honey or Karo syrup carried in a small plastic bottle for such emergencies. In the absence of this potion, part of a candy bar or a couple of lumps of sugar make a reasonably effective substitute.

Snakebite

Symptoms of poisonous snakebites are almost instantaneous acute pain; considerable swelling; oozing fluid from the wound; weakness and labored breathing.

Many times you'll be close enough to your dog to be aware that a snake has hit him. If you possibly can, kill the snake and identify it as poisonous or non-poisonous. In the event you're not sure, check the

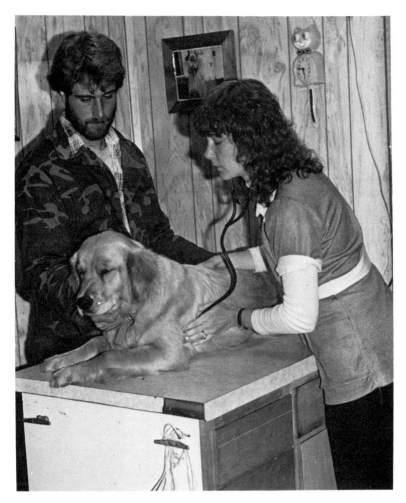

A dog injured in the field should be taken to a veterinary hospital as quickly as possible for a thorough examination and treatment. Here, Dr. Jill Endler Hanson checks a golden retriever for a concerned duck hunter.

bite area on your dog. A poisonous snake leaves two distinct fang punctures whereas the non-poisonous variety leaves multiple scratch-like toothmarks in the shape of a U. In the latter case, merely cleanse the bite area with antiseptic.

If your dog has suffered the bite of a poisonous snake, keep him as quiet as possible while affixing a snug one-inch bandage between the bite and his heart—assuming the bite is on his leg. Bear in mind that the bandage is not a tourniquet, but rather something to slow down the flow of venom, so it should be snug, not tight. Do not give your dog any stimulants; keep him warm and, above all, still, and get him to an animal hospital immediately.

Oh, yes, bring the dead snake along for positive identification.

Drowning

The likelihood of your dog drowning may seem slim, but if, through sheer exhaustion in rough waters, swift current or any similar situation, he does drown, you'll have to revive him as quickly as possible. First, pick him up and hold him by his hind legs for about half a minute to encourage the water to drain from his lungs.

Next, to give him artificial respiration, lay him on his side, place your hands on his ribs just back of his shoulder blades, and push down with a quick, firm motion. Release the pressure right away and repeat the motion with rhythmic regularity every four or five seconds until your dog is breathing naturally again by himself. Keep him warm and calm.

In order to administer proper first aid to your dog in the field, we mentioned earlier the need for a couple of first-aid kits, one you can slip into your jacket pocket and the other to be stored in the car. The one for your pocket must, of necessity, be very basic. It should contain:

Pair of tweezers
One roll, 1″ gauze bandage
One roll, 1″ adhesive tape
Four 3″ square gauze pads
Small tube of 2 percent yellow oxide of mercury
Small (3 oz) plastic bottle of honey/brandy mixture
Pocket-sized first-aid manual

The first-aid kit carried as regular equipment in your car can and probably should be of the "people" variety to which you should add or make sure it contains:

Pair of tweezers
Pair of small scissors
One roll each, 1″ and 2″ gauze bandage
One roll each, 1″ and 2″ adhesive tape
10 3″ square gauze pads
Six Q-tips
Small bottle of hydrogen peroxide (3 percent strength)

Small tube of 2 percent yellow oxide of mercury
Small bottle of sterile distilled water
Small bottle of boric acid

The most vital thing to remember when an accident befalls your gun dog in the field is to avoid panic. I realize that it's easier said than done, but try to keep as calm as you can. If you're hunting with a friend, keep him calm, too, by having him read instructions to you from the manual in your pocket kit.

It must be pointed out that the recommendations given here for first-aid care in the field have been gleaned from a number of sources and are necessarily general in nature. It's absolutely essential that you get your injured gun dog to the nearest veterinary hospital as soon as possible after an accident occurs. When it comes to your best and most faithful gunning partner—your gun dog—any risk to his safety and well-being is too great to chance not getting professional help right away.

12

Focus on Fall

PICTURE YOUR GUN DOG

FEW FOLKS TODAY have to be sold on the fact that good photographs provide lasting satisfaction. Photography has become so much a part of modern living that a camera routinely goes along on even the most ordinary outing. In fact, any pictureless occasion seems more the exception than the rule.

Automation, of course, has contributed immensely to both the ease and popularity of picture-taking at home or away. The fantastic technology incorporated into present-day cameras, lenses, and even film has made it a cinch for anyone, including the most fumble-fingered among us, to take goof-proof pictures.

Naturally, then, the dog-owning sportsman can always be counted on to produce an oversize album crammed with great photos of his canine pride and joy at work in the field, right? Wrong. Unfortunately, a majority of gun-dog owners would be hard pressed to come up with even half a dozen reasonably decent, much less truly excellent, pictures of their four-footed hunting partners plying their trade in the field.

How come? Well, part of the excuse—and Lord knows, it's all too familiar to most of us—is the immutable fact that "Ya just can't hunt and take pictures at the same time." But this common dilemma is not without a solution. Almost unthinkable as the suggestion surely will

To preserve some pride-filled moments for later enjoyment, you won't regret putting the gun aside for a few minutes during the hunt in order to take pictures of your dog doing his thing afield.

be at first, the answer is simply to put aside the gun, at least briefly, during each outing and concentrate on taking a few pictures.

Even if you stingily ration your camera time to a few minutes out of every hour or so, you'll probably be pleasantly surprised at the opportunities afforded you to snap interesting and possibly highly exciting pictures that capture the real essence and spirit of your gun dog at work.

Obviously, for openers, a good camera is a must, and most experienced photo buffs agree that a single-lens-reflex (SLR) camera with interchangeable lens capability is the best type to choose for all-around use. Select any name-brand 35mm SLR such as Canon, Pentax, Nikon, Olympus, Minolta, or Konica and you'll be on safe ground. They're all good, and which one you choose depends on what combination of features appeals most to you.

Almost certainly the one you buy will feature an electronic built-in exposure metering system that enables you to concentrate on picture composition without worrying about dial and knob manipulation to set proper exposure. It's definitely advisable, though, to make sure the camera also has a manual override for those occasions when you'll want to set the exposure manually.

Most SLR's come fitted with a standard lens, usually a 50mm, in speeds expressed as F stops, such as F1.4, F1.8, F2.8, etc. The F stops indicate the lens's light-gathering capability: the smaller the number, the more light the lens admits at its largest aperture, or F stop. The faster the lens, the less light it requires to take a picture at any given shutter speed.

By all means, buy a camera fitted with a standard lens of the fastest speed you can afford. The combination will serve you well for most family and scenery snapshot situations. And, let's be realistic, to justify buying a good camera, you'll have to take all sorts of pictures besides those of your gun dog. Just as soon as you can manage it, plan to acquire a good-quality zoom lens with a focal range from 70 or 80mm to 200mm.

Since every 50mm of lens is equal to 1X magnification, the 200mm end of the zoom lens gives you 4X magnification. Put another way, it means you can get four times closer to your subject without budging from your tracks. And the versatility of this focal-length zoom lens will

A good zoom lens will let you close in tight on your subject to catch details that are often missed with a standard lens.

add immeasurably to your ability to frame and compose all your photos in an interesting manner.

Initially, you should buy a skylight or UV filter for each of your lenses. This kind of filter is practically clear and, while having little effect on your pictures, it does protect your lens from damage.

One other accessory you'll want to consider sooner or later is an auto winder or motor drive. For fast-action sequences, one or the other is an absolute necessity. Both units cock the shutter and advance the film automatically after every shot. A fairly light-weight attachment, the auto winder advances the film at between 1.5 and 2 frames per second, normally speedy enough for most amateur photography. The motor drive is a much faster, more sophisticated device, zipping the film along at up to 5 frames a second. But it's also a lot heavier and substantially more expensive.

Just as important as using the right ammunition for the kind of game being hunted is choosing the right film for the job. If you're primarily interested in color prints, then a "negative" film such as Kodacolor will be your best bet. However, if slides that you can show in a

There's no need to wait until the hunting season opens to start photographing your dog. Training and exercise sessions provide fine opportunities to practice with a camera and to get both candid and posed shots of your canine hunting companion.

There's action in immobility when a pointer is frozen on birds. Such a photo speaks eloquently of the dog's performance and the thrilling action to come.

projector are your first choice, you'll want one of the "positive" films like Kodachrome.

Next is the choice of high- or slow-speed film, customarily speed rated by an ASA or ISO number. The smaller the numeral, the slower the film. In general, films with high ASA ratings—200 to 400—should be used for fast action and low light. Slower films, which provide less grain, richer colors, and more detail, are best used for posed shots and in bright sunshine.

High-speed films do very well in combination with a telephoto or zoom lens, enabling you to set your shutter speed at $\frac{1}{250}$ or even $\frac{1}{500}$ of a second to avoid the possibility of camera shake and blurred pictures.

Once you've bought your camera and interchangeable zoom lens, plus three or four rolls of fresh film, the smartest thing to do is get comfortable with the new rig. Several readings of the instruction manuals—one for the camera and another for the lens—will help familiarize you with the equipment's basic functions. But it will be the hands-on experience of shooting a few rolls of film that will really put you at ease with your new camera gear.

Don't make the mistake of waiting until hunting season opens to start getting some decent shots of your gun dog. Training and exercise sessions can offer excellent opportunities for getting both candid and posed pictures of your gun dog at work. And they also serve as extra practice sessions with your new camera, rehearsal periods for improving your techniques before the gunning season.

Although action photos have the most appeal to everyone, tremendous excitement can be generated in a so-called static shot. A pointer intensely frozen on game, nostrils flared, forepaw cocked, body half-crouched, muscles taut, and tail slanting skyward, certainly exudes pent-up tension and impending action. So, too, a close-up head study of a golden retriever against a duck-blind backdrop, his eyes riveted on the horizon, intently watching incoming waterfowl, graphically conveys the promise of imminent action. Such photos, because they can be set up with relative ease, deserve more attention than they generally get from dog owners.

Avoiding some of the most common faults of most gun-dog photos will speed you on your way toward good and eventually even better shots of your own dog. One of the most flagrant spoilers is the taking of pictures strictly from a people point of view or, rather, from a person's eye level. Think about it for a minute. Virtually every dog photo you've ever seen that had that certain something, that indefinable quality of true-to-life warmth, charm and appeal, had at least one common denominator: it was shot at the dog's eye level.

Squatting on your haunches or even getting right down on your belly when photographing your dog will perk up your pictures remarkably. And often a lower-than-subject level can achieve unusually dramatic results. Try, for instance, getting your chin as close to the ground as possible while snapping a picture of your dog on point. This bird's-eye view will make him look and seem more dominant and lend a distinctly bold touch to the scene.

Boldness, of course, can also be attained by shooting from different angles. Extreme close-ups, too, sometimes can produce a bold effect. And speaking of close-ups, another serious flaw in many ordinary snapshots of gun dogs—and of people, too—is not getting close enough to the subject. Good advice, then, is when you think you're close enough, get even closer before you snap the shutter.

Only by filling as much of the frame with your subject as possible can you succeed in getting a photo with sufficient detail in it to be of real interest. And with a zoom lens of 70-200mm, there's just no excuse for not taking frame-filling shots under most circumstances.

Except for certain special effects, it's probably a wise idea to keep your shutter speed set no lower than $\frac{1}{250}$ of a second. At this speed

To be sure of getting good action shots of your dog in the field, you should plan to shoot film unsparingly. A single truly memorable action photo per roll of film is a realistic average.

you'll generally freeze most action and preclude camera movement as well. Even for your hand-held posed or static shots, especially with the 200mm end of the zoom lens, it's safer to shoot at ¼₂₅₀ of a second for no-blur insurance. A potentially great picture can become ho-hum if it's fuzzy.

Lighting, certainly, is critical to any good photograph. Used properly, lighting can create and capture a wide range of moods. When time permits, take an extra minute or two and study the effects certain lighting will have on your canine subject. Shift from one angle to another and check each one through the viewfinder to zero in on the best effect.

Another thing to bear in mind on the subject of light: don't keep your camera cased just because the sun refuses to shine. Beyond October are a bunch of gray hunting days, any one of them offering many good picture possibilities. Fast films, of course, are the perfect solution for these low-light situations. And, if really pressed, you can always fight back by pushing your ASA 400 film to 600 or even 800. Just don't forget to let your film processor know what you did when you take the film in for developing.

For the amateur, there's no sure-fire formula for coming up with prize-winning gun-dog action photos, at least none that I've ever managed to stumble across. The closest I've come to a meaningful clue is to shoot film lavishly and then shoot some more for insurance. It takes a lot of frames and even more rolls to produce a couple of really good pictures of the kind you can be proud of.

13

Advanced Performance Afield

HOW CLOSE IS TOO CLOSE?

"HE'S AN IDEAL shooting dog," Bill enthused, "thorough as a vacuum ...never strays out of gun-range on me all season long. That way, even if he bumps some of his birds, I can still get a crack at 'em just the same."

Bill had chattered so much about the pointing dog he'd brought along that I insisted we work his dog on the first four pheasants put out for us at the shooting preserve that morning. It was 8:30 when our hunt began. Three hours later, dragging our tails, and with only two of the four birds accounted for, I suggested we break for lunch.

Throughout the meal, Bill droned on, obviously happy with the performance his "close-working" shooting dog had turned in and the results of the morning's hunt. Deliberately, I managed to avoid serious comment on either count. Yet, the bare facts couldn't be overlooked; Bill and I had covered almost as much ground, and worked just about as hard, as his dog had during that interminable three-hour hunt.

After lunch, with four more pheasants released for us, we started out again, this time "resting" Bill's dog and using one of the preserve veterans. This dog, the same breed as Bill's, was one I'd hunted over before. By no stretch of imagination could he be considered a big-going dog, but he had just about double the range and speed of Bill's pooch.

A pointing dog that always hunts underfoot, no matter what the cover conditions, just isn't doing his job. **Photo by Sid Latham.**

Cutting the dog loose, we watched him make his first cast, which carried him just short of the field's northern fencerow before we'd gone a quarter of the way; the look on Bill's face told me he expected the worst. The time was 1:39. Exactly fifty minutes later, we slid pheasant number three into our game pocket and began searching for the fourth. At 2:45 it was all over. All four birds had been collected; we were pleasantly tired, but not bushed; the job had been accomplished in half the time of our morning's hunt; and the results were doubly fruitful.

An indictment of close-working shooting dogs? Not at all. For the preserve pooch we used was just that. But Bill's dog, despite his owner's classification, was a graphic example of the pottering grass-prowler type of pointing dog that too many novice owners erroneously but enthusiastically embrace as the practical epitome of the term "close-working."

The idea that a pointing dog that works at ultra-modest speed, never ranging more than half a gun-shot away, increases the hunter's chances to fill his bag under most conditions and circumstances has become an uncommonly popular notion. Of course, in the case of a pointing dog who seldom points, but generally bumps his birds, it has understandable merit.

But, the man who owns this kind of poor pointing dog performer might better devote additional time and effort to training him to be properly staunch on point, or trade him in for one of the flushing breeds. For, if his so-called pointing dog seldom bothers to point, then the man has nothing more than a flushing dog anyway.

Assuming, however, that his dog is reliably staunch on most of his birds, the man who steadfastly insists that he never hunt outside of gun range cheats both himself and his dog every time they venture into the field. After all, it is the pointing dog's job to find birds for the gun, not vice versa. Yet, if the dog is consistently required to hunt only within a thirty- to forty-yard radius of the gun, it's obvious that the gunner himself will have to do a lot more walking in order to get his dog into birds in any given cover.

Saving steps for the gunner is a definite part of the pointing dog's primary bird-finding function. And if the hunter has to trudge within easy gun-shot distance of every likely piece of cover his dog investigates, a good deal of his time and energy will be used unproductively. For it's a cinch that a majority of those covers, no matter how likely looking, won't actually have birds in them.

How much more effective, to say nothing of being less tiring to the gunner, is the pointing dog that's permitted to range freely, within the limits of his own natural range and pace, while the hunter maintains a comparatively straight course? With this sort of pointing dog, a hunter has only to walk up to each point his dog establishes, not to every spot his dog searches.

Even the true "close-working" pointing dog adjusts his range to the cover, ranging further than gun-shot distance in open areas.

It's hardly our purpose to make a case for the big-going pointing dog. For, except under specific conditions — notably the wide-open quail country or the sprawling prairie haunts of the sharptail grouse and Hungarian partridge — the ultra-wide-ranging dog is as much as extreme as his opposite number.

Nor are we advocating the middle-of-the-roader, the dog of medium range and pace. Rather than questioning what constitutes ideal pointing dog range, the point here is how close is too close? Hunters who, like my friend Bill, have come to misconstrue the term "close-working" to mean keeping the dog virtually underfoot, regardless of terrain and cover, simply are not getting the most out of their dogs. For, with the exception of heavy cover hunting for grouse and woodcock, any pointing breed must, of practical necessity, work beyond spaniel range (thirty-five to forty yards) in order to do his job properly for the gun. Moreover, any pointing breed which, without training deliberately designed to restrict him to ultra-close distance, never voluntarily exceeds spaniel-range, just doesn't have enough of what it takes to do a practical job.

The true "close-working" pointing dog lacks nothing in the way of enthusiastic hunting desire, drive, stamina, or nose. Thus, he's not inclined to potter around every wisp of scent he encounters. Nor will he dawdle at every clump of grass or brush pile where, had a bird been concealed, it would have been flushed by the hunter's approach anyway. Such, unfortunately, are the hallmarks of the grass-prowler.

The close worker differs from his medium- and wide-ranging counterparts principally in his constant awareness of the person he is hunting *with* and for, not from any overdependence or inhibited desire to find and point birds. Physically, he may not be built to run as far or as fast as some other dogs, or even some members of his own breed. Or, he may merely be smart enough to synchronize his running gear with his scenting capabilities. In any event, the combination of psychological and physical qualities that contribute to his naturally close-working affinity in no way diminishes the effectiveness of his work.

If for all of these reasons his range and speed are less spectacular to watch than that of bigger-going dogs, the close-worker is nonetheless an ardent bird-finder, under any conditions and circumstances. He'll seldom hesitate to adjust his pace and the distance at which he works from the hunter, according to the dictates of the cover he's in. Put him in the thickest alders, where scent hangs heavy on dank air, and he'll tread more cautiously, well within gun range. But, once the cover

Unlike the "grass prowler," a good close-working pointing dog doesn't dawdle at every grass clump and brush pile. This close-ranging Brittany shows no lack of enthusiasm, style, or nose as he stacks up on a pretty and high-head point. **Photo by Evelyn M. Shafer.**

opens up, perhaps to a sparser mixture of popple or birch, or to a field dotted with brush and weed patches, he will open up, reaching out beyond gun-shot distance to hit the birdy spots and save time and steps for his boss.

He's definitely not a "mile-away" dog...ever; but neither is he just a "gun-shot in front" dog at all times.

REFINEMENTS OF TRAINING

Few people would willingly trade a dollar bill for anything less than a hundred cents. Yet, in effect, thousands of hunting dog owners shortchange themselves every year.

What's more, they do it deliberately, by ignoring the last lap of formal training, that final phase that lifts a dog out of the unfinished, run-of-the-mill category and into the ranks of the really polished performers. And the saddest part of it is that such owners cheat themselves, not from an inability to add the final refinements of training, but usually only because they may believe such finishing touches to be frivolous.

"Why bother to teach my Brit to honor another dog's point? That's just field trial nonsense . . . who needs it in an honest-to-God practical shootin' dog?" How many times we've heard that comment made, in one form or another, around the old pot-bellied stove! Or a similar pronouncement that "being steady to wing and shot's the last thing I want in my dog. The steady dog loses more crippled birds than any shot-breaker ever would."

Of course, anybody who has ever spent much time around a group of dog-owning hunters has no difficulty recognizing such familiar quotes. But the problem arises from the new or relatively inexperienced hunting dog owner's willingness to accept—if you'll forgive the pun—such dogma as gospel.

Well, let's flip it over and see. First of all, a definition of the refinements of training that make for a fully finished dog is in order. Although varying to some degree, according to the type of dog concerned —pointing dog, flush dog, or retriever—the refinements are amazingly similar in principle. Basically, they reflect an additional measure and form of control that is outside the dog's instinctive behavior.

For example, it's perfectly normal for the pointing breeds to point; for the spaniel or flushing dog to flush; for the retriever to pick up and bring back. These are basic characteristics, carefully nurtured in each particular type of dog over many generations of the utmost breeding selectivity. They are not taught by the trainer, only cultivated and guided under proper circumstances.

It is not instinctive, however, for the pointing dog to remain indefinitely immobile, or for the flush dog to sit, or for the retriever to stay, once the quarry is flown and/or shot out of the sky. Quite the contrary, in fact. Yet, in each instance, the dog that has been fully finished will respond to the trainer's demands to remain steady to wing and shot. Additionally, the pointing breeds can be taught to honor, or back, another dog's point on sight or command, though such response has no relationship whatever to the dog's natural instincts.

These, then, are the principal training refinements that characterize the fully finished hunting dog. There can be no doubt—even from the most extreme dissidents—about the esthetic appeal such training produces. But, more than simply being pretty to watch, these refinements have a practical value to the hunter in the field.

Consider, for instance, the business of backing, or honoring, another dog's point. On the face of it, there would seem to be no practical reason to require one dog to freeze in his tracks the instant he comes upon another dog on point. But let's set up a typical quail hunting situation to illustrate the significance backing can have on the game bag.

Dog A, a pointer, has established a staunch point on quail, on the west side of a strip of millet. A slight northeast breeze carries bird-

Honoring, or backing another dog's point is not only pretty performance, but highly practical as well. Since it's not instinctive, it must be taught to the pointing dog as one of the refinements of training.

scent to the pointer as he awaits the arrival of the guns. Meanwhile, dog B, a setter that has been working to the east of the millet patch, swings toward it on a line that carries him just inside its northern edge.

Halfway along the patch, the setter spies dog A, but instead of stopping immediately to honor the point, continues running his original line. Since the breeze is wrong for the setter to wind the covey being pointed by dog A, he blunders in too close, bumps the birds, and spoils a nice chance for the gunners who are still too far away to shoot.

Under these or similar circumstances when two dogs are working simultaneously, who can seriously believe that honoring is a frivolous bit of field trial fancy?

Steadiness to wing and shot, too, is a training refinement that has demonstrably practical advantages which, in most instances, far outweigh the arguments against it. What being steady to wing and shot means, simply, is that the dog will hold a stationary position and await the command to proceed, instead of dashing off in hot pursuit at the flush of the bird and the sound of the gun. It has application to all types of hunting dogs, with the exception of hounds.

In the case of the fully finished flush dog—springers and cockers, as a rule—the steady dog is required to sit, or "hup," the instant he puts his bird to flight. He remains in the sitting position, while the gunners shoot, and waits for the order to fetch if the bird has been dropped, or to resume hunting if the quarry has escaped unharmed.

"Okay, so it's good to look at," you say, "but what possible difference can it make in my game bag?"

First, suppose the flush dog, hunting within good gun-range as he should, routs out a cock pheasant that angles off low to the ground. If the dog is steady, he immediately sits, and the guns go to work. No problem. But what happens with an unsteady dog? He's off like a shot, tagging along just a few feet beneath the bird. Shoot, and you may pepper pooch as well as pheasant. So, you hold fire and kiss the rooster goodbye...a good opportunity lost.

Let's carry it a step further, with another possibility. Same place, same unsteady dog, same low-flying cock bird. Barreling along with his full attention glued on the rooster he's chasing, the dog, now forty-five to fifty yards away, wouldn't smell a skunk in full bloom. If there are any more pheasants in his path, you can wave them farewell, too, as they boil up out of range of your gun.

Lack of steadiness can be just as detrimental to the retriever man. The lab, chessy, or golden that bounds out of the blind at the first sound of gunfire or the first fall can louse up the shooter's chances at another batch of waterfowl that might be on their way in to stool. And the unsteady retriever operating from a boat has caught more than one duck hunter off balance and succeeded in dumping him in the drink.

For many of the same reasons cited for the flushing dog, steadiness to wing and shot is an important asset in the pointing breeds. The unsteady pointer that breaks and goes with the first flutter of wings or the crack of the gun also risks bumping additional birds ahead of him.

Granted, it may be less of a problem, percentage-wise, with pheas-

Professional trainer Ed Frisella of Peace Dale, R.I., checks to make certain setter in foreground is honoring brace-mate's find on a covey of bobwhites.

ants, grouse, or woodcock, which are not ordinarily found in groups. But it can be catastrophic in hunting any birds that covey, such as quail or Hungarian partridge. For after breaking up a covey, the singles hunting can be turned from a dream into a nightmare with an unsteady dog that breaks wing or shot with each flight.

The only argument against breaking wing or shot is the standard contention that the unsteady dog can get to a downed bird faster, thereby giving a crippled bird less chance to gather his wits, run off, and hide. While this is true as far as it goes, it tends to presuppose that the hunter racks up a high percentage of crippled birds that he has to worry about saving. If that's the case, the cause of conservation might be better served if that kind of hunter simply concentrated on practicing a little more to improve his skill as a wingshooter.

In our opinion, there is no really practical reason for the average hunter to shun the refinements of training that can turn his shooting dog into a well-polished, fully finished field performer. Not only will he gain more satisfaction from his dog, but very likely more game, as well.

A yearling pointer gets a lesson in becoming steady to wing and shot. As bird flushes, trainer fires blank gun and commands, "Whoa," while helper yanks back on check cord to restrain dog. **Photo by Dave Petzal.**

The moment of truth for every gun dog is his in-season performance on wild game. But the open season shouldn't signal a halt to continuing your dog's field education. Photo by Sid Latham.

IN-SEASON TRAINING

The start of the hunting season too often seems to signal a temporary moratorium on the proper handling and mannerly performance of the average gun dog, just at the time such factors become most crucial to what gun dog ownership is really all about. It defies all logic when even the most conscientious amateur trainers, who unstintingly labor to improve their dogs' field performance at every off-season opportunity, backslide into an "anything goes" attitude the moment the shooting begins.

Oh, sure, at least a dozen different excuses might be dragged out to explain the phenomenon. Embarrassment at having to admit and correct a dog's blunders in front of other people might account for the acceptance of sloppy hunting field performance from a dog. The real or imagined resentment of companions at sacrificing precious hunting time to canine correction might also bear the blame. And there's even the possibility that, being a bit too eager to collect every duck, pheasant, quail, or rabbit the law allows, a hunter will condone shoddy work for the sake of an extra shot.

Like most excuses, though, none of them justifies the neglect of an important phase of your dog's practical education: learning to handle wild game properly for the gun during the open season. In-season training can certainly be viewed as the "moment of truth" for every hunting dog. After all, hours of care, yard-training, schooling in hand and whistle signals, and tutoring on planted game have been painstakingly directed toward the single goal of molding your dog into a capable, efficient, and gratifying adjunct to the gun in the taking of wild game.

There can be no logic, then, in the attitude of the owner who devalues his sizable investment of time and effort by suddenly calling a recess on training and discipline during the open season. Instant correction—which doesn't always necessarily mean punishment—when he makes a mistake, is no less essential to your dog's learning experiences when you're out to kill game than it is during off-season training sessions. Any infraction or miscue that you wouldn't permit in a training workout certainly shouldn't be tolerated during a hunt either.

Of course, some people contend that "the hunting field is no place to indulge in dog training. Either hunt or train...but don't try to do both." To the extent that an owner knows his dog to be so inexperienced as to turn a hunting trip into a training session, such people are right. The owner of such a dog certainly shouldn't inflict his pupil on his companions under the guise of a serious hunt. That would be deliberately misleading and totally unfair, giving other members of the hunting party ample cause to be resentful.

However, friends who have been advised beforehand that they'll be gunning over your young or unfinished prospect should certainly expect and understand that the hunt will be interrupted—often, if necessary—to correct the mistakes of a dog that's still learning. If they don't, they're not really the sort of friends most men care to hunt with anyway.

While an older dog's minor transgressions—especially the accidental ones—can often be overlooked for the expediency of the hunt, you can't afford this luxury with a young, inexperienced gun dog. He's still in the impressionable stage, and habits, both good and bad, are formed by repetition. Permit him to make a mistake with impunity and he'll go right on repeating the same error, each time fixing the habit more firmly until it becomes so ingrained that breaking it later on will be extremely difficult.

Mistakes demand instant correction if your dog is to progress rather than backslide. A willful flush and chase by this young pointer won't win him any bouquets from his owner.

Admittedly, you'll face some problems, and they'll vary, not only with the age and degree of field training of the breed involved, but with the individual dog and even the game being hunted. But for virtually every problem encountered, there's a solution. Whenever your dog makes an accidental mistake, you should call him back—or catch him, if necessary, and bring him back—to the place where he committed the error. Then, if it's possible to repeat the situation, have him do whatever he blundered at over again correctly.

For example, let's say that your pointing dog began making game, then moved in too fast and too close and inadvertently flushed a bird. Of course, you can't duplicate the flush, but you can bring the dog back to the exact spot where it occurred and, setting him up on point, make him stand fast for a minute or two while cautioning him to "whoa...whoa...whoa." No punishment is needed in this case, since the error he committed was not deliberate. Had it been a willful mistake, however, you'd have to chastise him right at the spot and then set him up on point, letting him remain there as you repeat the "whoa" command firmly.

What do we mean by chastising? Even that will vary, depending on how tough or soft a temperament — the dog's, that is, not yours — is involved. A big verbal commotion and a couple of light taps with a switch or flushing whip may be ample punishment for a timid dog; whereas, for a hardhead, lifting him off the ground, by the loose skin on his back and neck, and shaking him vigorously may be just barely harsh enough to get your message across. Obviously, only you will know your dog well enough to choose the severity of his punishment.

Let's take anouther example. Suppose your retriever is on his way back with a downed pheasant and accidently flushes a second bird. He may drop the one in his mouth to chase after the other bird. Okay, you call your dog back to the spot where his mistake was committed, where he dropped the bird he was fetching. Then after a suitable reprimand, make him pick up and hold the bird, in a standing position, while you return to your original spot and signal him to fetch to you. When he's taken a few steps toward you, signal him, by voice or whistle, to sit—which is what he should have done when the second pheasant flushed. After holding him in the sitting position for a minute or so, release him to complete his original retrieve and receive a rewarding pat of approval.

"All that's fine," you say, "but how can I keep my dog under the same kind of control while we're out hunting as I have during training

Taking the time to overcome errors by your dog may cut into your hunting one year, but will more than compensate you in future seasons. Here a two-year-old setter is encouraged to retrieve a woodcock.

sessions? I can't hunt him with a choke collar and a fifty-foot check cord, yet, when I remove them, he may run too wide for me to control him. If that happens in the hunting field, how can I catch and correct him?"

A fair question, since many a young dog is inclined to range beyond good control of his handler and, recognizing the fact, generally takes advantage of this edge to do whatever he pleases, at least for awhile. The problem is, of course, to provide some means of restraint, less cumbersome than a long check cord, to prevent the dog from extending his range just beyond that psychological point at which he knows you've lost control.

The electronic shock collar is one answer, but many hunters shy away from using it on dogs that react adversely. Any of several other contrivances that hunters used long before the advent of the shock collar can also solve the problem, or at least lessen it. All of these old standby methods involve affixing something to the dog's collar to slow him down. It may be a three-and-a-half-foot length of heavy chain or a similar amount of ordinary rubber garden hose, which drags on the ground between his legs and restricts his range and speed.

A third technique similarly utilizes a burlap sack, in fifty-pound size. With one corner of the bag tied to the dog's collar, the other three form a triangular shape that drags on the ground for him to step on with every third or fourth stride. Unless the dog is smart enough to pick up the bag in his mouth—and we'd like to own the dog that masters this trick—it will keep him from taking off beyond controllable range, while not seriously hampering his ability to hunt.

Still another variation of this type of range-restricter is one that our longtime friend, the late Pert Prince, used successfully in training countless field trial pointers and setters. Pert call it a "bolo," and though it was probably a name of his own invention, the device did indeed resemble, in miniature, the *bolloderos* of the South American gauchos. Simply described, it consisted of two differing lengths of light but tough plastic rope suspended from a snap. At the end of each rope was a solid rubber ball, approximately two-and-a-half inches in diameter. The ball on the longer rope touched the ground with about six inches to spare, while the other hung about six inches shorter.

When attached to the dog's collar, the weight of the balls was sufficient to keep them swinging and periodically wrap one or the other of the plastic ropes around the dog's front legs...thus beautifully slowing him down and keeping him close enough to maintain good control.

Since lack of control is the key factor in a majority of hunting field difficulties, any of the above described measures should offer you a start toward solving a host of miscellaneous problems in training your dog during the hunting season. For with your control factor reinforced, your dog won't be so likely to commit deliberate errors, and the accidental ones can be corrected more easily, since he'll seldom be beyond your control.

14

Your Gun Dog, Off-Season

YEAR-ROUND PSYCHOLOGICAL TRAINING

TRAINING A GUN dog takes in a lot of territory—yard-breaking, car-breaking, teaching hand and whistle signals, retrieving lessons, field work—all of it vital to attaining your goal of producing a practical hunting field assistant. But a gun dog's ultimate value and performance can be strongly influenced by still another factor, one that's most often overlooked or, perhaps, not even dreamed of by the average owner.

Psychological conditioning is what we've chosen to call it, though "rapport" probably capsules its essence as well as any word can. It consists not of any single ingredient or formal training lesson but rather of a combination of simple everyday things which, taken as a whole, can create a closer psychological bond between dog and master.

The Germans, while having no monopoly on psychological conditioning, provide a fine example of the successful results obtainable with their dogs from its application. Consider the hallmarks of most German-trained gun dogs: intelligence, devotion, and responsiveness, qualities that translate into efficient service to the gun. Style aside—for there are many Americans who contend that much is to be desired from them in this regard—the German-trained hunting dog has an enviable record of serviceability that's hard to match.

How does the German owner achieve such a consistently high level

Permitting your dog to spend more time with you is the basic idea behind psychological training. This setter who's so attentive to his owner at home will doubtlessly be more biddable in the field as well.

of success with his field dog? Obviously, scrupulous training — and plenty of it — is a significant element. But there is something else that goes into it, too. Invariably, the German sportsman tempers his dog's formal training with liberal amounts of informal psychology.

The average gun dog in Germany is permitted — no, encouraged — to become virtually his master's shadow. Where the owner goes, so does his dog. A walk to the village, a visit to a neighbor's home, a trip to the big city market, a Sunday picnic with the family, are all occasions for the owner to be accompanied by his dog. And almost no opportunity is overlooked to foster this intimate companionship

Though one might suspect that such familiarity could also breed contempt, and possibly lead to a general softening or complete breakdown of discipline, the exact opposite holds true. No matter how close the attachment he forms with his dog, the German owner is canny enough not to permit an order to go unobeyed or a misdeed uncorrected. Although essentially a relaxed association there is never any laxity condoned in the dog-and-master relationship, a relationship that, in time, produces the highest degree of mutual respect and understanding.

The dog obeys not merely because he thinks he must, but because he has been psychologically conditioned to the point where he wants to obey and thereby please the master he loves and respects. Ultimately, both the desire and the knowledge of how to do this become so inseparably fused within the dog's behavior pattern that they become almost instinctive responses. The resultant rapport, when transferred into the hunting field, makes the German-trained gun dog infinitely more biddable, hence more functional to the gun.

How can such psychological conditioning be applied to American gun dogs? It might be argued that conditions are different in America. The pace and way of life here are faster, more frantic, less relaxed. Many a gun dog owner in America simply can't devote as much time as he might like to his gun dog.

True enough, yet, with few exceptions, anybody who owns a field dog and has time to hunt will discover that he also has far more opportunities for psychologically conditioning his dog than are immediately apparent.

Actually, the whole idea is not so much a matter of spending more time with your dog as it is permitting your dog to spend more time with you. There's quite a difference. The former sense implies that an owner must somehow make the time—sacrificing something else that he could be doing—to devote exclusively to his dog. The latter, on which psychological conditioning is based, means simply that the dog is allowed to become more a part of the owner's normal routine.

Psychological training promotes greater rapport between owner and dog and stimulates the dog's eagerness to please.

Thus, even the busiest person need not drastically intrude upon his regular schedule in order to do the job effectively. Almost anyone giving it a few minutes' thought will be able to come up with a couple of dozen possibilities that lend themselves to including the company of his dog.

For example, how many times a day, especially on weekends, do you hop in the car and run downtown...to the cleaners, to the drugstore, to the bakery? Each trip constitutes a separate opportunity, and only a few seconds extra trouble, for the dog to go along. Nor should it present any great difficulty to have Rover lying quietly near your side while you're washing the car, painting the back fence, weeding the garden, tinkering in the garage.

Ideally, psychological conditioning should be a year-round proposition. But even if a man can't meet the "ideal," he can at least make a stab at including the practice in his pre-season get-ready program come September. And five or six weeks of intensive effort can make a noticeable difference in the field later on.

Perhaps a few words of warning are in order for those who might be inclined to oversimplify the meaning and purpose of psychological conditioning.

Merely spending considerable time or living with his owner is, in itself, not the complete answer for any dog. Witness the average house pet who, too frequently, through the owner's laxity or laziness deteriorates into a spoiled, overfed, obese, unmannerly clod that is utterly beyond training. In such instances, it is surely the owner—not the dog—who has been psychologically conditioned into acceptance of a completely bass-ackwards relationship.

The entire philosophy of psychological conditioning hinges on properly combining frequency of opportunity for personal contact and companionship with gentle but firm, almost subtle, control. While the dog shares the company of his owner—as he eagerly longs to do—he should be learning that this reward is earned mainly by his responsiveness and good behavior. The master must be alert and quick to provide guidance and correction. If the owner is slovenly or inconsistent, how can the dog be expected to be much different?

Sure, it will take some extra concentration on your part at first to make the results worthwhile. But when you discover the benefits, even after just a few weeks, you may decide that psychological conditioning belongs in your training schedule not just on a pre-season basis but each and every day of the year.

Exercise should begin with brief daily sessions, gradually working up to the thirty-minute run that will harden your dog into good hunting shape by opening day. **Photo by Dave Petzal.**

PRE-SEASON TUNE-UP

Each year, as the lazy days of summer wane and the arrival of September stirs the first faint thoughts of the coming hunting season, sportsmen around the nation begin their annual ritual of getting ready. Cleaning rods are re-introduced to grease-lined gun barrels, the thirsty leather of upland boots is quenched by multiple dubbings, shotshells are sorted—the 12's from the 20's and the 6's from the 7½'s—and brush pants, wool shirts, game vests, and caps get a shake or two, a quick inspection, and a satisfied nod that once again indicates dry-cleaning can be put off for still another year.

And watching all this, with perhaps an occasional sniff and a flurry of tail thumping in anticipation of what's to come, is old Queenie or Jack, ahead of whom lies a different, but equally necessary routine of getting ready for the new season.

After the long summer layover, often spent building up excess fat and flabby muscles and searching for nothing more physically taxing than the nearest patch of shade, no gun dog can hope to dive right into a hunting season of long, rigorous hours afield. Conditioning your dog, though a relatively simple procedure, involves pretty much the same principles an athlete must observe in getting himself in shape.

Exercise of the proper type to melt away excess pounds, harden soft pads, tone flaccid muscles, and improve wind and stamina must be given in sensible doses. Just as the athlete is careful never to overdo, to stiffen, to tax and tire himself with too much, too fast, so, too, must you regulate your dog's conditioning program for best results.

If your dog gets no summer exercise beyond a couple of daily trips to the fire hydrant on the corner, ten or fifteen minutes of running, once a day for the first two weeks, makes a good beginning. In fact, if he's really hog fat—for that you should slap your own wrists—it would be wise to limit him to the lesser side of ten minutes for the first week, and work him up to the full fifteen only toward the latter part of the second week.

Increasing these regular exercise periods by a couple of minutes every other day for the next three weeks will enable you to work him up sensibly to the thirty-minute daily run that he'll need in order to become hardened into really good hunting field shape. If you begin early in September and stick faithfully with your routine, you should have your dog well-conditioned in a matter of five or six weeks—plenty

Left: *Basic obedience to commands often needs review. A few minutes spent each day on his yard-training lessons will soon have the average gun dog responsive again.* **Right:** *Pre-season review should include brushing up on all commands. Here, setter gets a lesson in walking at heel.* **Photos by Dave Petzal.**

Retrieving dummy and blank cartridge gun add zest to backyard refresher course after basic obedience review has sharpened your dog's responsiveness. **Photo by Dave Petzal.**

of time for a mid-October opening day.

What's the best method of exercising the dog during this conditioning period? Actual field work, of course, is the most ideal. But if you don't have access to the acreage needed on a daily basis, the next best thing is regular roadwork. This can be accomplished in either of two ways. If you can get someone else to do the driving, you can work the dog right from the tailgate of your station wagon, on a fifteen- or twenty-foot rope. With this system you can vary the pace from a brisk trot to a short run, and actually time and regulate your outings precisely. Obviously, for safety's sake, you'll have to choose a decent road that's off the main routes.

If you can find neither a driver nor an old quiet road, you can always resort to working your dog from a bicycle. If fact, the bike provides a distinct advantage over the station wagon, inasmuch as peddling it will help you get in better condition, too.

As important as pre-season physical conditioning is, it represents only part of getting your dog ready for the full season ahead. Since his brain is probably as rusty as his body, his response to commands will almost certainly leave a lot to be desired. While this is particularly true of the kennel dog, who's had a virtual vacation from discipline over the summer, the house dog often displays exasperating disregard for discipline once outside the confines of the home.

Since such deportmental backsliding is not at all uncommon in the average gun dog, you should plan to include a review of your dog's yard-training lessons, as brief or extensive as the situation demands.

Putting him through a full course of basic yard-training certainly can't hurt him, if you can spare the ten minutes' extra time it takes every day for a week or so. By sharpening his attentiveness to your directions, you'll be assured of his prompt, enthusiastic response to commands in the field, right from opening day on.

By yard-training we mean simply the basic obedience lessons by which you first taught the dog to "Sit," "Come," "Heel," "Stay," and "Whoa." Reviewing each of these commands, with your dog on leash or check cord to give you control and enforce his compliance, should enable you to spot the ones he shows hesitancy in obeying, so you can devote extra effort to them.

It's also a good idea to review the voice, hand, and whistle signals you ordinarily employ when working your dog on game. Some of these, such as the signal to whoa or sit, plus the recall and go on commands, can be gone over right in your backyard, again with the use of the check cord and leash. Sooner or later, though, you'll have to get him out in the field to review these signals under more realistic working conditions.

Before jumping right into the serious business of these outings, though, the dog should be permitted a few minutes freedom to romp, stretch out, and burn up some of his initial excess nervous energy. Then, when you call him in to snap on the check cord and get to the task at hand, he'll be more willing to settle down to business.

With his physical conditioning, yard-training review, and field refresher projects completed, or at least well under way, the remainder of your pre-season preparations are mostly simple chores, none of which can't be easily accomplished well before the season opens. Doubtless the most pressing of these miscellaneous but important details is a thorough check of your dog's general health by a veterinarian. No matter how efficient your conditioning and obedience programs may be, your dog cannot attain his physical and mental peak in anything less than perfect health.

For example, worms can seriously drain an otherwise healthy and well-conditioned dog of much of his normal vitality and endurance. Since microscopic examination is the only way to determine the presence of the more debilitating types of worms, a sample of your dog's stool must be taken to your vet for analysis. He'll prescribe the proper treatment for any kind of worms your dog may have.

At the same time, it is a good idea to have your vet look over the dog thoroughly and, if the animal is in good health, provide you with a certificate to that effect. Such affidavit, together with certification that the dog has been inoculated against rabies, is of multiple value to the shooting dog owner. Besides being a rigid Customs requirement to transport a dog across international boundaries, a health and rabies certificate can save you considerable trouble should your dog get involved in a scrap with another dog, or take a nip out of somebody. It's equally important if you plan to breed your dog, for most professional breeders insist that all bitches sent to their kennels for stud services be accompanied by a health certificate.

All these details are, of course, important throughout the year, and no dog should have to wait until just before opening day of the hunting season to be checked by a veterinarian. Even if he seems quite up to snuff, he should be checked at least twice a year, for worms if nothing else.

At least ten days to two weeks before opening day, an inspection should be made of your dog's nails; those that are overly long, cracked, or ragged may then be properly trimmed. Regular canine nail-clippers are the best tools available for this job, which should be done gingerly, taking only the thinnest sliver of nail at a time, to avoid trimming into the quick. A dog's nails are of the right length when, with the foot placed firmly on level ground they do not quite touch the surface.

Longhaired breeds—like setters, springers, and cocker spaniels—should be stripped of excess hair on ears, tail, legs, and underparts, to prevent undue matting and the tendency to burr-up in heavy-cover hunting. And, lest you hesitate on the grounds that such stripping will mar your dog's appearance, forget it: in the course of a full season in the field all that flowing coat eventually will be stripped out by brush and brier anyway.

Doing it beforehand may detract momentarily from the dog's comeliness, but it will certainly make the job of combing and de-burring him after a day's hunt a lot easier on both of you.

With the accomplishment of these last few details, plus a few additional ones that every individual case may suggest, you can take justifiable pride in the completion of a job well done. For, in meeting squarely your obligations to your canine field companion, you'll have proven yourself not only a responsible, devoted owner, but a smart one as well. Your dog may not be able to say thanks in so many words, but his performance in the field, from opening day straight through the entire season, will speak volumes of appreciation to an owner who cared enough to make sure his pal was thoroughly prepared to do his job right.

Commercial shooting preserves offer a post-season bonus of up to fourteen weeks of hunting. Whether used to provide extra work for veteran gun dogs, like this springer, or to continue training the young bird dog, preserves are a real boon to sporting dog owners.

OFF-SEASON BONUS FOR BIRD DOGS

Commercial shooting preserves have proven to be a boon not only to sport-starved shooters in heavily populated metropolitan areas, but also to bird dog owners seeking to stretch their dogs' field work over a more substantial portion of the year.

No longer can a man blame aborted seasons and token bag limits for his dog's inadequacies in the field. No longer must he resort strictly to backyard artifices in attempts to produce in his dog the natural responses that only work under actual field conditions on live game can perfect. For, with seasons ranging up to six months in length, and the only limit on birds imposed by man's pocketbook, paid shooting preserves today are at the dog owner's beck and call in all but a handful of states.

So much has been written on the subject of controlled-shooting areas, their rates and method of operation, that it would seem foolish to suppose any reader is not well acquainted with these aspects. However, the full potential offered the dog owner by such establishments has barely been touched upon.

Fundamentally, shooting preserves provide the dog owner three advantages: (1) a pre-season jump of as much as six to eight weeks on the regular public open season, during which time he can work the kinks out of an older dog or essay the field training of a young one; (2) a place to work his dog, undisturbed by outside distractions, in a diverse variety of natural covers, with the assurance of contacting game under natural, partially- or fully-controlled conditions; (3) an extension of his dog's field work by as long as three-and-a-half months after the close of the regular open season.

There is no gainsaying the value of the pre-season tune-up preserves afford. Yet, even more significant to the average bird dog owner are the after-season opportunities. At a time of year when a majority of the upland bird seasons are but a fond recollection, the controlled-shooting grounds represent a whole new lease on life. After an entire open

Staunchness on point is just one of the many lessons a dog can be taught on the grounds of a commercial shooting preserve. Here, author demonstrates proper technique to encourage staunchness in an English pointer. **Photo by Dave Petzal.**

Planting birds in specific covers gives the dog owner the kind of controlled training situations he could not possibly duplicate in the wild. **Photo by Dave Petzal.**

season's hunting, the properly observant owner has had ample time to study his dog's overall performance and to spot consistent mistakes, delinquencies, and weaknesses in handling game, all of which demand the kind of corrective training—on live game—that ordinarily would have to be postponed til the following year.

Fortunately, the latter part of December and the months of January and February conventionally seem to be the least busy times of year for preserves in all but the southernmost parts of the country. Thus, during these months many paid-shooting establishments not only welcome but seek the patronage of sportsmen primarily concerned with working and training their own bird dogs. This is especially true of the smaller operations that impose no minimum either in daily fees or bag limits. If a man has shown himself to be a good customer by occasionally sending or bringing a few friends there to hunt, the welcome mat will always be out.

Just how effectively the dog owner goes about using these bonus post-season opportunities is, of course, up to the individual. Where the fully finished gun dog is concerned, it may be simply a matter of giving him extra work on birds over a longer portion of the year. For the younger dog that may require special or additional training in some specific phase of game-handling, the work may be fashioned along whatever lines are necessary. Suppose, for instance, you have a young dog that flash points but refuses to hold, and boldly rushes in to flush before you can get near enough for a decent shot. Such a pupil is badly in need of staunching on point, a facet of training easily undertaken on the controlled-shooting area. The situation calls for the use of a single "planted" bird (bobwhite or coturnix quail serve nicely) and a fifty-foot check cord.

With the latter attached to the dog's collar, he can be circuitously led to the vicinity of the "plant," which should have been made earlier, out of sight of the dog. Allow the dog to work the area until, catching the scent and pinpointing its source, he establishes a momentary, or flash, point. Having taken up slack in the check cord meanwhile, you're now in a position to restrain the dog's attempts to dash in on the bird, while simultaneously cautioning him to "Whoa." Still keeping him in check until you reach his side, you have but to re-set and style him in the pointing stance, soothing him meanwhile with hands as well as voice. Once he's grasped the idea and re-established a fairly solid point, a few gentle nudges applied to his rear, to push him off balance or move him closer to the bird, will invariably stiffen him into unyielding staunchness.

Teaching a dog to remain steady to wing and/or shot can be accomplished with essentially the same procedure. Nor is it necessary in the process to kill the bird each time. If bobwhite quail are used — and we strongly recommend them for this type of training — the same bird may be flushed, marked down, and re-located two or three times before it's finally brought to bag. Because preserve quail seldom make long flights, they're ideal for such multiple use by the sportsman-trainer.

Besides being less expensive than pheasants, quail have other merits too. We discovered one of these advantages accidentally a couple of years ago, when necessity truly proved to be the mother of invention.

For three successive weekends a hunting buddy and I patiently hand-planted bobwhites in a remote sector of Mike Pender's Twin Elms Game Farm at Golden's Bridge, N.Y., in an attempt to coax a solid point out of my friend's young setter. The pup, about fourteen months old, had all the prospects of becoming a nice shooting dog. He exhibited strong desire to hunt; to search out all types of cover, at close-to-medium-range; to obey hand, voice, and whistle signals with instant response. He was adequately dependable in every respect save one: he apparently thought that pointing, even for an English setter, was rude.

Lord knows how many quail we planted for him. But in no time he showed how savvy he was, quickly learning to follow the scent-trail of whoever planted the bird and running directly to it with a minimum of effort. Each time he "showed" us where the bird was, but he refused to point it in the acceptable sense, preferring to walk around it. If we cautioned him sharply to "Whoa," he'd either sit or lie down near it and wag his tail. He was not a true "blinker," yet we couldn't fathom his failure to point. Then, suddenly, an idea took form. Due to to unnatural man-scent unavoidably left on planted birds, even those handled with gloves, some dogs tend to be slightly soft in pointing them. Maybe it was this man-scent that was disturbing our pupil. On this premise, and because neither of us had gloves, we took the next quail to the middle of the field. Now, out of sight of the dog, we chucked it into the air in the general direction we hoped it would go. Luck was with us; it did not fly far before pitching down into some grassy cover at field's edge. Marking it well, we sauntered back to the car, smoked two cigarettes, then turned the dog loose.

Without hesitation, he made like a bat out of hell for midfield, following our scent trail, of course. But, once there, finding no "plant," he began hunting, quartering nicely into the wind and eventually making game where our handflown bobwhite had landed a few minutes earlier. When the bird's body-scent hit him square in the face, he froze almost in mid-stride, jacking up on as solid and intense a point as a man could ask. We had it made!

From that day on, we've continued to fly most of our preserve quail, finding that even the older dogs seem to slide into their points a lot harder on birds so released. The reason is simple: the bulk of the human scent is air-washed from the birds in that short initial flight. And, while it's equally true that the flight somewhat reduces the amount of natural odor the bird gives off, waiting about ten minutes before loosing the dogs is apparently enough to offset this. Not to be overlooked either, is the fact that the flighted quail in seeking its own hiding place, leaves some natural ground scent about the area for the dog to pick up. The system, which we call "flight-planting," also eliminates the possibility of a dog's trailing the bird-planter instead of searching for the bird in a natural manner.

Without the protracted seasons and the unlimited supply of live game birds that the regulated-shooting ground provides, such advantageous training situations would be impossible to create. Certainly, such ideal contact with game, under controlled circumstances, in natural covers, could hardly be duplicated in the wild. Add to these obvious benefits the fact that long after the public open seasons end, commercial shooting preserves are still going strong. Right through the month of March in most states, you can continue to work or train your dog on quail, pheasant, or chukar partridge, rapidly advancing his education and practical experience, instead of relegating him to a spot on the hearth and idly dreaming of what you'll be able to do with him during those far-off golden days of next October.

If you don't know of any shooting preserves in your area, a postcard request addressed to the National Shooting Sports Foundation, Inc., 555 Danbury Road, Wilton, CT 06897 will bring you a complimentary Preserve Shooting Directory with state by state listings.

THE MERITS OF FIELD TRIALS

"Field trials? What good are they, outside of playing nonsensical games with a bunch of fancy-pants dogs you wouldn't even dare to take out hunting anyway?"

Sound familiar? Sure it does. Anyone who's ever hunted behind a dog has probably heard similar expressions of contempt for field trials and the dogs that run in them. At one time or another, maybe you've even joined the bad-mouthing chorus, without knowing exactly why, except that, well...that's what Joe Jones is always saying, and he's been hunting for years, so he must know what he's talking about.

Did you wonder, though, just how well acquainted with field trials Joe Jones is? Pinned down to an honest answer, he, like so many who shoot off their mouths more effectively than they do their shotguns, would probably do a bit of squirming before admitting his limited, if any, firsthand field trial experience.

Yet, because of all too many Joe Joneses, a large percentage of the hunters who every year swell the ranks of new gun dog owners automatically acquire a strong prejudice against field trials without ever having had an opportunity to find out what they are all about.

Given a chance to learn the score for themselves, such sportsmen would probably be surprised to discover that field trials, instead of being "just a lot of nonsense," actually contribute substantially to the betterment of many of the hunting breeds. There are, in fact, few really popular hunting breeds in this country today that do not owe to field trials a good share of credit for their development and present high standing with the gunning public.

All field trials, of course, are not alike. There are as many different types as there are different breeds. For instance, there are trials for retrievers, for spaniels, for beagles, for fox and coon hounds, and for pointing dogs. There are big trials and small ones, professional and amateur, specialized and non-specialized, formal and informal. Most of them are further broken down into various stakes, such as puppy, derby, all-age, and gun dog categories. Although the rules, procedures, and conditions under which various types of trials are run may differ to some extent, the majority of them have at least one aspect in common: the recognition of dogs that conform most closely to the ideal performance standards of their particular jobs.

Since the standards as well as the test of ideal performance are formulated by human beings, field trials, like everything else in this world, are not infallible. As their harshest critics are quick to point out, some have strayed so far from standards even remotely applicable to practical hunting dog performance that they must be regarded strictly as "games."

The fact that such events are lumped under the general heading of field trials is unfortunate. Some consolation exists in knowing that they are in the minority. Most field trials are run under conditions designed to approximate as closely as possible those that sporting dogs would encounter in the normal course of their work. But it would

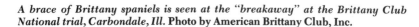

A brace of Brittany spaniels is seen at the "breakaway" at the Brittany Club National trial, Carbondale, Ill. **Photo by American Brittany Club, Inc.**

Gallery members usually ride along behind dogs, handlers, and judges at a National Pointing dog trial.

be naive to expect to run a large number of dogs under optimum natural conditions and, at the same time, provide each one exactly the same opportunity to demonstrate the full scope of his abilities under judgment.

Reasonable concessions and some degree of controlled or artificial situations, therefore, must enter into the field trial picture in order to provide a fair basis for comparison of all entries. Artifice is present in greater or lesser degree in all field trials, depending upon the type of dogs involved and the special difficulties encountered in setting up equitable tests on game.

As for their effect on the ultimate performance the dogs turn in, there is scant excuse to quibble. For in most cases, except for the knowledge that a course may be "seeded" with planted birds, or a water retrieve may be made on a conveniently pre-killed duck, the dog work is little different than it would be under natural conditions in the field. The important thing is the appearance of realism not to the spectator, but to the dogs. In this respect most field trials succeed admirably.

What good are field trials, generally, and how can they possibly affect the average gun dog owner?

As we have already mentioned, virtually *all* field trials contribute something to the overall improvement of the hunting breeds. All of them, right through the local, county, state, and regional trials clear to the top-notch championship affairs of the national circuit, benefit the working sporting dog. How?

Perhaps the best way to illustrate what we mean is to consider one particular type of trial. Let's take a look at the big national pointing dog trials to see what makes them tick. In these events, with competition of the keenest order, only the very best performers can hope to make the grade. Here, dogs are expected to achieve the nearest thing to absolute perfection.

Stamina is tested in grueling three-hour heats, and dogs must pace themselves intelligently for the long pull, in order to finish as strongly as they started. They must show an abundance of natural abilities, including insatiable desire to hunt, good range and speed, instinctive bird-sense, superior nose, and plenty of style and intensity on point. And complementing these natural qualities, they must display a willingness to handle easily without undue loss of independence and initiative.

Failure in even a single instance, obvious weakness in any one quality, and a dog is generally ruled out of contention, so fierce is the competition.

As a result, the national championships draw only the cream of pointing dogs from all over the country and sort from these but a few winners — great dogs that reflect the very finest qualities obtainable in their respective breeds. And if any doubt exists that top quality is not the rule, it can quickly be dispelled, not by any high-sounding idealistic principles, but by cold, hard economics.

Thousands of dollars must be invested in the training and campaigning of dogs for the big circuit. Handlers' salaries, travel expenses, entry fees...all mount up to formidable proportions. And few owners, breeders, or trainers can afford the luxury of fooling with prospects that simply don't measure up to the performance standards they know exist in the nationals. There is no money, prestige, or satisfaction in losers. Hence, economics proves an efficient benefactor in safeguarding the continuing high quality of which the nationals are justly proud.

Undeniably, then, the nationals make their most significant contribution to the improvement of the hunting breeds by uplifting and maintaining a set of high standards toward which all breeders and trainers can aspire. In so doing, of course, it is not unusual for breeders to seek out national champions as studs for their most promising bitches. And it is, in fact, through the recognition and subsequent demand for such superior performers as stud dogs that better bloodlines become more widely disseminated throughout the country. The average hunting dog buyer eventually reaps the benefits fostered by field trials when he purchases a puppy whose potential in the field is virtually insured by ancestry of proven quality.

What holds true for the major trials also applies on a lesser scale to

Under the watchful eye of mounted judge, a German shorthaired pointer holds staunchly as his owner-handler prepares to flush and shoot bird. Such "shoot-to-retrieve" stakes are increasingly popular at one-course trials for pointing breeds. **Photo by Gaines Dog Research Center.**

most other field trials. And while their rules, procedures, and qualifications may be less stringent, these "minor leagues" are frequently the development grounds for future champions.

Typical of the smaller events run by local clubs is the one-course pointing dog trial. The grounds used for such contests may cover as much as several hundred acres, with the boundaries largely determined and defined by the terrain. Entries are drawn from a hopper the night before the competition, and dogs are run in pairs, or braces, with bracemates selected purely by chance from the random drawing.

Next morning, after checking the board on which each brace is posted, the two handlers running the first brace approach the starting line, where they await the judges' order to cast off their dogs for the half-hour heat. Customarily, there are two judges, who are on horseback both for mobility and better observation.

After the dogs are cast off, the handlers proceed, followed closely by the judges around what is known as the back course. This terrain is selected to provide an ideal variety of natural cover conditions. As a rule, it is not seeded with birds, so that the entries are judged solely on how they hunt. The qualities looked for are good range and pace, style and ground pattern, intelligence in seeking birdy objectives, and responsiveness to handling. Each judge carries a booklet listing entry names and brace numbers, in which he can make notations on performance.

The back course is laid out so that it will take approximately twenty-two minutes to hunt. At its end is the bird field, where the dogs spend the remaining eight minutes of the half-hour heat attempting to locate and point birds that were planted shortly after the brace's breakaway on the back course. The bird field generally is situated in a hollow to

Informal contests, such as this "shoot-to-kill" stake, give the average owner and his dog a chance to taste the thrills of field trialing. **Photo by WPG Club of America.**

give the gallery spectators a good view. Each handler carries a blank cartridge gun, and whenever his dog points a bird the handler, after receiving the judge's acknowledgment, flushes it and fires.

During the eight minutes in the bird field, each handler tries to keep his dog hunting in a different sector, so that he'll have a chance to find and point his own birds rather than use up time honoring his bracemate's points. Judges evaluate bird field performance primarily on a dog's ability to find, his style and intensity on point, and his manners. The number of birds found is taken into consideration, but does not necessarily effect the eventual order of first, second, and third place winners.

The smaller trials — whether for pointing dogs, spaniels, retrievers, or hounds — are no less valuable for the fact that they bring together many men and women who love and admire the work of functional sporting dogs. Friendships are made between people with a common interest; ideas are freely exchanged; bloodlines and training discussed; breeding programs laid out; dogs bought, sold, or traded...all toward the end purpose of getting good dogs.

You need not be a participant in order to gain a great deal out of attending a trial every now and then. If at first you're a trifle hazy about what goes on, there is always someone in the gallery willing to take time to explain procedures and answer your questions. Once you understand what to look for, you'll be amazed at how much enjoyment can be derived from watching good dogs perform and then trying, as is the time-honored prerogative among the gallery, to second-guess the judges.

Additionally, there is always the possibility of being bitten by the field trial bug; many a casual observer has found himself suddenly hooked on the infectious enthusiasm and spirit of competition that pervades even the smallest field trial gatherings.

Yet, whether you become an active trialer or simply an occasional spectator is incidental to the more important fact that you've taken a look for yourself at what field trials are all about. Only then, without second-hand prejudice, can you reach a fair answer to the question, "What good are field trials?"

YOUR DOG CAN COMPETE

HUNTING REMAINS ONE of the few activities of modern-day life in which competition—the compulsion to best one's fellow man—is intrinsically out of place. The real values of hunting somehow prohibit reducing the sport to the level of a superficial contest to fill the bag faster and with fewer shots than your companions. Invariably, those who approach hunting competitively will find scant personal satisfaction in "victories" when no one else is competing.

Since field trials are run virtually the year round, they extend your dog's work far beyond normal seasons' duration. This wirehaired pointing griffon gets in some water work at an early fall trial. **Photo by WPG Club of America.**

But if taking of game in the field properly transcends any semblance of a contest, sportsmen unquestionably satisfy their competitive instincts in various specific aspects of their favorite sport. For example, trap and skeet originated and were developed not only to provide fun, but also to determine which hunter was the best wingshot. Likewise, the issue of who owned the best retriever, hound, spaniel, or bird dog gave birth to the contests we know as field trials.

Contrary to the idea shared by many nonparticipants, however, every field trialer is far from a "do-or-die" type out to win honors and glory or spend the next week sulking over his failure.

In fact, increasingly today, field trialing is widening its appeal as a distinctly recreational form of hunter-dog relationship separate from, but closely akin to, that enjoyed in the hunting field. Without compromising the traditional standards of excellence sought in the major trials, more average dogs and owners are being introduced to trialing through the incorporation of additional special stakes.

Amateur events for puppy, derby, and shooting dog as well as restricted breed stakes—the first three barring professional handlers and the last excluding the most consistent winners, English pointers and setters—are being carded more frequently in the programs of burgeoning numbers of field trial clubs in all parts of the nation. On the up-swing, too, are "shoot-to-retrieve" stakes and "fun" trials, designed to attract the interest and active participation of hunters who, though they love and enjoy working their dogs, would normally hesitate to enter highly formal competition.

Since some of these special stakes carry no official recognition by the American Kennel Club, the American Field, or similar registry organizations for various breeds, they are conducted under less exacting rules than would apply in formal competition. Judged with a far more lenient eye toward minor faults, the dogs in these stakes need not show the high degree of training and performance demanded in officially recognized trials. So, while nonentities in the record books, these special stakes offer excellent opportunities for the average hunter to enter his dog in competition while becoming acquainted with the thrills and satisfaction of field trialing.

Bird dog events, such as the "shoot-to-retrieve" stakes, not only offer the same basic rewards found in the hunting field, but also the extra exhilaration of having an impartial judge confirm what you'll be boasting about to your hunting buddies for years: namely, that Rover does turn in a pretty decent, if not damn good, job in the field.

What does it matter if his win is uncounted in the annals of field trial history? In a "shoot-to-retrieve" stake, you've had a good chance to come home with the bacon (usually a pheasant or two) and perhaps a ribbon as well, to commemorate the occasion.

Even if your dog didn't rate a prize for his efforts, both of you have experienced the fun of trying: the dog has had an extra workout, and just possibly you've picked up a little more know-how about dog handling and proper performance along the way.

With the exception of killing game, "fun" trials offer the same benefits, whether they be for pointing, flushing, hound, or retriever breeds. As the very name implies, their true purpose and major emphasis is one of pleasant recreation rather than hard-fought competition. If they are approached on such basis, no man need feel that he or his dog is unqualified to participate.

Nor is participation in these informal types of competition without other merits besides recreation. The observant field trialer, watching and listening intently, can hardly fail to add to his store of knowledge of canine field performance. A remark overheard here and there; a handler discussing his own or his dog's mistakes; the group reaction of the gallery to a particularly good or glaringly poor piece of dog work—all help to increase the onlooker's awareness of many aspects he might never have noticed before when afield with his dog.

Chalk up on the credit side, too, the number of new acquaintances you can make at a trial. The sociability of field trialers is well-known,

Sociability of galleryites at trials is well known. New friendships and the exchange of information and ideas are valuable bonuses derived from field trial attendance.

and rarely can anybody hang around watching the proceedings without being drawn into conversation with some of the gallery. Formal introductions are seldom long in coming and, as the potato-chip TV commercial attests, one inevitably leads to another. Fast friendships have been known to materialize out of common interests far less intense than those shared by gun dog owners.

From such friendships often spring valuable exchanges of ideas and information. Hints for dog training: tips on how, when, and where; equipment that worked well, and some that didn't—all these are discussed among friends at field trials.

Some gun dog owners eschew field trials solely on the basis that they prefer hunting to running their dogs in competition. Certainly, no one who enjoys shooting game would argue the point. But you can only hunt for a relatively short portion of the year, whereas one of the significant advantages of field trials is that they are conducted virtually the year-round.

In other words, they not only don't have to interfere with regular hunting activities, but can actually serve to extend your gun dog's field work far beyond the limits of the public or preserve hunting seasons. It is not uncommon, in fact, for smart gunners to rely heavily on field trials to sharpen up their dogs in the month or so preceding the open season each year. And just as many take advantage of trials to keep their dogs in shape long after the gunning season is just a happy memory.

Of course, there will always be some people to whom field trialing—in any form—will never appeal. By nature, some folks simply are not built to feel at ease in, or enjoy, any sort of group activity. For most, though, field trials have much to offer. Whether your motives are to satisfy the compelling urge to compete; the means of providing more work for your dog off-season; or merely enjoyment of additional outdoor recreation, trials can fill the bill.

And any single outdoor sport that's completely compatible with such widely divergent interests is certainly worth investigating.

15

Seasons Relived

KEEPING A FIELD-DOG DIARY

LOOKING BACK at the hunting season just past always brings happy memories. Recollection can miraculously retrieve the irretrievable—like the unmistakably birdy aroma of a damp alder patch and the abrupt muting of a gently tinkling bell whose very silence sounds an urgent call to action. A shotgun's roar—the smell of gunpowder—wispy brown feathers drifting earthward. Good days. Days brimming with excitement, with action. These are the kind all gunners remember best.

Human nature prevailing, the rosy-hued remembrances always eclipse the less successful, the uneventful experiences, the slow days, easy shots missed, bumped birds, sudden downpours, cripples unretrieved, dogs lost hour upon interminable hour. Yet these moments, too, rightfully belong to the season, the whole season. They provide the balance that gives the highlights special meaning.

Some hunters, blessed with almost total recall, need nothing more to summon up the joyous—and sometimes not so joyous—occasions of seasons past. Others, less fortunate, rely on a written record of each gunning trip's happenings in a hunting log, or diary, to sum up and help remember each season's delights.

But, oddly, few hunters carry the diary idea the one extra step that adds an entirely distinct dimension to it and creates an invaluable

Action-filled days afield with your dog can be lived only once, but they can be recalled countless times. A field-dog diary will help to vivify and preserve those recollections.

reference of practical information. Of course, as this chapter's title suggests, we're talking about keeping a field-dog diary. Aimed primarily at the canine aspects of each hunt, it can serve a number of useful functions besides entertaining and nostalgic post-season reading.

If well organized and kept up, a field-dog diary can document and reveal a great deal of pertinent information about a gun dog's progress afield. Especially valuable in tracking a young dog's headway, it should set forth a concise description of his overall performance on each trip, detailing his superior work along with his inconsistencies and his errors, both accidental and deliberate.

By periodically reviewing recent entries, you'll find that patterns of problem behavior will become evident while still in the formative stages, enabling you to plan corrective action for future trips or training exercises. The entry of various salient facts can make it easy to recognize certain conditions and circumstances, or combinations thereof, that contribute to good or poor field work by your dog.

Certain factors that produce odd or inconsistent behavior in the game hunted also may exert a negative influence on your dog's natural abilities and performance. Without benefit of a well-kept field-dog diary, the significance or even the existence of such possibly critical factors might well elude a majority of gun-dog owners.

Peripheral advantages of keeping a field-dog diary include the recording of good game covers and an accurate tally of game bagged in them. Not surprisingly, covers that produce well for several successive years often begin to peter out almost without our noticing. Unless we know for sure that they're giving out on us, we tend to sentimentalize, I suppose, and continue returning to them season after season, wasting valuable hunting time for little or no reward.

How a field-dog diary is organized, and what goes into it, is critical in making it a valuable tool. Borrowing a bit of computerese, "Garbage in—garbage out" is equally applicable to a field-dog diary. And while "programming" might be considered as carrying the analogy a bit too far, a good field-dog diary certainly should be well planned.

The inclusion of certain basic information for each entry is essential in order to establish the sort of fundamental statistics needed for season-long analysis. Along with the day and date, the time that the hunt began and ended should be noted. The temperature range, barometric pressure, and type of weather experienced—sunny, cloudy, showery, snowy, windy, calm, etc.—are significant factors that should not be overlooked.

Recorded in the summary information at the top of each entry should be a notation on the areas hunted, with specific names and/or locations of covers so they can be pinpointed for future reference. The game, by species and number, started and bagged also should be entered. In addition, a one- or two-word evaluation of your dog's overall performance—such as "excellent," "good," "mediocre," "erratic," or "poor"—should be included. Generally, it's a nice touch to list the names of any companions who hunted with you, too.

All of the foregoing is designed to provide you with each trip's pertinent data at a glance. Next, what is needed is a more detailed account of the hunt, with particular emphasis on how your dog worked in the field. In writing down your impressions, consider such things as: Did he bump any birds and, if so, how many? As far as you could tell, were they deliberate or accidental flushes? Was his nose up to par? Did he seem to have trouble accurately locating his birds? What kind of scenting conditions prevailed? Was he handling kindly, or was

"Scenting conditions were near perfect this morning," your field-dog diary might record, "and Flash retrieved every bird like a veteran although he just turned two years old." Those are the types of diary entries that are a pleasure to read long after the season.

he just a bit "deaf" to your directions? (Obviously, while these considerations apply to pointing dogs, corresponding information would be entered for whatever type of gun dog you own.)

A few astute observations about how the game acted will prove worth recording. If grouse seemed extra spooky, for example, then perhaps your pointing dog should be exonerated for some of the flushes you may have perceived as being deliberate. On the other hand, you may have found that the birds held tighter than normal and made your dog look spectacular in the morning, but terrible later in the day when they suddenly turned hawky.

Instances of strange behavior by game over the course of an entire season—or even several seasons—may well be explained by virtue of a series of consistently similar circumstances noted in your field-dog diary. For that reason, any odd or unusual occurrences definitely should be included in your entry for each trip, since they may have some later-realized significance in analyzing variances in your dog's performance.

Naturally, you can make your chronicle as intricately detailed as you want, or as brief as seems feasible to provide the sort of basic, practical reference that makes keeping the diary worthwhile. But I would caution against over-ambition initially, in trying to make it so extensive that you risk losing interest in keeping it up-to-date because it becomes too much of a chore.

Any kind of journal, of course, can be improved substantially with the addition of some visual aids. So, you should seriously consider dressing up your field-dog diary with a few good color or black-and-white snapshots. (Remember our advice in Chapter 12 about taking the time to capture your gun dog at work on film.)

Action shots make superb additions, but don't neglect those moments when your dog and you and your gunning companions stop for a five-minute rest. Or those tailgate lunch breaks when your dog gets every third bite of everyone's sandwiches. Mood and candid shots add a lot of interest and appeal to a field-dog diary, as does the occasional inclusion of a grouse, woodcock, or pheasant feather for decoration.

Just how practical and easy it is to keep a field-dog diary is determined to a great extent by its physical configuration, type, and size. A common school kid's composition book can be made to serve the purpose, and its size is adaptable to the photos and decorative additions just mentioned. Those fancy leather-bound "Personal Di-

An ideal field-dog diary should accommodate photoprints as large as 5x7 inches. The diary can be not only a log but an album in which to preserve pictures like this one of a hunting companion, a favorite springer, and a trio of cock pheasants.

ary" books, generally a little bigger than 5 × 7 inches, are a bit too scanty—unless you write very small—and even a wallet-size snapshot would use up almost a whole page of space.

Our nomination for the ideal field-dog diary has to go to a looseleaf folder that accommodates typewriter-size (8½ × 11-inch) paper. Fancy, in leather or simulated leather, or plain, in heavy cardboard, whichever way your preference runs, such a looseleaf binder offers several functional advantages. Not only is it possible to add pages as needed, but they can also be typed, thus contributing to legibility, neat, attractive appearance, and more efficient use of space.

If you don't type, this size and type of binder affords ample room for handwritten entries, as well as photos as large as 5 × 7 inches. And, should you really want to get spiffy about it, you can have your neighborhood printing shop run off a ream of 8½ × 11-inch inserts you design yourself. These, of course, would include pre-printed summary data, such as day, date, temperature, etc., with spaces for you to type or write in the information.

Whatever size and style and detail your first field-dog diary encompasses, one thing is fairly sure: it will prove valuable to you, even after just a single season. And in years to come, it will provide a treasure well worth your efforts in happy memories vividly preserved.

Part V

Your Dog at Home

16

A Formula for Multiplication

AN OBJECTIVE LOOK AT CROSS-BREEDING

IF ANYTHING CAN stir the hunting dog owner's imagination, it's the prospect of cross-mating his dog with some other hunting breed. Spurred by the desire to produce a better field dog for his own use, the more a sportsman contemplates the idea, the more intriguing becomes the notion that he may end up creating an entirely new and, perhaps, sensational shooting dog breed.

Our mail, as gun dog editor of a national magazine, periodically brought us letters from readers seeking confirmation of the feasibility of cross-breeding. Occasionally pretty far out, a majority of these inquiries reflected the serious consideration the writers had given to their projected combinations.

Typical of such mail was one gentleman's conviction that crossing his springer spaniel, Flush, with Lottie, an English pointer, was sure to produce pups better than any of the other local quail and pheasant dogs. Flush, it seemed, at age three was a "natural" on ring-necks, while five-year-old Lottie could always find a covey of bob-whites, no matter how scarce pickings were. Surely, crossing these two, and combining the best qualities of both, would result in cracker-jack gun dogs that would point quail and flush pheasants and make all the other dogs look like amateurs by comparison. The gentleman went on to wonder if anyone had ever tried the springer-pointer cross to obtain pups with both flushing and pointing instincts.

Although the letter writer's idea seemed perfectly sound, he — as did all those with similar cross-breeding inquiries — received our standard advice: Forget it.

Why? Well, the most significant reasons can be grasped merely by taking a look at cross-breeding in the past and examining not only its results, but its goals and methodology.

Undeniably, our modern hunting breeds are the products of cross-breeding, but it's equally true that very few of the crosses involved immediately produced all the desired results, much less the distinct breeds as we know them today. Nor can the fact be overlooked that in only a couple of isolated instances was the development of any of the modern gun dog breeds accomplished by a man of modest means, working alone and with limited facilities and breeding stock. To the contrary, tracing the known history of today's hunting breeds reveals that they were originated chiefly through the efforts of men of sub-stantial wealth, who owned extensive kennels and had nothing but time on their hands.

In the expansive kennel facilities maintained by the well-to-do

Although most of today's hunting breeds like this German shorthair pointer are the result of cross-breeding, none was perfected without long and painstaking further selective breeding programs.

European sporting gentry, each experimental breed cross was usually initiated not with just one pair of dogs, but with several. Moreover, crosses with many different breeds could be achieved simultaneously, with the progeny discarded or retained and bred again, depending on whether the pups displayed the physical characteristics and hunting traits desired.

When an eminently good cross was effected—and the failures outnumbered the successes by a wide margin—it usually required years of careful selective breeding to weld the resultant desirable qualities into a fixed pattern that would faithfully transmit itself to each succeeding generation. And even after years of apparently "breeding true," such crosses were not always immune to throwing an occasional odd mutation. Some of these, of course, being recognized as assets, were seized upon and, through additional selective breeding, incorporated into successive generations. The basset hound's crooked forelegs and the Brittany spaniel's taillessness provide two of the most graphic examples of fortunate mutations.

As obviously important as were money, time, and suitable kennel facilities, they were only part of the overall considerations contributing to the successful cross-breeding programs of early-day breeders. Cross-mating strictly on a whim or a wild idea, just to see what would happen, was seldom practiced. Instead, most trial crosses invariably were backed by a good deal of thoughtful planning, a liberal sprinkling of common sense, and a well-formulated goal.

That goal may have been to put more "nose," or scenting ability, into an otherwise satisfactory hunting breed. Such was the aim of the Germans when they crossed the St. Hubert hound into the old Spanish pointer to produce the German pointer. Later, when the keennosed German pointer was found to be too cumbersome, an infusion of English pointer blood served to achieve the two-fold objective of producing a somewhat smaller, moderately faster breed we now know as the German shorthaired pointer.

Another example of cross-breeding for a definite effect can be cited in the golden retriever. Though the forebears of the golden were highly regarded during their first decade in England, it was the consensus of many sportsmen that the breed might be improved by a reduction in size. Outcrossing to the bloodhound, and subsequent selective breeding, not only afforded the desired size reduction, but at the same time produced a sharper nose and finer, darker coat in the breed.

The history of the development of our modern gun dogs is replete

The springer spaniel, a flushing dog that specializes on ringneck pheasant, would lose his biggest advantage—the ability to push running birds into the air —if he were changed into a pointing dog by cross-breeding.

A natural impulse to freeze immobile on point at the scent of birds characterizes the English pointer. Combining this with the opposite instinct to flush would serve no useful purpose and probably produce neurotic pups, torn between both instincts.

with such examples of purposeful cross-breeding. But the main point each of the notably successful crosses illustrates is the importance of planning with a clear-cut set of realistic objectives in mind, and executed with a well-educated guess as to what type of breed to cross in, in order to produce the desired results. Selective breeding, coupled with the all-important influence of time, ultimately makes the big difference in refining and standardizing the results.

With so many varieties of pure-bred gun dogs available today as a result of the painstaking cross-breeding experiments of yesteryear, casual crossbreeding has, in our opinion, little to recommend it to the average hunting dog fancier today. Especially since the amateur so often becomes victim to his own enthusiasm and winds up trying senseless cross combinations which succeed only in increasing the world's population of lovable but otherwise useless mongrels.

As a perfect case in point, let's hark back to that earlier mentioned example — crossing Flush the springer, with Lottie the English pointer. What such pups might look like, I can't say from experience. Yet, for at least one even more important reason, mating these two breeds would be inadvisable. The springer spaniel flushes his birds in front of the gun, while the English pointer freezes into immobility when birds are located.

Just imagine a puppy combining, on one hand, the instinct to rush in boldly and push up his bird and, on the other, the natural inclination to freeze in his tracks at the first strong scent of birds. If the pup were a perfect fifty-fifty blend of both parents — which does not necessarily happen in cross-breeding — then two of his most rudimentary instincts would be constantly at odds with one another. He would not, as our correspondent believed, alternately point quail and flush pheasants.

Suppose, however, that one instinct, say pointing, were a trifle stronger in such a pup, than the desire to flush. At best, then, the pup's natural pointing inclination would still be weaker than that of the English pointer half of his parentage, and since he could not be used very satisfactorily as a flush dog either, he'd be far less practical, reliable, or effective in the field than either of his parents. Hence, if no improvement results, what could possibly be gained by crossing a springer and a pointer?

Though our advice to the average gun dog fancier is to eschew cross-breeding and stick to the proven pure-breds, this is not to say that all cross-bred hunting dogs are necessarily valueless, or that thoughtful cross-breeding has no further place in today's gun dog world. Indeed, perhaps one of the most notable recent examples of meritorious cross-breeding can be found in the work of W. E. (Ned) LeGrande and the Red Setter Club of America, with the fast-fading field type Irish setter.

In a valiant attempt to salvage that breed's once proud field heritage, drastically dissipated by years of breeding for bench quality alone, in 1951 LeGrande crossed one of his best field-bred Irish setters, Willow Winds Smada, with the noted English setter field trial winner, Illsley Chip, in order to rejuvenate the Irish's waning hunting instincts. By selecting the best pups from this litter and breeding them and their progeny back to full-blooded Irish setters from field stock for four generations, LeGrande's dogs were again eligible to be registered as pure-bred Irish setters.

The success of the venture speaks for itself in the increasing number of field trial laurels the LeGrande setters and their progeny have accumulated over the ensuing years.

Another frequently seen cross-breed that generally acquits himself in the field about as well as either parent is the "dropper," a pointer-setter cross. Quite common in the south, the "dropper" just as often as not is the result of accidental rather than planned cross-breeding. He is unusual in that, to a striking degree, he may resemble either his pointer or setter parent, but seldom, if ever, is an obvious combination of both. Therefore, in the average litter of droppers one is likely to see several pups that look like pointers, several that could easily pass for setters.

Since both parents are pointing breeds, with similar hunting styles, dropper pups suffer no conflict of instincts, and ordinarily, with proper training, can be expected to mature into good, or at least serviceable, bird dogs.

Again, though, it must be observed that, except for accidental mating or unusual difficulty in locating a suitable mate of the same breed, deliberately crossing your pointer with a setter, or vice versa, has no special merit to recommend it. By and large, the sportsman who intends to breed hunting dogs can render a far worthier contribution to the gun dog fraternity, and derive infinitely greater benefits and personal satisfaction from it, by taking up the challenge of producing better pure-breds.

PLANNED PARENTHOOD

Sooner or later there comes a time, providing nature's processes haven't been thwarted by spaying, when every hunter wants a litter of pups from a good hunting bitch. Perhaps she may be the best shooting dog he's ever owned and he simply wants to make sure he has one of her pups to carry on after she's gone. Or, possibly his gunning partners have urged him to breed her so that they might have some of her pups to shoot over in the future.

Whatever the motivation, when the idea takes hold, there is no use fighting it; the thought of having a litter of pups out of one's very own bitch is a contagion cured only by fulfillment.

If the decision to breed the bitch on her next heat has been prompted primarily by the proximity of a male owned by Joe Doakes, the results may fall short of what they could be. For, unless Doakes' dog measures up to at least a few important criteria of sound breeding, not only will the bitch be cheated of her opportunity to reproduce her full potential, but, likewise, the breeder will be shortchanged in the quality of the puppies he seeks to obtain.

Breeding is not an exact science. At best, it is always something of a gamble. However, there are certain tried and relatively proven principles that, if followed with reasonable care, can usually eliminate some of the most common risks. In choosing a proper mate, it's important to secure a dog with as few faults as possible.

Since no dog is perfect, the main thing to be sure of is that the male doesn't have the same faults as the bitch to which he'll be bred. To do this, it is necessary, first, to admit that your bitch has her faults, and second, to be able to recognize them.

The faults most easily perceived are the major physical ones, defects that might include improper size, bad conformation (sway-, hump-, or roachback), poor feet, straight shoulders, legs too short or too long, and any other points that differ sharply from the accepted standard of the breed in question.

Breeding two dogs with similar structural defects greatly intensifies these bad points. Thus, if your bitch is slightly swaybacked and the dog you use to breed to her is similarly built, their puppies will exhibit the fault in increased measure. Nor, is it possible—however logical it might seem—to counteract such a fault in your bitch by breeding her to a sire with the same fault exaggerated in the other

The potential sire should be chosen on the basis of sound physical structure, good temperament, intelligence, and natural field talents. This Weimaraner displays fine physique and plenty of pointing instinct.

extreme. In other words, you cannot eliminate the swayback defect by breeding to a humpbacked sire.

Although the major physical characteristics are important considerations in choosing a sire, others, far less discernible to the unpracticed eye, are also significant. Good temperament and intelligence are qualities vital to the total makeup and potentialities of every hunting dog. Each complements the other and plays an important role in fitting the dog for his ultimate work in the field.

For example, temperament — the dog's natural manner of reacting to everything about him — determines his ability to take training in stride. The temperament of the bold, independent dog qualifies him as a far more suitable candidate than the timid prospect. And the intelligent dog learns much faster and with greater ease than does his less bright brother.

Added to the considerations of temperament and intelligence of the potential stud dog are the talents he displays for his particular function in the field. Is he blessed with a good nose? Does he work with enthusiasm, always eager and intense, showing spirit and style, yet handling kindly for the gun? Will he point, if he's supposed to? Retrieve, if that's required? Give tongue, or remain silent, if that's his job? Each of the necessary natural traits that enable him to do the job for which he was bred will be passed on to some degree to the pups he sires. Therefore, the closer he is to being ideal in each respect, the better the chances that such desirable qualities will be strongly transmitted to his offspring.

What about pedigree, the certified tracing of his family tree? Will it really matter much in affecting the quality of the pups he produces? All other things being equal, that is, proper attention having been paid to the selection of a stud of sound physique, temperament, and intelligence, a dog's pedigree, or bloodlines, can exert considerable influence on the caliber of the puppies produced (see Chapter 1, "Plain or Fancy").

Whether or not your bitch's bloodlines include any champions or notable field trial performers within three or four generations, if her own talents in the field satisfy you, then she probably is worth mating. Any bitch worth breeding at all is worth breeding to the best sire obtainable.

Why? Dogs, like most domestic animals, invariably breed downward, that is, without the practice of judicious selectivity, succeeding generations tend to deteriorate in quality. However, use of the proven performer and producer affords the selectivity necessary to maintain, or even improve, quality.

You may not be at all interested in breeding to obtain field trial

The more closely related the sire and dam, the greater the probability of the pups' uniformity to their parents. Note the similarity of these two wirehaired pointing griffons — the son is pointing while the sire backs. **Photo by WPG Club of America.**

prospects, but the sire with a respectable trial record offers concrete proof that he has enough of what it takes to meet the high standards imposed by stiff competition. Since, as a rule, these standards call for the display of qualities in excess of those ordinarily demanded in the average gun dog, field-trial-stud sired puppies are generally more than sufficiently endowed with the right ingredients to make the grade in the field.

Aside from indicating performance value, a dog's pedigree provides a key to the matching of bloodlines. By comparing your bitch's lineage with that of a prospective stud, it is possible to duplicate bloodlines more closely. Generally, the more closely related are the stud and your bitch, the greater the probability that their pups will be more uniformly similar to their parents.

When to breed your bitch depends, of course, on her heat cycle and your plans and facilities for raising the litter. Most bitches come in season, or heat, twice a year, at six-month intervals. If yours was last in heat, say, in September, she would normally be due again in March. With the gestation period of sixty-three days, a bitch bred in mid-March would whelp (give birth) in mid-May.

Next in importance to lining up well in advance the best sire obtainable is the matter of having a clear arrangement—preferably in writing—about the stud fee. Sometimes a cash stud fee, payable at time of service, is requested by the sire's owner. Usually a return service proviso, if the bitch fails to whelp, is included in the contract.

Often the stud fee will consist of a puppy proposition, the most common arrangement calling for the stud dog owner to receive first choice pup of the litter. However, since any number of variations are possible in arranging the stud fee, it is always advisable that the terms be spelled out in a written agreement.

It would be grossly unfair—and we've seen it happen—for the bitch's owner to agree verbally to a puppy proposition, only to change his mind after the whelping and expect the stud dog owner to accept a cash settlement...something like betting on the winner after the race is over.

Once your bitch has been successfully bred, be sure to continue to keep her isolated from all other males for the remainder of her heat. The normal heat period lasts twenty-one days. She can be bathed, checked for worms, and wormed if necessary shortly after her season ends. Her regular diet will suffice for the first three weeks after breeding, but should gradually be increased and supplemented with vita-

Make certain the stud fee arrangement is spelled out in writing before your pups are whelped. Trying to switch from a puppy proposition to a cash fee at the last minute—even if the litter is small—just isn't cricket. **Photo by Evelyn M. Shafer.**

mins and calcium gluconate during the last three to four weeks before whelping. It will pay to have her examined by a veterinarian at least once during her pregnancy.

Reading our next subject, which deals with care of the bitch during pregnancy and preparations for whelping, will stand the prospective "grandfather" in good stead while he's waiting for the blessed event. Finally, when that long-awaited moment arrives, and those six or eight little squealers are lined up at their feeding stations, who could blame you for wanting to bust your vest with pride? Both you and that good hunting bitch of yours will have established a new and even closer bond of affection through her new brood.

BEFORE AND AFTER THE BLESSED EVENT

The air reeks of stale tobacco smoke. In the ashtray a mound of twisted butts bears mute testimony to the agonizing vigil. Earlier charged with nervous anticipation, the atmosphere now exudes only numbness. The gaunt and haggard figure, pacing the floor no longer, responds dazedly to the appearance of the white-garbed figure and the words: "Congratulations...it's a boy."

Everyone's familiar with the cliché of the expectant father, a poor wretch who suffers painfully through the blessed event and winds up more in need of medical comfort than the female of the species who just gave birth.

Although awaiting arrival of a litter of pups can occasionally provide some anxious moments, if everything has been properly prepared, no such harrowing vigil need attend the average canine blessed event. Proper care and feeding of your bitch during her pregnancy are important to her well-being. During the first three to four weeks after breeding, she will usually continue eating no more than her usual amount and won't require any change in diet. But her appetite will increase progressively from that point on, and she should receive larger portions and more protein daily. Often, if her appetite seems to exceed even the extra amounts of food given her at regular feeding time, a second meal may be called for earlier or later in the day.

In addition to having a vitamin-mineral supplement added to her diet, she should also receive calcium phosphorus or calcium gluconate, which in powdered form can be sprinkled on her food or mixed with milk. Tablets also are available should she stick up her nose at chow that's been doctored with powder.

Throughout the pre-natal period your bitch should be exercised regularly. You don't have to baby her in the early stages, but during the last three weeks before whelping, as she becomes obviously heavier with pups, her exercise should be frequent, but mild, with no jumping or hard running permitted.

Sometime before the expected arrival of the pups – and the normal gestation period is sixty-three days – a few other important details must be arranged. The first of these involves construction of a whelping box, a contraption infinitely simpler to build than to describe.

Basically, a whelping box is nothing more than a wooden container with floor, sides, and no top. Its dimensions will depend on the size of the breed for which it's designed. Generally, it need not be much bigger than the regular box or dog bed in which the bitch can sleep comfortably. The sides should be low enough to permit the future mother to negotiate them without difficulty, yet high enough to keep puppies penned in for a couple of weeks.

Along the box's interior sides, about four to five inches above floor level, a guard rail should be mounted. The object of the railing is to prevent a puppy who gets between Mom and the side of the box from inadvertently being crushed or smothered. One-by-four planking serves the purpose very well.

A few layers of newspaper, placed on the bottom of the box, provide suitable bedding as well as insulation against a chilly floor. Next, a warm, draft-free spot, away from most family traffic and undue disturbances, should be chosen for placement of the whelping box. The expectant mother can be made to feel a lot more secure in her new maternity ward if she is encouraged to sleep in it for a week prior to actual whelping.

When arrival day nears, the bitch will show obvious signs: loss of appetite, a general restlessness and an inclination to tear up the papers in her whelping box. She should not be permitted to go outdoors unattended, lest she decide to wander off to find a whelping spot of her own selection.

About an hour after going into labor, the normal bitch will deliver her first pup. The remainder of the litter should arrive — one at a time, of course — at fairly regular intervals. If the owner is in attendance and observes what appears to be very obvious straining, or undue delays, he would be wise to telephone for veterinarian assistance at once.

Not infrequently, an owner will tire of waiting for something to happen, go off to bed, and arise the next morning to discover his bitch blissfully nursing a full litter that arrived without fanfare during the night. When it happens this way, it truly can be called the most blessed of events.

As each delivery is completed, the bitch will begin licking the pup to cleanse and simultaneously stimulate it into activity. It's imperative that the puppies begin suckling as soon as possible, for from the colostrum obtained in the first-day milk they receive temporary passive immunity to distemper and other diseases.

In extra-large litters, where pups outnumber "faucets," the owner must do a bit of traffic-directing to make certain that every pup gets his share of nursing. The easiest way to avoid confusion is to place the "haves" in a separate box for a few minutes, while the "have-nots" take their turn at the fountain.

The single most important factor in successfully raising a litter is to keep the pups warm and well protected from drafts. A constant temperature level of 72 to 75 degrees is ideal, and many breeders utilize an infra-red lamp, suspended at the proper height above the whelping box, to maintain it.

Aside from feeding the bitch — extra meat and plenty of fresh milk will be called for — and letting her out regularly to relieve her customary needs, there is little else the owner need do during the first couple

A six-week-old setter pup tugs at his mother's tail. Just about fully weaned by this age, pups can shortly be separated from the bitch.

of weeks. The puppies' eyes will remain closed for nine to fourteen days, and they will do little except nurse, relieve themselves, and sleep during that time. Their ears will begin opening a few days after they can see.

As the pups enter their fourth week, the weaning process can begin. By then, normally healthy pups are very active and growing at an amazing rate. Even the best of brood bitches will commence showing considerably less enthusiasm for nursing pups after the first month. It is then that the pups should be taught to lap warm milk, gradually thickened with Pablum or cereal and, eventually, with commercial dry meal and finely ground cooked meat.

Most puppies, if properly started, can be fully weaned by the age of six or seven weeks. They can, and should, be separated from their mother when they have reached this stage. They will then have to be fed three or four times daily, cleaned up after, and played with several times each day. Patience will begin getting thin; it is time to place the care of each of these lively guys and gals in other hands—each, that is, except for that one particular puppy from which you just can't stand to be parted.

If you have consulted your vet—and you certainly should have—he will have wormed the litter and given each pup a temporary distemper shot by the time they are ready to leave home. Now your only task is to place each puppy in the hands of people who will love, appreciate, and care for them as ardently as you have done.

You'll be surprised at how carefully each would-be owner who comes to inspect your pups will be scrutinized. It cannot be any other way. The intensely personal concern for the welfare of these little "kids" that you have solicitously nurtured from birth comes surprisingly close to parental love. If you think that's just sentimental hog-wash, just wait and see for yourself!

Finding suitable homes for your litter can offer some difficulty. Assuming you bred your bitch at the instigation of several of your hunting buddies, placement of the pups should be easy. Otherwise, you will be faced with giving the pups away or trying to sell them. In either event, you will probably have to do some advertising. The classified ad columns of the outdoor magazines provide one good medium. Your local newspapers offer another. Area sporting goods dealers, too, are generally willing to pass the word along to their customers that a litter of good hunting breed pups is available.

Nor should you overlook pet shops. Often the larger ones are willing to serve as brokers in the sale of several pups. Some, in fact, may offer to buy entire litters—if the price is right—for eventual re-sale.

A pair of seven-week-olds rushes to the feed pail as Ma looks on, resignedly waiting her turn. Between now and their tenth week is the best time to sell pups.

With all the rest of the litter sold, these two setter pups, at eleven weeks, are the ones the owner can't seem to choose between.

In the latter instance, of course, the pet shop assumes all the gamble of being able to sell the pups, so their purchase price from the breeder is apt to be fairly low.

Most amateur breeders, however, are not seeking a profit from a litter of pups. They are primarily interested in securing a good pup for themselves out of their favorite shooting dog. If they can improve their chosen breed a bit and succeed in producing a few puppies of the type that can provide some other hunter the joys of shooting over a first-rate gun dog, then their efforts will have been in keeping with the finest traditions of the true hunting dog enthusiast.

Who can deny that the inner satisfaction of having produced a litter of puppies as good as — or maybe better than — what you began with is the breeder's real reward from any blessed event?

17

Additional Food for Thought

CANINE MYTH-QUOTES

IN AN AGE of mass communications media, all of them striving to dispense up-to-the-second information on everything from world news to aboriginal cookery, you'd think superstitions would be unable to survive.

But many myths persist, and several of them are concerned with man's best friend, the dog. It's ironic that man's very first domesticated animal—and the one that to this day shares the closest kinship with him—should still be the source of so many grievous misconceptions. True, some of these old wives' tales are believed by fewer persons each year than was once the case. That they should find credence with any dog owners, however, demonstrates the continuing need to debunk such fiction with fact.

Probably the dubious distinction of leading the parade of canine noxious notions falls to the one that states: mis-mating a purebred bitch to a mongrel ruins her for further breeding; all her future litters, no matter how pure their sire, will bear the mark and influence of the mongrel stud. Where and when this fallacy began is not known. Possibly, it originated as a result of the fact that a bitch can conceive by two different dogs, if the successive matings occur during a single ovulation period. Consequently, a purebred bitch who got involved with a mongrel suitor just before, or right after, breeding to a purebred male, could whelp two types of pups in a single litter. Naturally, this would give rise to her owner's conviction that her previous litter of mongrels had, indeed, left their mark upon her for life.

Nonetheless, whatever its origin, telegony (the book name for the influence of one stud upon the progeny of future mates to the same bitch), has been scientifically proven to be absolutely without basis.

An equally prevalent fallacy holds that "pre-natal influences are significant in determining a pup's inherited characteristics or behavior." From this belief stem a number of erroneous notions, including the old chestnut: "If a pregnant bitch is hunted as often as possible — right up to the last minute before whelping — her pups will be imbued with an extra share of hunting desire and ability."

This has about as much factual foundation as the idea that "A bitch startled by a loud noise will whelp gun-shy pups."

A ten-week-old Brittany spaniel pup shows inherited soft mouth in retrieving live bobwhite quail without ruffling a feather. But only the genes passed on by his parents, not their cumulative field experience, can be credited for his precociousness. **Photo by American Brittany Club, Inc.**

The science of genetics has shown that genes alone determine inheritance. Like tiny computers, these genes have been programmed with all the necessary information to "construct" the new offspring. Aside from disease or accidental injury (non-hereditary factors), nothing can alter the pattern that the genes' memory banks have begun building at the instant egg and sperm unite.

The unborn pups, therefore, are merely nourished, but otherwise not further influenced, by their mother during the gestation period. The parents' total contribution to the pups' inherited makeup is fully decided from the moment conception occurs. Whether she is periodically glad or sad, frightened or pampered, hunted or not hunted will, of itself, exert no further bearing on her unborn pups.

Along the same general line, some persons believe that a better trained and more experienced gun dog will, in later years, tend to produce more naturally gifted puppies. Training and field experience, of course, are acquired, not inborn, traits and cannot possibly be transmitted from one generation to the next. If acquired talents were transmissible, man would long ago have been able to breed pups that required no training at all. Such puppies, having inherited all the cumulative skills and learning acquired by their forebears, would by now be pretty fantastic gun dogs, easily worth their weight in uranium — or perhaps only a dime a dozen, since they would be so commonplace.

One of the older superstitions now pretty well laid to rest by time and common sense found the faithful hunter sprinkling a pinch of gun powder over the rations of all newly acquired pups, to prevent gun-shyness. The same recipe was supposed to serve equally well as a curative.

Since only a small amount of black powder was ever used, the practice seldom did any serious or long-lasting harm to the dog. It may have had some value as psychological fodder for the owner's peace of mind. It did not, of course, cure or prevent gun-shyness in the dog, any more than it would have cured flinching had the owner eaten it.

Foolish as it may strike us, sprinkling gun powder on a dog's food is not so far removed from another practice still indulged by some dog owners, today. This notion has it: "Feeding your dog an occasional rabbit, pheasant, or whatever primary game you seek, will maintain his interest in, and even improve his performance on, that particular game." This procedure may well have been Indian in origin, coming from the old Shoshone superstition of eating the flesh of a fox to gain cunning, that of a bear for strength, that of a wolf for courage. That

Permitting a young dog to chase, catch, and maul a bird or two can hypo his eagerness to hunt. However, regularly feeding him the game you seek will have no bearing on his ability to hunt.

it is still employed is testimony enough that some hunters remain awfully gullible, if not downright superstitious.

Permitting a young bird dog to catch, kill, and maul or even partially devour a grouse, quail, or pheasant can sometimes hypo his eagerness to hunt. Under certain circumstances, especially where a youngster is a bit bird- or gun-shy, encouraging the act of chase, capture, and mouthing will prove inspiring to a reticent pup.

But this is a far cry from simply feeding occasional game to a dog throughout his lifetime in hopes of improving his abilities as a hunter of that specific game. One might wonder, does the pheasant-eating nightclub habitué become an accomplished pheasant hunter for all the birds served to him under glass?

On the subject of eating, man has really concocted some doozies about how his best friend is affected by various foods. One of the most commonly accepted of these fantasies declares: "Dogs can get worms from eating certain foods." The offensive items cited depend mostly upon the "expert" dispensing the advice, but they range widely, taking in most anything from meat and milk to potatoes and parsnips.

With the exception of uncooked pork from a hog infected by trichinosis, no fresh, pure food can of itself cause a dog to get worms. In order for that to occur, the food would first have to come in contact with a worm-egg-infested kennel run or be soiled by a dog so infected.

"Show me a vicious dog and I'll show you a dog that's always been fed raw meat," is another food-inspired fallacy still in general circulation. Fed a balanced, nutritionally sound diet, a dog can be given any amount of supplementary meat—raw or otherwise—with absolutely no effect to his natural temperament.

The list of superstitions, fantasies, and strange notions of which our canine population is victim could be expounded almost ad infinitum. "Mutts are much smarter than purebreds…Mongrels always outlive bluebloods…You can tell a purebred by the color of the inside of his mouth." These and countless other pernicious pearls swell the already overloaded roster. But we trust the point has been made clear.

Most myths become recognizable for what they are when a little common sense is applied to them. Next time someone volunteers as gospel a gem of canine counsel that has a vaguely hollow ring, think it over. Check it out in a reliable, up-to-date manual, then re-check with a knowledgeable dog man, such as your vet.

Many of the old wives' tales you hear are harmless, but some are not—and it is the latter that, if taken seriously, just might adversely affect the care and training you give your gun dog.

CAN DOGS THINK?

Can dogs think? Do they actually have any reasoning power at all? Most scientists ridicule any such idea, pointing out the fact that the cerebrum—the portion of the brain that in humans does the thinking—is grossly underdeveloped in the canine. Everything the dog does, they contend, he does without thinking. He only reacts to various stimuli and conditioned reflexes and instinct; he does not reason, simply because he is, they tell us, incapable of reasoning.

Dog owners, on the other hand, are not quite as sure about this as the scientists. True they lack the same degree of clinical detachment, but they do not lack for incidents that seem to call the scientists' findings into question.

Anybody who has hunted with dogs for any length of time has surely witnessed at least a few occasions, and heard of many more, in which a dog's behavior gave cause to wonder about a canine's ability to "think."

How, for example, does one explain the incident of the veteran pointing dog who, in field trial competition, remains rock steady to wing and shot, but consistently breaks to retrieve in the hunting field?

The dog in question, the late Plantation Danny Boy, a setter owned by the writer, acquired a total of more than twenty-two recognized wins in field trial shooting dog stakes. In such competition a dog must, among other things, demonstrate that he's completely steady to wing and shot, which means simply that he must not move at the flush of the bird or the shot that follows, until ordered to do so.

Under judgment in trials, Danny was a statue on point. Take him hunting, though, and he'd break point at the first flutter of wings, fully expecting the bird to drop at the shot he knew was forthcoming.

By human standards of reasoning, his behavior was not at all illogical: In trials, he knew the birds weren't killed and couldn't be retrieved; he therefore remained steady. In short, it might be said that he recognized and played by the rules of competition. Of course, to him, they were not rules *per se,* but they were nonetheless part of a definite pattern to which he had been conditioned by long experience.

Flanked by gunners, the author's setter, Plantation Danny Boy, points covey of Hungarian partridge near Winchester, Ontario. Rock-steady under judgment in field trials, Danny consistently broke wing and shot when hunting.

Yet, how did he know when he was entered in a field trial rather than just out for a hunt? Doubtless, the analytical scientists could cite a number of "stimuli" to account for Danny's ability to differentiate. They might, for instance, point to the large gathering of cars, people, other dogs, plus the judges on horseback at a trial, all of which normally are absent during a regular hunt.

In truth, however, we often used to hunt Danny on a commercial shooting preserve, where all of these specific stimuli were present: clusters of cars, lots of people, other dogs, and sometimes even a horse or two. Under such nearly identical circumstances as might be found at a trial, Danny would blithely proceed to "go hunting" without so much as a single "thought" that he might be in competition.

How could he possibly perceive the difference, based solely on existing stimuli, instinct, or conditioned reflexes? To save the frustration of further wear and tear on the scientific mind, we might introduce what could be considered another significant clue: in field trials a .22 caliber blank revolver is used instead of the shotgun always carried on a hunt. Could it be that Danny, devoid of any powers of reasoning, learned to recognize the shotgun and isolate this one factor from all other stimuli, and thus differentiate between a field trial and a hunt? Indeed, if such were the case, wouldn't we have to credit him with some form of thinking ability that enabled him to sift through all the evidence, disregard the very similar aspects, and isolate the one different factor that held the answer?

There are many instances that would seem to counter the theory that dogs do not think. One we have never personally witnessed, but have no reason to doubt, is the claim by three different individuals of our acquaintance that their dogs would leave point, return to find their owners, and then lead them back to the place of the original point.

What would motivate a dog, once having found game, to leave it to search for his overdue owner and, finding him, literally lead him by the hand back to the spot where the game was waiting to be bagged? Could we call it instinct? Hardly. A conditioned reflex? Not likely.

The dog's act of finding and pointing the game is, of course, instinctive. Holding point indefinitely for the arrival of the gun is nothing but the result of training, a so-called conditioned reflex. But since, to our knowledge, it is impossible to train a dog to abandon game temporarily and deliberately return to it later with his master, such an act would clearly seem indicative of some sort of logical sequential thought.

Could it be that this beagle wants to go chasing rabbits and is trying to tell his boss to get going? You bet your boots he knows what he's trying to say. **Photo by Gaines Dog Research Center.**

Most duck hunters can quickly call to mind numerous examples whereby the actions of retrievers seem to belie the scientific consensus that canines are devoid of a thinking apparatus. From a blind situated on a spit of land where the river bent sharply, almost doubling back on itself, we have seen retrievers exhibit a mental agility that, if not attributable to logical reasoning, could only be termed the most remarkable kind of perception.

After a multiple fall to the front of the blind, seeing a dog race directly to the rear and plunge into the water on the other side is a rather startling occurrence. That is, until the realization suddenly dawns that the dog, having watched several ducks fall, has calmly figured out that the bend of the river and the speed and direction of current flow would necessitate pickup of one of the ducks beyond the river bend behind us.

Once again, in such a situation the scientist might specify conditioned reflex as the simplest explanation for the retriever's educated behavior. Retrievers, like any dogs, he could explain, learn by experience, and the subject dog or dogs undoubtedly were merely falling back on some previous experience to expedite the seemingly "thoughtful" maneuver. Perhaps this is the most accurate explanation; still, doesn't the ability to relate past experience to present situations constitute one of the most fundamental types of reasoning?

In the average dog owner's everyday routine there are probably as many as three or four instances that reflect his dog's ability to think. For example, the dog's deliberate and persistent rattling of an empty water dish that eventually results in the owner's refilling it with fresh water. Or the house dog's appearance at the boss's easy chair, leash in mouth and forepaw extended, that plainly says, "Come on, Boss, I gotta go."

Certainly, unless such acts have obviously or painstakingly been taught, they demonstrate a dog's power to reason that a particular action will produce a specific desired effect. Admittedly, pretty basic, it is nonetheless, by scientific definition, one of the first precepts of logic.

Recently, in talking to a friend at a field trial, the discussion turned to the subject of cures for dogs that were overly noisy in a kennel. "A good dousing with a garden hose," someone offered, "is the best cure for the problem."

Our friend agreed that water would usually dampen the spirit of even the most confirmed kennel barker. In fact, he told us, he had gone so far as to install a remote control shower in his kennel. All he had to do when one of his dogs began vocalizing was flick a switch that turned on the shower, dousing the offender and sending him scurrying for cover inside the doghouse.

"Worked fine with every dog but one," our friend said. "That one was a real oddball; he loved standing under that cool shower, especially in hot weather. I watched him a couple of times, to make sure I wasn't imagining things, and you know what that son of a gun learned to do? Whenever the heat was bothering him too much, he'd simply walk over, stand under the shower fixture, and begin barking his head off, knowing that I'd turn on the shower to shut him up. When he'd cooled off enough under the shower, he'd just stop barking and saunter over to the shady side of the run to take a nap."

Do dogs think? Well, by golly, if they don't, they certainly give a pretty good imitation of it...and give us a lot to think about in the process.

Two gun dogs are twice as effective, twice as practical, and at least four times as lovable as one. **Photo by Dave Petzal.**

WHY NOT TWO?

Few serious hunters have not, at one time or another, wistfully contemplated the advantages of owning a second hunting dog.

To the bird hunter who puts in a dawn-to-dusk day in the field, the comforting knowledge that he can switch to a fresh dog when the first one begins to tire can spell the difference between a highly productive or a so-so afternoon. Casting off a pair of beagles or bassets not only doubles the hound man's effectiveness, but provides twice the satisfaction that comes from 100 percent more "music." Two retrievers can mean having one for a morning duck hunt and one for an afternoon's go at upland birds. A brace of spaniels can be similarly employed or merely alternated, like bird dogs, for a full day of fast action in the uplands.

Whatever the breed or type of dog involved, there is no gainsaying the fact that two are twice as effective, twice as practical — and at least four times as lovable — as one. Yet, contrary to what would appear a logical conclusion, keeping and caring for two dogs does not necessitate twice as much effort. Oddly enough, in fact, the extra time and work involved in owning two dogs is little more than most hunters devote to caring for one.

Aside from the more obvious benefits just cited, there are several other reasons for the serious hunter to consider owning a second gun dog. One of these — perhaps the most common — is the sad but necessary matter of having a replacement to take over when the first dog passes on or simply becomes too old to put in a full day's work afield.

Some sportsmen, in understandable but nonetheless impractical deference to the "old fella," delay acquiring another dog to take his place until the first one dies or has to be completely retired. Then, forced to begin from scratch in training a young pup, they lose an entire hunting season, or even two, in getting their replacement ready.

Far more sensible, and really no less sentimental, is the hunter who obtains his potential replacement at least two or three years before his present dog reaches the age of full retirement. By so doing, he insures his future gunning without interruption and, at the same time, can enjoy the benefits of two dogs for at least a single season or more.

In addition, this often simplifies the task of breaking in the second dog, since the youngster has the good example of the veteran to follow for part of his basic education. With the aid of the "old fella," teaching a pup some of the fundamental commands, such as "Here," "Sit," "Stay," or "Kennel," can be accomplished in amazingly short order. Instant response by the old dog to basic obedience orders frequently carries greater weight with the youngster than even your own best instructional efforts. And should the pup err momentarily, the reliable

A pair of Labrador retrievers can offer a man one dog for duck hunting in the morning and another for flush dog chores on upland birds for the rest of the day.

responsiveness of the veteran nine times out of ten will bring the puppy back on the beam a lot quicker than the boss could — with less danger of spirit-breaking, too.

When to acquire a second gun dog, of course, depends solely on the individual hunter's judgment and circumstances. Naturally, since these vary widely, compromises must often be made. Yet, where at all feasible, we've always held to the belief that owning two dogs of three years' age difference was just about optimum. These are the advantages: being able to alternate two dogs on a day's hunt; knowing that the older, more experienced dog can always be pressed into service when needed, in a difficult or challenging situation; yet enjoying the luxury of giving the younger dog needed experience after a bird or bunny has safely been tucked away in the bag.

The fact that the three-year-old has really begun to come into his own in the field when the second dog is acquired is of tremendous psychological significance to the hunter. The three-year-old knows his job, is dependable, and will continue to gain polish while the puppy begins undergoing his training. The contrast between the two is apparent, refreshing, enjoyable; there is no impatience, no undue pushing of the pup's education, for the hunter's need of productive results is satisfied by the older dog.

While the older dog's performance mellows and improves, the younger one learns unhurriedly, ripening eventually to maturity in plenty of time to complement for several seasons the work of his veteran counterpart. And in the process the hunter inevitably derives the satisfaction of watching the natural, unrushed development of a second hunting dog.

The three-year age difference is also most beneficial from the standpoint that the hunter will have the simultaneous services of two experienced dogs over a longer span of seasons. The first dog will only be six by the time the second begins hitting his stride. Should some minor injury temporarily sideline either dog during the height of the gunning season, the other one can then be relied upon to carry the full workload.

Now, let's get down to the specifics of how much more trouble it is to keep a second dog. As mentioned earlier, two dogs involve little more time or effort to own than one. First of all, there's feeding. Pouring and mixing meal for two takes just a couple of seconds longer than fixing for one. Then you have to walk out to the kennel, to the back porch, or wherever with the feed pan. It certainly won't require any

A second hunting dog doesn't mean twice as much care and effort for the owner. Feeding, watering and exercise require neglibly little more time and work for two dogs.

extra time or measurable energy to carry two pans instead of one.

It's the same thing with replenishing fresh drinking water. Logically, you'll have to obtain a larger receptacle; but toting or hosing twice the volume of water still takes negligible extra time or effort.

Exercise? Unless it's done strictly from a leash, you might spend a couple of minutes more rounding up two dogs instead of one. But the difference between fifteen- and eighteen-minute romps can hardly become vital to the average person's schedule. And even if a leash is required, five extra seconds spent attaching a tandem collar snap to a single lead will solve the problem of walking both dogs simultaneously.

Since feeding, watering, and exercising make up the lion's share of day-to-day dog care, it's easy to see that whether you do it for one or two makes very little difference.

There are certain aspects, of course, that will require almost twice as much time and effort. Grooming, for example, has few shortcuts; only by working a little bit faster and fussing less can two dogs be attended in somewhat less than twice the time normally devoted to one. However, it is proper to point out that most breeds of field dogs require so little grooming as to make this a relatively minor facet of their care and maintenance.

Even in the matter of transporting two dogs to and from the field, the hunter's task is no more difficult or time-consuming. He may need an extra dog crate — although if he employs a station wagon barrier he won't need another — but aside from taking up a little more space, the second dog offers no special problems to transport.

The question of expense, of course, is most likely to arise in the form of the anticipated protests from your spouse. However, with a bit of imagination and fast arithmetic — the kind that works in a new table saw — any man worth his salt should be able to override such protests.

Take, for example, the matter of transporting two dogs, say to the vet's for shots. By taking them both in the same car, the cost of gasoline, oil, and depreciation is cut in half, 50 percent for each dog. So far so good — most spouses can recognize a half-price bargain when they see one.

The fact that it has cost you twice as much to have two dogs inoculated becomes a minor detail when you use arithmetic to rationalize it. You simply explain to the wife that, although the vet charges $25 apiece for shots, he also gets $25 for an office visit. With two dogs, you got twice the value of an office visit at half the cost.

If really backed to the wall, there is always one tactic that can save the day. With straight face, expressing all the angelic naivete you can muster, merely remind her of how astute her own arithmetic was the day she got you to propose by telling you that "Two can live as cheaply as one."

SUMMER AND WINTER HEALTH AND COMFORT

The seasonal extremes are potentially the most hazardous and least cordial to a dog's general health and comfort. During summer and winter the gun dog owner should be alert to the need for the extra care so important to his dog's physical and psychological well-being.

For the neglected gun dog, summer can be purgatory. Left to the mercy of sweltering sun and stifling humidity, hounded by swarms of flying insects and badgered by crawling parasites, the kennel dog, especially, can only look forward to a summer in abject misery. His indoor counterpart, though somewhat better off, might also wish for a more considerate owner. Far from pampering, applying a little "summer comfort" constitutes no more than reasonable humane consideration for the gun dog who does his best to serve you all year long.

Properly providing for his summertime comfort will take a little initial sweat and elbow grease on your part. But, if the effort can't be dispensed as a labor of love, it can at least be chalked up to practical necessity, as good insurance against poor condition that will be a detriment to your dog come hunting season. The recipe for summer comfort is hardly complex, but it does take in numerous ingredients, principally involving cleanliness and grooming, feeding and exercise.

Whether your dog is housed in a kennel or shares the family quarters, one of the first steps toward his summer comfort should be a haircut. For the shorthaired breeds—labs, German shorthairs, vizslas, etc.—this will be little more than a good session with stripping comb

A canine haircut, really a once-over-lightly trim, with stripping comb or electric clippers is one of the first steps in providing for your dog's summer comfort. **Photo by Dave Petzal.**

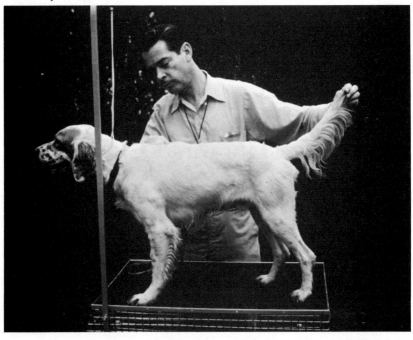

Removal of excess coat helps owner spot skin irritations and parasitic infestations more easily. Electric clippers are ideal tool for the job. **Photo by Dave Petzal.**

and brush to eliminate dead excess hair from the coat. The longhaired breeds—setters, spaniels, goldens, and the like—will need a light, overall trim, taking about a quarter of an inch of coat length in the process. A stripping comb will do, but electric clippers are the ideal tool for the job.

The folks who argue that a haircut has no cooling value to a dog are right. The pores of the canine skin differ considerably from those of humans. Unlike ours, the dog's skin pores release only minute amounts of body heat through evaporation; most of the dog's sweating is done through his tongue. But the canine haircut provides comfort in other ways. Principally, dispensing with superfluous coat during a time of year when that coat is least needed enables an owner to spot more easily the presence of skin irritation or parasitic infestations. Not only can they be detected more readily, they can also be treated more expeditiously when the coat is sparse.

Moreover, the removal of excess coat makes less of a task out of the more frequent groomings the dog should receive during the summer months. The combined effects of a light trim and regular brushings help stimulate the growth of a healthy new coat by the time the fall gunning season rolls around.

The trim and brushing should be followed by thoroughly soaking the dog in one of the commercial dog dip mixes designed to rid him of all external parasites. Sold in highly concentrated form, these solutions are made to be mixed with water and are easy to prepare. Dipping is quick and simple when done properly. The best utensil for the purpose is a fifty-gallon steel drum or clean G.I. can of sufficient

Whether kenneled or housed indoors, the dog and his quarters should be thoroughly disinfected to rid both of insect pests and parasites.

proportions to dunk the dog right up to his neck or shoulders. When placed in the prepared mixture, the dog is able to stand on his hind legs and place his forepaws over the edge of the container's rim for support.

Taking care to protect his eyes, nose, and ear canals, you can then scoop the solution over the head, neck, and outer ears and give the submerged portions of the dog's body a few brisk rubs to make sure the coat is thoroughly soaked. The entire procedure takes no longer than six or eight minutes.

After dipping, it's not necessary to dry the dog; simply let him shake—he will anyway—and walk him around in the sun for a few minutes. When his coat is dry, follow up with a quick brushing, and he'll not only look and feel clean and refreshed but will also give off a pleasant odor.

In fact, the aroma, which lasts for a week to ten days, will repel fleas, ticks, mosquitoes, and other insect pests during that period.

Kennel dogs should be dipped approximately every other week for maximum comfort and freedom from parasites; house dogs need be dipped only every three or four weeks during the warm months. Incidentally, the dip solution can be saved and re-used, often for the entire summer, if a lid is kept over the container to prevent evaporation.

Before each dipping session, the solution should be stirred briskly and a few more drops of concentrate and water added, if necessary, to replenish the mixture.

On the same day the dog receives his trim and first dip, his quarters should be thoroughly cleaned and sprayed with a suitable disinfectant and tick-and-flea killer. Take care in reading the labels of any sprays before using, to determine that they contain no ingredients harmful to pets. Obviously, it does no good to dip the dog and skip disinfecting his sleeping and living quarters, or vice versa. If fleas and ticks are eliminated from one and not the other, the dog will quickly become re-infested, and all your efforts will have been for nought.

Extra special care must be given to cleaning the doghouse and kennel run. A cement run is the best type, since it is easiest to keep clean, disinfected, and sweet-smelling in hot weather. However, if the dog is kept in a pen with plain earthen or gravel surface, the run should be soaked down with a strong solution of salt water at least once a week. The saline mixture discourages fleas and kills their eggs as well as those of parasitic worms. For most effective results, earthen runs should be turned over and graveled runs raked prior to sprinkling the salt water.

In summer, a length of canvas draped over kennel top provides dog needed shade from hot sun. Side drapes offer extra shade and, in winter, act as windbreaks. **Photo by Dave Petzal.**

Besides cleanliness, shade is one of the most important considerations for the comfort and well-being of the kennel dog in summer. If his enclosure has the advantage of natural shade from a nearby tree, the problem has been solved. But if his run is out in the open, in the direct rays of the sun, some form of artificially provided protection becomes a must.

A drape of heavy duck canvas placed across a portion of the top and one side of the fence will serve as well as anything. It is not necessary, or even advisable, to shield out the sun entirely. Some sunlight — preferably that of early morning and late afternoon — should be available to the dog. So adjust the width and placement of the canvas in accordance with your kennel's dimensions and east-west exposure.

An adequate supply of fresh, cool water is as much a comfort as a necessity for both the kennel and indoor dog during the warmer months. Diet, or rather the amount of food given, is significant, too. Generally speaking, a reduction of about 25 percent of the winter volume of food given the kennel dog will adequately sustain him during the summer. Cutting down on the fat content of his rations by about a third will keep him from gaining more weight than he should. Remember, though, that every dog is different, and it is up to you to watch your dog's diet carefully while making whatever adjustments seem appropriate.

No less important in summer than at any other time of year is the matter of providing the dog with proper exercise. The major difference, however, is that in warm weather the dog should be exercised in the cool of early morning or late evening, times that fortuitously can be worked into the average wage-earner's schedule. Additional exercise, for dogs who naturally take to water, can be obtained by swimming, one of the best of all possible summer conditioners.

A word of warning for the gun dog in summer. A car parked in the direct rays of the summer sun, with windows rolled up tight, will become a death-trap for a dog in amazingly short order. Always leave all car windows open at least an inch-and-a-half to two inches from the top and park in a shady spot. Don't forget, the sun moves and so does the shade; never leave your dog in a parked car any longer than a half-hour without checking on him.

Going from one extreme to the other, winter, is of course, a time for buttoning up, fortifying against the elements, and awaiting the arrival of spring. For the kennel dog, the cold months are potentially the dreariest and loneliest of the entire year. During no other season does he receive so little companionship, attention, or exercise.

Properly winterizing the kennel dog consists first of providing him with adequate protective shelter. It should be draft-free, large enough for comfort but small enough to be kept warm by the dog's own body heat. Many doghouses, especially the homemade kind, are constructed of wood. Since wood can rot, split, expand, and contract, cracks are bound to appear. These should be filled with plastic wood compound and painted — with a non-leaded paint — to seal out cold air.

The base of the doghouse should be elevated several inches off the ground, so that air can circulate beneath the floor and prevent dampness. A brick placed under each corner of the house is the most common method of providing elevation. A double floor, with a two-inch air space between it and the exterior flooring, offers adequate insulation for the base of the house.

At the entrance, either one of the various two-way swinging doors now being marketed or some sort of breeze-break should be installed. The simplest form of baffle is a slab of plywood catercornered across the inside front of the entrance, and extending a few inches above the doorway's highest point. The most practical and efficient baffle arrangement consists of a detachable entrance extension. Even the dog owner who complains of being "all thumbs" can build one in a couple of hours. In design, it is essentially like a box with one end knocked out and an opening cut in one of the sides near the closed end.

By means of hooks-and-eyes — one at the top and another at the bottom on each side — the open end can be secured to the doorway of the doghouse for the winter. In effect, the extension provides a sort of closed porch, the end and sides of which prevent any drafts from blowing directly into the regular entrance port. An old piece of carpet, or a double thickness of burlap, tacked over the outside entry point of the extension serves to block out additional breezes that might chill the interior.

In severe winter climates, an insulated doghouse is distinctly in order. Most of the modern varieties now available are made of metal or plastic compounds that include built-in insulation. But even the less expensive plywood types can be insulated by a handy and ambitious owner who is willing to rebuild the entire interior.

You can give your kennel dog extra protection from howling winds and driving snow in two ways. The first involves the simple precaution of facing the doghouse entrance in the opposite direction from the prevailing winds. The second is to attach a tarp or strip of heavy canvas around the outside of that portion of the kennel fence that the doghouse entrance faces. The same canvas strip used to give shade in summer can double in spades for the winter and, therefore, amortize its purchase price twice as quickly.

The inside of the dog house should contain fresh, dry bedding of the sort that your dog can snuggle into to keep warm on the coldest days and nights. Ordinary straw makes about the best winter bedding obtainable. It has the proper consistency for burrowing and its peculiar body-heat-holding qualities are unequaled by any other material yet grown or manufactured. The fact that it's both economical and generally available adds to its desirability.

After seeing to his primary requirement of protective shelter, the next most important consideration is your dog's winter diet. Generally speaking, the colder the climate, the greater the percentage of food energy he'll require just to maintain body heat. He'll therefore need larger quantities of his regular ration, in addition to supplements of higher-energy-producing foods.

Animal fat in either liquid or solid form must be included in the dog's daily diet. A good feeding rule for the kennel dog in winter is a 25 percent increase in his portions plus the addition of two tablespoons of rendered fat daily. Since climatic factors must be considered, along with the normal variance in the needs of individual dogs, you obviously should not hew to a hard-and-fast rule on winter feeding. Instead, judge your dog's personal requirements by observing his overall condition and varying his diet accordingly.

Adequate amounts of fresh water, too, are no less important to your dog during the cold months. Unless an electrically heated bucket is used, there is no easy solution to the problem of avoiding freeze-up of the dog's drinking water, with the resulting necessity of making three or four trips to the kennel each day to replenish his supply.

A possible alternative is to attach the water bowl or bucket, by means of a sturdy bracket, to the inside wall of the doghouse, where freezing will be prevented or at least slowed considerably. Every precaution must be taken, however, to insure against spillage, for soaked bedding would constitute a far greater health hazard to the dog than would temporary thirst.

Although thoughts of frigid digits, numb knees, and frosty feet can cool any owner's desire to venture from the hearth, the kennel dog's daily exercise should not be neglected. Turning him out to stretch his legs and flex his muscles is just as necessary to his mental state as to

Summer or winter, adequate protective shelter for the kennel dog consists of a good doghouse, preferably well-insulated. Facing house entrance away from prevailing winds and canvas-stripping kennel fence affords additional winter protection.

his physical condition. Even a five- or ten-minute exercise period twice daily will tend to break the monotony and loneliness of kennel life during the long cold spell.

Grooming a kennel dog in the dead of winter would be regarded as sheer idiocy by some folks. Yet much of the practical merit in its practice is purely psychological. Bringing the dog into the kitchen, basement, or garage for a nightly ten-minute grooming where it's warm and cheerful gives his spirits a tremendous lift.

Not only is the change of scene from his kennel beneficial, but the idea of spending a little time with his owner will mean more to him than a hefty chunk of beefsteak. Even these few minutes of personal contact each night will prove sufficient to instill in him the sense of belonging that every dog must have, but which is most often lacking in the kennel dog...especially during the winter.

Actually, that's about all there is to providing proper winter care for the kenneled gun dog...if most people are willing to go to as much or more trouble winterizing a car to keep it serviceable, you can hardly mind some extra effort to do the same thing for your own gun dog.

One thing is certain: Rover won't hesitate to show his appreciation ...but we've never yet seen an old Ford wag its tail for a considerate owner.

CANINE VACATION

The time when the family annually eschews life in the old home-stead for the myriad summer delights so enticingly pictured and de-scribed in the brochure on "Vacation Lake Lodge" will come.

Mom and Dad will shed the routine and cares of the work-a-day world, roast marshmallows and wieners over open fires, drink in the aromatic pungency of the silent forest's majestic pine and hemlock, tread old Indian trails, and watch Junior and baby Sally splash ecstat-ically in the cool, emerald-green, trout-teeming waters of the natural man-made Lake Whateveritis.

Certainly, if Dad is the stalwart kind, the model husband and father that his wife thinks he ought to be, he'll spend his whole vacation with his family, reveling in each precious moment of togetherness. On the other hand, if he's only average—and, therefore, mildly heart-less, unthinking, and selfish—he may be fortunate enough to have rescued at least a small portion of his holidays for that hunting trip he dreams of taking in the fall.

In any case, the family vacation is often a must, and with it comes the need to arrange Rover's vacation. With but two alternatives open—to take or leave him—the decision should be made well in advance of the family's scheduled departure.

There are, of course, two schools of thought on the question of whether to take Rover along on your vacation or to farm him out to a boarding kennel. Each has its own merits; we intend to espouse neither. Surely the alert, perceptive man of the house, being fully aware of his own future hunting vacation plans and the delicate psy-chological balance on which they hinge, is the best judge of which course to pursue.

Our advice, therefore, will confine itself to a few suggestions and helpful tips for taking or leaving your hunting dog when family vaca-tion time arrives.

The first thing to establish if you decide in favor of including Rover on your trip is whether or not he will be welcomed by the management of your vacation hostelry. Just because there is an old English sheep-dog nuzzling an adoring youngster in the cover photo of a lodge's brochure, don't take for granted the fact that guests' dogs are wel-come. Check it out by letter with the manager. The same holds true for any places at which you may stop overnight along the way. Fortunately, this aspect is no longer the problem it once was; by writing to Gaines Professional Services, P.O. Box 877, Young America, MN 55399 and enclosing $1.50, you can obtain a copy of "Touring with Towser." This handy directory contains a listing alphabetically, by state, of hotels and motor courts that accommodate guests with dogs. Simply checking it out against the route you will take enables you to plan your stopovers accordingly.

Once Rover's welcome is assured, your next thoughts should turn to organizing and stocking up on all the provisions he'll need while he's away from home. Food comes first. Take enough of his usual ration to see him through the duration of your trip. In addition, take along some extra chow for emergency. You never know when a change of plans may extend your stay, and re-stocking Rover's larder may prove difficult.

Naturally, you'll need his feeding and watering pans, a can opener, and a fork or spoon for mixing feed. It's most practical to pack all his supplies beforehand in two corrugated boxes. In the larger one the bulk of his chow can be stored; the smaller one should be reserved for utensils and sufficient rations to feed him only the meals he'll need en route. In this way, the smaller carton can be placed in a conveniently accessible spot in the car, after most of the other loading has been done.

If he's going on vacation with you, Rover will travel much better in his own carrying crate, which will also double as a doghouse at your destination. This Kennel-Aire crate,with grooming top and grooming arm attachments, serves both functions. **Photo by Dave Petzal.**

Some advance thought should be given to just how Rover will travel. Your carrying crate may take up a little more precious space, but in the long run it will prove well worth it in safety, security and peace of mind on the road. The carrying crate also has the advantage of doubling as a doghouse in which Rover can sleep after arrival at your final destination. Fitted out with his blanket or pad, the crate then becomes a little bit of "home" to him in the midst of strange surroundings. Seemingly a small detail, it can spell the difference between sound sleep—his, yours, and the neighboring guests—and a difficult time at night.

A certain amount of caution, dictated by plain old horse sense, should be exercised when Rover participates in the normal activities of a family vacation. Even if he's familiar with boats, for example, it's generally unwise to venture forth on any deep-water excursions without first outfitting each member of the family with life preservers. If your dog has had no previous experience with boats, a few preliminary lessons—conducted in shallow water—are a must before permitting him to take part in any family boating activities.

Seldom is it a good idea, either, to let him run loose around your camp or cabin area, at least for the first full day. Until he becomes used to the surroundings, he should be kept on a leash or long rope. And at all times he should wear his collar, complete with license and identification and rabies tags.

Except in the most isolated vacation spots, there are bound to be other guests in fairly close proximity to your own accommodations; you owe them the same consideration that you extend to your neighbors back home. Morally, as well as legally, you're just as responsible for your dog's actions and behavior on vacation as you are at home.

Now let's consider what to do if you decide *not* to take Rover along with the family on vacation. In that event, you'll still have to do some advance planning. The first step, of course, is to locate a suitable place to board him. It's a matter of opinion, but trying to pawn him off on a friend or neighbor for the sake of saving a few dollars while you're gone just isn't a good idea. It is both a responsibility and a gross imposition; a favor that we, personally, would neither ask of, nor do for, anyone.

From the standpoint of peace of mind about your dog's safety, care, and general well-being, a professionally run boarding kennel is by far your best choice. Like any well-run business, a reputable boarding kennel will be properly staffed and equipped to provide your dog the

Vacation boating activities — with or without Rover — should always include the wearing of life preservers. Familiarizing your dog with good boat manners is best accomplished by a few preliminary lessons conducted in shallow water.

best of quarters and care. Should any emergency or question of your dog's health arise, the boarding kennels will have ready access to a competent veterinarian.

The job of finding a suitable boarding kennel should be taken care of as far in advance of your departure as possible. Your own vet often can provide the answer. He himself may have boarding facilities, or he can probably recommend one or two reputable kennels. Then, too, there are always the classified ad columns of your local newspaper or various magazines that specialize in dogs and kennel products and services. Should you strike out with all these services, Gaines Professional Services (earlier mentioned) will supply free of charge on written request a copy of "Where To Buy, Board or Train a Dog," a listing of kennels and services they offer.

When you've found a place to board Rover that sounds to your liking, don't hesitate to check it out personally. If it's close to home, there's no reason why you can't arrange an evening visit. If it involves driving some distance, plan a Saturday or Sunday inspection. Make certain the facilities are sanitary, clean-smelling, and reasonably roomy. Be sure your dog will be quartered in an indoor stall, with draft-free kennel box and fresh bedding, that provides access to an outside run long enough to give him moderate exercise. The inside area

Sanitary facilities, combining a draft-free inside stall with access to a roomy outside run, should head your check list of kennel necessities. Insist on separate runs, unless you're boarding more than one dog. **Photo by Dave Petzal.**

should be well ventilated and the outside run should offer some provision for shade from the hot sun.

Take particular notice, too, of the overall appearance and behavior of boarders; they should be lively—therefore, noisily interested in your presence—and look clean, tidy, well-fed.

Once you're satisfied with your choice of boarding kennels, have dates, rates, and any special instructions agreed upon in advance. An extra bit of precautionary insurance, one that most thoughtful owners concur is practical, is bringing Rover's shots—rabies, distemper, hepatitis—up to date before leaving him at the boarding kennel. Some boarding kennels make such procedure mandatory; as mutual protection, it leaves little to be desired.

Part of the services offered by some kennels includes pickup and delivery of your dog. Make certain of these arrangements beforehand. If you change your plans, or alter your time or date of departure, don't forget to notify the kennel, too.

Whether you take Rover or leave him, when you and the family shove off on vacation, depends entirely on you. Whatever your decision, like the well-known sign says...**PLAN AHEAD.**

Additional Suggested Reading

Inevitably, every gun dog owner will seek to broaden his knowledge of hunting dogs in general, and of his chosen breed in particular, by reading additional books. In fact, once having selected his favorite breed, no sportsman that we've ever run across has managed to get by without at least one good manual devoted exclusively to the step-by-step detail and instructional procedures of training his specific type or breed of gun dog. And, since opinions and training systems and philosophies vary — even for the same breed — most owners won't be content to accept just one, but want two or three, in order to compare and cull what seems best suited to their needs.

To these ends we've compiled the following list of books, categorized for convenience under the headings of pointing dogs, flushing dogs, retrievers, and hounds. We are not personally in agreement with everything said in every book listed, yet each one contains worthwhile information representative of the broad scope of thought and experience brought to bear on the wonderfully interesting world of hunting dogs.

POINTING DOGS:

Brown, W.F., *How To Train Hunting Dogs.* New York: A.S. Barnes, 1942

Davis, H.P., *Training Your Own Bird Dog.* New York: Putnam, 1948

Evans, G.B., *Trouble With Bird Dogs.* New York: Winchester Press, 1983

Falk, J.R., *The Complete Guide To Bird Dog Training,* Revised Edition. Piscataway, NJ: Winchester Press, 1986

Robinson, J.B., *Hunt Close.* New York: Winchester Press, 1978

Wehle, R.G., *Wing & Shot.* Scottsville, NY: Country Press, 1964

Winterhelt, S. and E.D. Bailey, *The Training and Care of the Versatile Hunting Dog.* Ontario: N.A. Hunting Association, 1973

FLUSHING DOGS:

Goodall, C.S., *The Complete English Springer Spaniel*. Middleburg, VA: Denlinger's, 1958
Pfaffenberger, C.J., *Training Your Spaniel*, New Edition. New York: Howell Book House, 1963
Radcliffe, T., *Spaniels For Sport*. New York: Howell Book House, 1969

RETRIEVERS:

Brown, W.F., *Retriever Gun Dogs*. New York: A.S. Barnes, 1945
Fischer, G., *The Complete Golden Retriever*. New York: Howell Book House, 1974
Free, J.L., *Training Your Retriever*. New York: Coward McCann, 1968
Morgan, C., *Charles Morgan on Retrievers*. New York: Abercrombie & Fitch, 1968
Wolters, R.A., *Water Dog*. New York: E.P. Dutton, 1964

HOUNDS:

Black, G.G., *American Beagling*. New York: G.P. Putnam's Sons, 1949
Duffey, D.M., *Hunting Hounds*. New York: Winchester Press, 1972
Whitney, G.D., *This Is the Beagle*. Orange, CT: Practical Science, 1955
Whitney, L.F. and A.B. Underwood, *The Coon Hunter's Handbook*. New York: Henry Holt & Co., 1952

GENERAL & MORE THAN ONE TYPE OF GUN DOG:

Duffey, D.M., *Hunting Dog Know-How*, Revised Edition. Piscataway, NJ: Winchester Press, 1983
Duffey, D.M., *Expert Advice on Gun Dog Training*. Piscataway, NJ: Winchester Press, 1977
Griffen, J., *The Hunting Dogs of America*. Garden City, NY: Doubleday, 1964
Moffit, E.B., *Elias Vail Trains Gun Dogs*, New Edition. New York: Howell Book House, 1964
Vine, L.L., *Your Dog: His Health and Happiness*, Enlarged and Revised Edition. New York: Winchester Press, 1975

Vine, L.L. *Your Dog: His Health and Happiness*. New York: Winchester Press, 1975 (enlarged and revised edition)

PAMPHLETS & BULLETINS, CARE, FEEDING, KENNELING, ETC.:

Countless books have been written on the topics of dog health, care, feeding, grooming, breeding, and kenneling. And, though it's by no means our intention to dissuade interested readers from further expanding their canine libraries, much of the same subject material is available free, or at nominal charge, in hundreds of pamphlets and bulletins produced by the nation's major manufacturers of dog foods. The following is a representative list of those companies that offer such materials:
Carnation Company, Friskies Pet Foods Division, 5045 Wilshire Blvd., Los Angeles, CA
Country Best, Agway, Inc., P.O. Box 1333, Syracuse, NY
Gaines Professional Services, P.O. Box 877, Young America, MN
Purina Pet Care Center, Checkerboard Square, St. Louis, MO

HUNTING DOG PUBLICATIONS

The American Brittany
The American Cooner
The American Field
Full Cry
The German Shorthaired Pointer
Gun Dog Magazine
The Gun Dog Supreme
Hounds and Hunting
The Hunter's Horn
Mountain Music
Retriever Field Trial News
The Weimaraner

BREED REGISTRIES

American Kennel Club, 51 Madison Avenue, New York, NY. Registers all recognized purebreds.
The Field Dog Stud Book, American Field Publishing Company, Chicago, IL. Registers all purebreds, but specializes in pointing breeds.
United Kennel Club, Kalamazoo, MI. Registers all breeds.
Full Cry Kennel Club, Sedalia, MO. Registers all coonhounds.

DOG EQUIPMENT AND ACCESSORIES

Canine accessories and training equipment are vital to the sporting dog owner. Where to obtain these specialty items, however, is often a problem to the uninitiated. Although there are innumerable sources, large and small, here is a sampling of those we've dealt with and found highly reliable:

GENERAL

Dunn's Supply Store, P.O. Box 449, Grand Junction, TN 38039
E-Z Bird Dog Training Equipment Co., Box 333-A, Morganfield, KY 42437
Gun Dog Supply, Box 320, 116 East State Street, Ridgeland, MS 39157
Hallmark Supplies, Main Street, Menomonee Falls, WI 53051
Happy Jack, Box 475, Snow Hill, NC 28580
Hulme Sporting Goods & Mfg. Co., Box 670, Paris, TN 38242
Nite Lite Co., AR 72830
Sporting Dog Specialties, Inc., Box 68, Spencerport, NY 14559
Tidewater Specialties, U.S. Rt. 50, Box 158, Wye Mills, MD 21679

DOG CRATES & STATION WAGON BARRIERS

Kennel-Aire Mfg. Co., 6651 Highway 7, St. Louis Park, MN 55426
K D Kennel Products, 1741 North Broadway, Wichita, KS 67214

KENNEL FENCING & PANELS

Bob Long Kennel Runs, Route 3 North, Gambrills, MD 21054
Brinkman Mfg. & Fence Co., Route 8, Huntoon & Auburn Road, Topeka, KS 67220
Crest Kennel Co., 1900 West Bates Avenue, Englewood, CO 80110
Econ-o-Ken'l, 6400 East 35th Street, Kansas City, MO 64129
Mason Fence Co., Box 711B, Leesburg, OH 45135

DOGHOUSES

Canine Pal Sales Co., 421 East 39th Avenue, Gary, IN 46409
Dogaloo Co., 6817 North 22nd Place, Phoenix, AZ 85016

Index